planning and analysis in health care systems

London Papers in Regional Science

Pion Limited, 207 Brondesbury Park, London NW2 5JN

edited by M.Clarke · London papers in regional science 13 · a pion publication

planning and analysis in health care systems

Pion Limited, 207 Brondesbury Park, London NW2 5JN

Copyright © 1984 by Pion Limited

ISBN 0 85086 108 X

Printed in Great Britain by Page Bros (Norwich) Limited

Contributors

J R Beaumont   *Department of Geography, Birkbeck College, University of London, Malet Street, London WC1E 7HX, England*

R G Bevan   *Centre for Research in Industry, Business and Administration, University of Warwick, Coventry CV4 7AL, England*

M Clarke   *School of Geography, University of Leeds, Leeds LS2 9JT, England*

S E Curtis   *Department of Geography, Queen Mary College, University of London, Mile End Road, London E1 4NS, England*

M Dear   *Department of Geography, McMaster University, Hamilton, Ontario L8S 4K1, Canada*

A M Kirby   *Department of Geography, University of Colorado at Boulder, Boulder, CO 80309, USA*

G Leonardi   *International Institute for Applied Systems Analysis, 2361 Laxenburg, Austria*

L D Mayhew   *International Institute for Applied Systems Analysis, 2361 Laxenburg, Austria*

J Mohan   *Department of Geography, Birkbeck College, University of London, Malet Street, London WC1E 7HX, England*

T Rathwell   *Nuffield Centre for Health Services Studies, University of Leeds, Leeds LS2 9JT, England*

E J Rising   *Department of Industrial Engineering and Operational Research, University of Massachusetts, Amherst, MA 01003, USA*

R S Segall   *Department of Industrial Engineering and Operational Research, University of Massachusetts, Amherst, MA 01003, USA*

A Sixsmith   *Department of Geography, King's College, University of London, Strand, London WC2R 2LS, England*

A H Spenser   *Department of Geography, National University of Singapore, Kent Ridge, Singapore 0511*

A G Wilson   *School of Geography, University of Leeds, Leeds LS2 9JT, England*

K J Woods   *Department of Geography, Queen Mary College, University of London, Mile End Road, London E1 4NS, England*

Contents

Introduction

M CLARKE
University of Leeds

This volume, the thirteenth in the London Papers series, consists mainly of
papers presented at various meetings held in 1982 and 1983 of the British
Section of the Regional Science Association. In addition, a few papers
have been specially written for this volume so that it represents the wide
range of regional science contributions to the general problem of health
care planning and analysis. However, as is the tradition in regional science,
the papers do not provide a concensus of ideas relating to how planning
and analysis should be undertaken. On the contrary, they offer a number
of different approaches and viewpoints on how regional scientists can
contribute to this important subject area. As a consequence, the reader
will detect a diverse number of philosophies and methodologies adopted
and developed by the various contributors. This is an encouraging sign.
As Arrow has pointed out, "If one thing is clear in any dynamic branch
of scientific activity, it is that the ratio of complaints to accomplishments
is roughly a constant" (Arrow, 1980, page 265).

That the analysis of health care issues is an important research area and
that regional scientists have an important contribution to make should be
fairly obvious, but it could be argued that, with a few notable exceptions,
it has remained a relatively underdeveloped field until fairly recently.
Expenditure on health care, as a proportion of gross national product,
varies quite markedly between developed countries, but the percentage is
always large. Furthermore, it is a self-evident but important fact that everyone at some stage in their life makes use of the health care system, and
therefore it can have a considerable influence on people's well-being
and quality of life. Consequently, its organisation, its availability and
access to different groups in society and over space, its quality, and its
cost are all factors of vital importance. In addition, there is no denying
that its funding, administration, and provision are firmly ensconced within
the political framework of any society.

There are a number of important research areas to which regional
scientists can contribute, and these will be elaborated in the papers
presented in this volume. One vitally important area, though, is that of
inequality in terms of access to and provision of health services. The
Black Report (Townsend and Davidson, 1982) found serious inequalities in
almost every aspect of health care in the United Kingdom, despite the fact
that the National Health Service (NHS) was set up on the principle of
equal access for all. And this situation will inevitably get worse as
government slashes the budgets of UK health authorities, which is having
the effect that decisions are now having to be made that are resulting in a
reduction in the level of care provided. Research is therefore required that

highlights existing inequities, that can examine the likely impact of proposed developments, or that can contribute to more effective organisation and planning.

This volume is divided into three subsections. In the first section two contrasting overviews of health care issues and the contribution of regional science are provided by Dear and by Clarke and Wilson. The second section focuses on primary health care, and the third on the problems of health care planning and analysis at the administrative level.

In the first paper, Dear offers a personal assessment of health care planning, in which he argues that the health of a population must be considered, not only in a medical sense, but also related to the nature of the social form and processes in which the population is embedded. Dear calls for a rejection of the highly disciplined approach to health care research in return for a single one which is located within a wider social context. Without this restructuring, he argues, much research that is undertaken will be largely irrelevant. This argument is then exemplified through a consideration of mental health care provision in North American cities. This is achieved through identifying the four groups of actors which control the way in which psychiatric care is provided, the professionals, the client, the community, and the planners, and the way in which these interact.

Clarke and Wilson adopt a more conventional attitude towards the integration of the various approaches to the planning of health care. They argue that a synthesis of existing methodologies is required. The failure of many existing methods in relation to problem solving has been through the lack of an adequate understanding of the nature of the health care system. Problems that arise often operate at different spatial scales and over different time horizons, and hence this will require a range of methodologies to be brought to bear. The lack of understanding of how the system functions can largely be put down to the inadequacy of existing information systems and the use of very crude indicators. After examining the range of techniques available and outlining a framework in which they can be viewed, they review a range of applications to allocation problems that have been reported in the literature. In the second half of the paper, an example of the type of synthesis they encourage is presented. This consists of a simulation model of a district health authority which has been designed to address a range of strategic planning issues. Finally, they outline the type and range of indicators that would actually be meaningful for health care planners. This is important because it comes at a time when a critical reappraisal of information generation and use is being undertaken within the NHS.

The next two papers are both concerned with the problem of primary health care. Curtis and Woods examine a range of issues relating to morbidity in London and how information on variations in morbidity can contribute to the planning of health care provision. The practical difficulties in assembling morbidity data are discussed and a variety of different methods are outlined. They then report on a number of local morbidity studies in London before presenting some early results of their own research in two contrasting London boroughs. The findings from their two surveys are compared both with each other and with national data. As expected, they find marked differences between morbidity in the two boroughs, and these are commented on in a concluding section. The paper provides further evidence that information on the need for health care and understanding of how this is related to various socio-economic factors are essential for effective planning.

The contribution by Kirby and Jones contrasts the difference between outbreaks of measles in the United States of America and in the United Kingdom. In the former, immunisation is compulsory for schoolchildren in most states, but in the United Kingdom it is voluntary and, as a consequence, variations in immunisation rates can be expected at the microscale and are probably related to local factors, particularly access to and the attitude of general practitioners (GPs). In their empirical analysis they attempt to extract the reasons for the low vaccination rate in the United Kingdom. Although no social data on patients were available, it appears that GP-related factors, such as case loads, lists sizes, etc, do correlate with the failure to vaccinate. Once again, the interplay of many macrolevel factors, such as resource availability, social processes, and attitudes, results in microlevel effects. In this case it is argued that compulsory vaccination is preferable to persuasion.

The final group of papers are essentially all concerned with the problem of allocating resources between different spatial or administrative areas and between different sectors of the health care system. Two major points emerge. First, that model-based analysis will often prove useful in guiding the allocation process. Second, a deep understanding of the planning process is essential if we are to appreciate how resources do actually get allocated. Optimal solutions may be one thing, but the political motives and the vested interests of those involved in the decisionmaking process often contribute significantly to the outcome of many planning decisions.

Bevan and Spencer first review the historical development of resource allocation and organisational structure in the NHS since its inception in 1948. This is followed by an outline and critique of hospital and service planning at the regional and district level. In recent years there has been the development of a formula-based method for the allocation of resources to regions. This method, known as the resource allocation working party (RAWP) method, after the working party that proposed it, is described and then criticised on a number of grounds. Methods for allocating resources subregionally are then discussed, these findings being the outcome of research with a number of regional health authorities in England. From their research they identify four models of resource allocation policy at this level. Finally, they turn their attention towards outlining possible improvements in allocation methods. For example, they advocate the use of spatial interaction models to determine the catchment areas for different specialities and for finance to be made available on this basis. Regional scientists can make important contributions through their analytic skills if they adopt a less naïve view of what planning and resource allocations constitute in the NHS.

Rathwell continues this general exposition of planning procedures in the health service by focusing on the problem of joint-care planning. Joint-care planning is an attempt to integrate the management of those services that are provided by both the NHS and local authorities in the United Kingdom that overlap and are directed at the same client group, for example the elderly and children in care. He focuses on a case study of joint-care planning for the elderly and the mentally handicapped in the north of England. What emerges is that the personality and commitment of individual committee members has a great deal of influence in relation to the decisionmaking process. The conflicts of interest that this generates are well exemplified, and it is demonstrated how, because of this, the rational planning paradigm is not adhered to. This is important to know, because the plans formulated by these planning teams result in the services that are provided to those in need. Mohan reinforces this view in a consideration of a particular problem posed for planners through the rapid subregional population growth experienced as a result of new town development in County Durham. He traces the historical background to the growth and location of new towns. The consequences of population expansion led to a political dispute between the area health authorities involved and the Northern Regional Health Authority. The use of analytic methods to determine the location of acute-care facilities is described and how the different parties involved derived different solutions to the problem. It is argued that in this case a wider range of issues than purely technical ones need consideration. Mohan then concurs with Dear that the development of a fuller understanding and interpretation of spatial processes and form fundamentally requires a consideration of the role of the state. This reflects a notable trend in regional science over the past few years towards the development of social theory and the role of the state.

The final three papers are all case studies of the application of optimisation methods to the problem of facility location. In the paper by Clarke and Wilson it was argued that, in many realistic planning situations, the range of possible alternative locations for new facilities is extremely limited and, in any case, the opportunity for the development of new facilities in the current environment is restricted. However, Beaumont and Sixsmith identify a particular problem that is readily amenable to this kind of analysis. The increasing proportion of elderly persons in the population has put pressures on the health system and this has often resulted in elderly patients being cared for on general medical or surgical wards, which are often not appropriate places for their needs.

The development of elderly severely mentally infirm (ESMI) units is a move towards providing purpose-built accommodation for a particular type of patient. Beaumont and Sixsmith look at the development of health policy for the elderly before examining the problem of determining the location of ESMI units in Lancashire. Their analysis is based on a number of different assumptions concerning the number and capacity of the units to be located. The results they obtain emphasise two important points—that optimisation methods may inform us as to where facilities might be located, but also that they provide us with further information about the system of interest. For example, they show that, with equal capacities, less densely populated areas have high accessibility costs, but, if capacities are allowed to vary, these costs are reduced. This, of course, is another example of the equity-efficiency argument that has interested regional scientists for many years.

The paper by Mayhew and Leonardi is a report on an extension of the health care modelling work undertaken at the International Institute for Applied Systems Analysis over the past few years. This work has been concerned with finding optimal resource allocations, in terms of acute-care facilities, over space. The particular model described in this paper is based on what they call the efficiency principle, which is designed to find optimal solutions such that the benefits associated with the patients' preference for treatment in given locations is maximised. The model is applied to the provision of health care services in Massachusetts, and a set of results are described. It is interesting to speculate as to what is the most appropriate spatial scale for the application of these models. Probably at a local level, for example, the district level in England and Wales, there is too little scope for reallocation and too many local factors to be accounted for. However, at the regional scale (for example, regional health authorities) they are probably more suited, and, if they do no more than provide planners with information as to how far the existing locational pattern is away from the optimal one, then this is useful. Incremental change may then be implemented which gradually progresses towards the optimal solution. The final paper by Rising et al uses the same spatial unit as above for the application of a different model of resource allocation, RAMOS. In this paper it is shown that the calibrated model provides a good description of patient flows in Massachusetts, but that much more model development needs to be undertaken if they are to be used in a forecasting mode.

That a wealth of diverse contributions should emerge from regional scientists on the issues of health care planning and analysis is hardly surprising, but it does reflect the continuing expansion of ideas and methodologies that now come under the umbrella of regional science. Good analytical and theoretical work is being matched pace for pace by philosophical, political, and ideological research. There is no reason for any incompatibility between the two. For example, quantitative analysis can begin to examine issues of inequality, distribution, and the impacts of policies on different groups of people. For their part, social and political theorists can provide us with a richer understanding of the processes that mould society. This can then be incorporated into model-based analysis to provide better descriptive and prescriptive tools. This type of eclecticism provides a major challenge to regional scientists in the future.

References

Arrow K, 1980, "Microdata simulations: current status, problems, prospects" in *Microeconomic Simulation Models for Public Policy Analysis* volume 2, Eds R H Haveman, K Hollenbeck (Academic Press, New York) pp 253–266

Townsend P, Davidson N, 1982 *Inequalities in Health: The Black Report* (Penguin Books, Harmondsworth, Middx)

Editor's note. Readers will notice that throughout this volume the word 'speciality' is used to describe distinctive medical departments within hospitals. The more common use of 'specialty' in the medical world does not appear to satisfy either *The Concise Oxford Dictionary* (sixth edition) or *Webster's New Collegiate Dictionary* (1981). In the former, specialty is defined as an instrument under seal or a sealed contract. Speciality, however, is defined as a special feature or characteristic; a special pursuit, product, operation, etc; or a thing to which a person gives special attention. In *Webster's*, a specialty is described as a distinctive mark or quality; a special object or class of objects [for example, a legal agreement embodied in a sealed instrument or a product of a special kind or of special excellence (fried chicken was mother's specialty)]; or something in which one specializes. Speciality is defined as a special mark or quality; a special object or class of objects; a special aptitude or skill; or a particular occupation or branch of learning.

Speciality, therefore, would best seem to describe the functions of those parts of a hospital devoted to specific medical activities, and has been adopted throughout this volume as a matter of consistency.

Health Services Planning: Searching for Solutions in Well-defined Places

M DEAR
McMaster University

1 Introduction

In this essay, I wish to develop the following argument. Three traditional research themes are evidenced in the literature on health services planning: disease ecology, access to health care, and administrative organization. I argue that these three research traditions are relatively independent and prevent an integration of health services planning with the wider social context within which it is embedded. A social theory of health would focus on three primary concerns: the origins and evolution of the institution of health care; the organization and practice of health care; and the political sphere. The potential of the social theoretic approach is demonstrated via the example of mental health care. The 'ghettoization' of ex-psychiatric patients is the sociospatial outcome of a complex interaction between four agents who are part of the psychiatric apparatus. Each agent uses space purposively to affect the required social structuring. The professional uses state-sanctioned principles of isolation to define a treatment space. The client undergoes an informal spatial filtering and establishes a coping mechanism in the inner city. The community seeks to protect its turf through the processes of residential differentiation. And the planner uses state-sanctioned land-use control to ensure conflict-free siting. This view of psychiatric care emphasizes the significance of the 'statization' of the psychiatric profession; the everyday experience of illness and its impact on client health outcomes; the pattern of community response and its effect on health outcomes; and the role of the planning apparatus in the supply of health care. The social theoretic approach requires a realignment of health systems planning towards a set of more realistic and relevant constructs. Let us now examine this argument in detail.

I recently declined an invitation to undertake research on the geographical distribution of physicians in Ontario. My reasons for so doing centered around the belief that the problem contained little in the way of new research challenges, and that I would merely be involved in a rather mechanical application of existing methodologies. This decision to ignore what is manifestly an important topic has subsequently caused me to reflect on the status of research in health services planning. It is not that there is anything intrinsically *wrong* about careful applied work, but why did I conclude that much contemporary research in health care delivery was devoid of theoretical challenge? What were the core issues that *ought* to be addressed in the discipline?

In this paper, I report some results of my reassessment of health services planning. This is a personal statement and it is highly abbreviated; I have not attempted to substantiate every argument and I have not provided an exhaustive review of the sources. The rest of the paper is divided into three parts. In section 2, I outline a critique of the current status of health services planning and argue for a social theoretic approach. In section 3, I examine the power of this approach, as exemplified by the case of mental health care. Finally, in section 4, I present a few concluding remarks.

2 The current status of health services planning
2.1 The search for solutions in well-defined places
The field of health services planning is extensive and ill-defined. The territory is contested by many academic disciplines, including geography and epidemiology, and by many professions, such as medicine and planning. As a consequence, the field is highly fragmented, although three broad themes have emerged to dominate the literature. These are: (a) studies in disease ecology, that is, the origin, transmission, and cure of disease (for example, see Meade, 1980; Pyle, 1979); (b) access to health care and the design of optimal systems to maximize population health—including the economics of health care (see the recent reviews by Drury, 1983, and Rosenberg, 1983); and (c) appropriate administrative structures for health care delivery (Donabedian, 1973, remains the primary source).

Most current research in health systems planning seems to be stuck in the well-worn ruts defined by these three analytical traditions. The same issues are constantly being reassessed, usually without reference to the wider context of health care delivery. Moreover, each research tradition, more often than not, seems totally oblivious of the other two. This entrenched independence of positions is well-exemplified in a recent review of medical geography. In examining medical geography's two main traditions of disease ecology and health systems planning, Mayer (1982, page 227) concludes that:

"As long as we recognize the manifold links between the two approaches, there is no need to develop 'one' medical geography. Its strength may, in fact, lie in its eclecticism".

Health services planning has evolved, then, into three distinct branches, each bearing relatively little reference to the other or to the wider context of illness and health. The situation is akin to that of an inebriated man searching for his lost keys under a streetlight. When it is pointed out that his keys were actually dropped in some darker part of the street, he replies that it is, nevertheless, much brighter underneath the streetlight. In health services planning, we have three confused people under separate streetlights, each searching for a single key which lies elsewhere in the street! The key is never glimpsed, nor does anyone think to ponder the whole.

Before proceeding, let me make it perfectly clear that I do not mean to imply that the three 'mainstream' research traditions identified above are in any way trivial. All three issues matter a great deal in determining the well-being of our populations. It is simply that an *overconcentration on these well-defined problem areas is preventing a necessary analysis of the wider context of illness, health, and society.* Now, we do obtain occasional glimpses of these 'darker fringes' of health services research. For instance, the inherent inequalities of the British National Health Service were recently revealed in the Black Report (Townsend and Davidson, 1982), and Starr (1982) has documented the evolution of the US medical profession to a vast corporate industry. These and similar studies point out the need to dissolve the unnecessary and confusing distinctions between the mainstream traditions in health services planning. They underlie the need for a social theory of health which will situate the single discipline within the wider context of concrete social relations.

2.2 Toward a social theory of health
There are few, if any, objective realities in health care. We do not doubt, for example, that there is a malignant disease, associated with an uncontrolled growth of tissue, which we call 'cancer'. However, our view of the symptoms of cancer depend upon how social values, attitudes, and personality influence our perception, interpretation, and response to the disease. In the case of 'mental illness', these sociocultural factors play a greater role. Even the term 'illness' has enormous implications for the way mental disorders are 'treated' by 'doctors' and perceived by a stigmatizing general public.

These examples illustrate the fact that everything involved in health care is, to a greater or lesser degree, a social construction. A proper theory of health care systems must accommodate the reflexive nature of the concepts of illness and health. Society has created these concepts and has designed systems of treatment and cure which reflect the prevailing social order which invented them. The health care system which we currently observe is the product of many years of sociospatial, political, and economic evolution.

A social theory of health implies an analysis of the health care system that is embedded within the wider logic of the contemporary social formation. Such a theory would have three primary concerns: the origin and evolution of the institution of health care; the organization and practice of health care; and the political sphere of health care.

The origin of modern systems of health care lies in the development of capitalism and industrial urbanization. The concentration of a newly urbanized labor force in dense settlements necessitated major state interventions to ensure the continuing health of workers (as well as of the wider populace). Given the significant leverage implied by this mandate, the medical profession continued its fight for professional sovereignty. It controlled the supply of and demand for health care and limited access to the profession. Increased professional power, coupled with growth in the demand for health care, led to an expansion of struggles over health in the political sphere. The subsequent history of the medical profession has been the story of an uneasy alliance between doctors and the state for the provision of something called 'health care'.

In the present-day practice of health care, health exists primarily as a commodity. Access to health care is achieved via a market which is, to a greater or lesser degree, state-regulated. The medical profession exists as a state-sanctioned institution charged with the reproduction of the labor force and the maintenance of nonworking groups. In return for this effort, the profession is granted a monopoly and a license over its own affairs. Its primary objective is self-reproduction; that is, to ensure the continued well-being of its members and its institutions. These potentially contradictory objectives often suggest that the central needs of the medical profession are not defined by the patients, but are instead those of its members. Doctors are thus implicated in the process of iatrogenesis—the creation of disease—as well as its cure. These twin objectives (reproduction of labor and self-reproduction) are also the source of constant dispute in the political sphere, including control over the 'territory' of medicine, doctors' income, and so on.

Contemporary political struggle over the practice of health care resulted in a series of corporatist-type social contracts between health professions and the state. A constant renegotiation of the territory of psychiatry in North America has, for example, led to an increasing 'statization' of the social relations of psychiatry, as the state has penetrated more deeply into the social fabric linking professional and client (Clark and Dear, 1984, chapter 4). Again, in the case of medical care in the USA, doctors are participating in the creation of 'corporate health care systems'—an industry increasingly run by corporations and the state in uneasy alliance with doctors. This has been made possible by increasing physician control of the health commodity, within a hospital system which is progressively being concentrated in fewer corporate hands (Starr, 1982).

Health systems are clearly undergoing major changes as they attempt to adjust to the current vicissitudes of capitalism. Attempts to restructure the welfare state, including efforts to reprivatize/recommodify the health care good, are destined to have major impacts on population health. The simple but powerful lesson of this critique has been to suggest that health outcomes are contingent upon those wider social changes. Moreover, a health planning discipline which ignores these issues is doomed to irrelevance.

In the remainder of this paper, via one extended example, I wish to develop the notion of a social theory of health systems. It will be possible, in this way, to indicate the theoretical and empirical potential of such an approach more clearly than if we persist with abstract formulations. At issue in this example is the use of space in the construction of the social relations of psychiatry. I wish to show how the social context of psychiatry, its internal organization, and political struggles over its outcomes came together in a purposeful manner to determine client well-being.

3 Spatial structuration of social relations in mental health care

The role of space in the structuring of social relations has recently resurfaced as a major focus of debate in at least three arenas. First, it is an important theoretical question in its own right; second, it represents a key element in contemporary social theory; and third, it is a primary connection in the explanation of many substantive processes, such as urbanization and urban planning. A great deal of theoretical 'heat' has been generated by these debates. However, it is my belief that relatively little careful attention has been devoted to the empirical relationships between society and space. In the remainder of this essay, I hope to begin to redress this imbalance. My point of departure is to restate and to provide specific answers for the central theoretical question—exactly how are social relations constituted through space?

At the risk of oversimplification, let me state my theoretical position as straightforwardly as possible. At the most abstract level, both the social and the spatial can be treated as theoretical or philosophical categories. At the level of the concrete, space is given meaning by social relations; but equally, social relations acquire a material presence through space. In other words, the majority of social relations become manifest only through some form of spatial organization, and they may even require a spatial dimension to become operational. This is especially true for collective and/or material relations (such as the relations of production), but may be less so for individual and/or spiritual relations (such as love). In between, there may be a variety of transitional arrangements, which show dimensions of both spatial and aspatial structuration. For instance, the family is organized around a partitioning of the living space for different functional purposes, as well as being a network of support and caring.

Given this emphasis, analytical focus should properly be placed upon *sociospatial* structures. The debate about the relative importance of the social and the spatial is entirely misplaced, and leads only to meaningless accusations of 'abstract reductionism' or 'spatial fetishism'. To discuss and to understand the concrete appearances about us, it is necessary to reject this dichotomy and to address the interrelationship between society and space.

To show how the social relations of psychiatry are purposively constituted through space, I shall focus on the concrete example of mental health care. This example is representative of a wider set of social institutions, characteristic of the health professions, the voluntary sector, and the welfare state in general. In the next section, I set out sufficient details regarding the problem of psychiatric care to motivate the discussion which follows. Subsequently, I trace the roles of four key actors (health professionals, clients, community, and planners) and their use of space in the structuring of the everyday relations of psychiatry.

One caveat is necessary. The approach taken here is deliberately both partial and simplified. To a large extent, the details of these arguments have already been presented elsewhere (for example, see Clark and Dear, 1984, chapter 4; Dear, 1981; Dear and Taylor, 1982). For the moment, my sole concern is a clear and simple demonstration of the significance and complexities of the interdependencies between social relations and spatial relations in a representative sector of health care.

3.1 Deinstitutionalization and the problem of planning for mental health
One of the most prominent outcomes of the deinstitutionalization of the mentally ill in North America has been the 'ghettoization' of the ex-patients. This is the tendency toward a pronounced spatial clustering of ex-psychiatric patients, usually in the core area of our inner cities. Ghettoization is a complex phenomenon—a result of a wide range of forces, including aspects of supply and demand for housing, and formal planning policy. For instance, the inner city is the place where there are: large properties available for conversion to group homes, etc; an established supply of transient rental accommodation; and established support networks (both of service facilities and of personal ties). Demand for housing and jobs by ex-psychiatric patients has led to: an informal (intracity) spatial filtering of patients to the core area; a significant amount of interregional migration (from rural areas to core areas of cities with major psychiatric hospitals); and the formal referral of ex-patients to core-area housing alternatives. These 'market' forces encouraging ghettoization have been reinforced by two other factors: an apparently extensive community opposition, which has effectively excluded ex-patients from most urban residential neighborhoods (especially in the suburbs); and the development of formal planning strategies which attempt to avoid community conflict over locational decisions by seeking out noncontroversial sites for neighborhood mental health facilities.

The mentally ill have been joined in the ghetto by a host of other deinstitutionalized populations, including the dependent elderly, the mentally retarded, the physically disabled, ex-prisoners, and addicts. The past decade has witnessed the development of a 'public city'—the spatial concentration of service-dependent populations and the agencies and facilities designated to serve them—on an unprecedented scale. As an urban phenomenon, the public city represents a significant structural change in the form of Canadian and US cities. As a social psychiatric phenomenon, the ghetto acts as a reservoir of potential clients and as a primary reception area for discharged patients. As more ex-patients arrive in the ghetto, so more services are needed to care for them; the new services themselves act as a catalyst in attracting further ex-patients, and so the self-reinforcing cycle is intensified.

The problem of planning for mental health care under the circumstances of deinstitutionalization is relatively simply stated. In essence it can be viewed as an assignment problem, in which client needs are matched with appropriate service settings. Client needs will vary along a spectrum from 'relative autonomy' to 'complete dependence', with several gradations between. Hence, at the autonomous end of the spectrum, a client may need only occasional home help, or meals-on-wheels; at the dependent end, a dangerous chronic schizophrenic may need total isolation. In between these experiences, another individual might be able to get by with only occasional counselling. Analogous to this taxonomy of client needs is a spectrum of service settings, ranging from the 'open-unrestricted' to the 'closed-protected'. Hence, one client may cope very well with living independently in an apartment, but another may require 'total' hospitalization. In between, such settings as group homes, clinics, etc represent degrees of protection in the service setting.

The effective delivery of mental health care depends (in part at least) upon maximizing the 'goodness of fit' between client needs and service settings. In principle, this fit ought to be achieved at the same time as the disruption to the client's everyday life and the degree of client envelopment in the system are minimized. The health care system ought to be designed to enable clients to move in and out of the various service sequences in the system with ease and without penalty. It is of special importance that we notice that progression through the open-unrestricted–closed-protected service sequence also implies a spatial sequencing. For instance, an autonomous client may well be able to live at home in the regular open environment of his or her own community. However, as the client moves toward the closed end of the spectrum, more 'medical' settings tend to replace the local neighborhood, until the hospital ward becomes the client's new community.

The effectiveness of this assignment process is severely compromised by the performances of the major agents which operate within it. The actual service outcome (for example, care or no care, and in what setting) depends very much on the way the four groups mediate the assignment process. These four are: professional, client, community, and planners. I now wish to consider the role of each in the assignment process, with particular emphasis on the purposive use of space made by all four in the structuring of the everyday social relations of mental health care.

3.2 Professionals
The care and treatment of the mentally disordered have always proceeded from fundamental principles of the isolation and separation of individuals in space. In penal systems, the most intense architectural manifestation of this principle was Bentham's 'Panopticon', which arranged individuals in isolated cells on tiered circles about a central observation area. More generally, the spatial separation of individuals for treatment requires four principles: (a) *enclosure*—the definition of a protected place of treatment; (b) *partitioning*—an elementary principle of internal spatial organization in which each unit has its specific place; (c) *functional sites*—in which internal architectural space is coded for several different uses, reflecting,

for instance, the need for therapeutic, administrative, and work areas; and
(d) *rank*—the definition of the place one occupies in a classification
hierarchy, in which status is not so much defined by place as by position
in a network of relations. These principles enable professionals to describe
a functional–analytic space and to allocate patients for treatment within
that space (compare Foucault, 1977, pages 141–147).

Every historical culture appears to have had its 'madness' and to have
devised some principles for the spatial isolation of the mentally ill. In
classical Greece, Plato advocated that atheists, whose lack of faith derived
from ignorance and not from malice, should be confined for five years in
a 'house of sanity'. In mediaeval Europe, the mad were driven out of the
city enclosures and forced to roam in distant fields. In addition, two
modes of ritual exclusion were developed: the 'ship of fools', where the
insane were entrusted to sailors of chartered ships and dropped off in
uninhabited places; and pilgrimages to holy places in the hope of recovery.
In the Renaissance period, the previous exclusionary practices were
replaced by a philosophy of confinement or separation. The 'great
confinement' of indigent, old, and physically and mentally disabled began
in mid-seventeenth century Paris. The purposes of the great 'hospitals' of
Salpêtrière and Bicêtre were economic, social, and moral. They were
intended to increase manufactures, to provide productive work, and to end
unemployment; to punish idleness, restore public order, and remove
beggars; and to relieve the needy, ill, and suffering while providing
Christian instruction.

The true birth of the asylum occurred toward the end of the eighteenth
century when the distinctive qualities of madness led to a call for separate
institutions for the insane. At Bicêtre, for example, the reformer Philippe
Pinel began the classification of patients and institutional space to calculate
needs, observe symptoms, and establish treatment. In England, the
principles of 'moral treatment' led to further classification and isolation of
patients, with concomitant change in hospital asylum architecture. During
the nineteenth century, there was a large-scale expansion of asylums
throughout Europe and North America, representing a decisive assumption
of direct state responsibility for mental health care. This expansion took
the form of massive hospital structures situated on extensive rural campuses.
Once again, a spatial exclusion was being practised, albeit with an entirely
defensible rationale for facilitating patient cure.

By the mid-twentieth century, asylums were overcrowded and were
reduced, in the majority of instances, to purely custodial care. Then, in
the 1950s, a revolution in mental health care occurred. This was the time
when a strong thrust toward a community-based mental health care was
being experienced. The pressure for a community-based care derived from
several sources, more especially the burgeoning evidence of the ill-effects
of extended hospital confinement on the patient, and the counterbelief
that a community-based care would aid in the normalization of the

mentally ill. At the same time, large advances in chemotherapy enabled the effective treatment and symptomatic management of chronic patients, without the need for confinement. These changes were sanctioned by government intervention, on a cost-sharing basis, to promote a nonasylum-based community mental health care. In both Canada and the USA, an infusion of federal funds enabled local officials to shift the fiscal burden of the cost of care, while simultaneously satisfying contemporary psychiatric and civil rights philosophies. The effect of the shift away from asylums to the community has been profound. In the USA, for instance, there were 559 000 patients in state and county hospitals in 1955; this dropped to 193 000 by 1975. The majority of patient care episodes now occur in community mental health facilities.

In short, the isolation of clients is still practised, but a new spatial partitioning has been devised, based in the 'community'. The partitioning uses spatial separation to control the clients of the psychiatric apparatus, so that the roles and activities within the larger social environment become manageable. Thus the social need for client treatment and differentiation has been translated into a policy of community-based isolationism.

3.3 Client

Upon deinstitutionalization, the person who is or has been mentally ill faces enormous challenges in everyday life. Many former patients view the prospect of discharge with sheer terror; in many cases they have simply not been provided with the skills that would enable them to cope outside the hospital. They face problems of social isolation, finding a job and a home, severe financial difficulties, and coping with their ongoing psychiatric and social service needs. In a survey of ex-psychiatric patients in the downtown core of Hamilton, Ontario, Dear et al (1980, pages 35–37) found echoes of all these difficulties in the ex-patients' own comments. On isolation: "I don't like going home [to my family] because as soon as I get there, everyone goes out and leaves me there alone"; and on housing: "It's hard to find a place to live—people avoid me". On coping with the apparatus of the psychiatric and social services, the ex-patients were vocal and specific in their opinions: "The psychiatric attention I get is not adequate. I feel funny after medication. They only cut down on medication; they don't explain anything; they keep secrets. .... I feel I'm being taken advantage of because of my situation. I took 35 or 40 shock treatments. I co-operated with the doctors when I didn't know what they were doing to me. .... I feel that the attention I get is almost excessive at times".

Similar problems are encountered by ex-patients in psychiatric ghettos throughout Ontario and Canada. A recent examination of one Toronto neighborhood incidates that most people live on welfare cheques of $258 per month (1982); room and board take up 90% of this. In this extreme poverty, an individual must fight to cope in the community, along with

the 14000 other patients who are discharged annually in Toronto. The
ex-patient's response is typically one of "rage at every misfortune that led
me here, rage at the doctors, the treatments, the pills. Rage at myself,
my weakness, my poverty" (quoted in Siggins, 1982, page 10).

The response of a significant number of ex-patients has been to
'ghettoize'. Ghettoization is an informal process of spatial filtering,
whereby a mobile minority (25%-50%) of the more severely disordered
discharged individuals gravitate toward areas of transient accommodation
in the core areas of Canadian and US cities. In effect, some aspects of the
hospital ward are being recreated in the inner city—a kind of asylum
without walls. The most significant impetus behind this agglomeration is
the search for a social support network. Many studies have suggested that
it is in the ghetto that ex-patients find help in the search for jobs and
homes, can locate other support facilities, begin or renew friendships, start
self-help groups, and operate newsletters. In short, the ghetto is very
functional for ex-patients; it is a spatially limited zone where individual
support is made possible through proximity. For the clients, the inner
city has become a coping mechanism.

3.4 Community
The success or failure of a community-based mental health care will
largely depend upon the community's attitudes toward the mentally ill.
Research on attitudes suggests that there exists a contradictory mixture of
sympathy and rejection. On one hand, we sympathize with the 'sick'
person in need of care; on the other, we seek to maintain our social
distance from the social outcast who manifests deviant behavior. This
confusion of motives was evident in a survey of community attitudes
toward mental illness (Dear and Taylor, 1982). Opinions about mental
illness resolved into four attitudinal dimensions: (a) authoritarianism,
which implied a view of the mentally ill as an inferior class requiring
coercive handling; (b) benevolence, a paternalistic kindly view of patients,
derived from humanistic and religious principles; (c) social restrictiveness,
viewing the mentally ill as a threat to society; and (d) a community
mental health ideology, representing an anti-institution bias in the care of
the mentally ill.

Little is known about the qualities which make for a good 'host' for a
community-based mental health service. It is generally acknowledged,
however, that successful resocialization of the mentally ill will require a
certain input from the community members. These services may include
assistance in shopping, or even home visits. Segal and Aviram (1978)
suggest that, for the chronic patient, the social support system offered by
an institution may best suit the rehabilitative needs of the client. For
others, however, there is a great potential for totally integrating the client
into the community. Segal and Aviram have determined three basic
components which act to produce a positive integration. In order of

importance, these are: (1) community characteristics, including positive response of neighbors; (2) resident characteristics, including client satisfaction with living arrangement and therapy, and control over financial arrangements; and (3) facility characteristics, including the facility as an ideal psychiatric environment and the integration of clients with residents from the external community.

The mentally ill, like other minority social groups, such as the poor, are restricted in their selection of residence, workplace, and recreational outlets. Their continued isolation can be interpreted as part of a wider system of sociospatial organization which causes the separation of antagonistic groups. Thus, just as the processes of residential differentiation cause the appearance of class- and ethnically-separated neighborhoods, so similar processes tend to isolate and exclude the mentally ill. The community which is in opposition to mental health employs two direct sources of power to exclude the mentally ill: the power of sociospatial exclusion; and the power of state authority, as manifest through planning policy (see next section).

The power of sociospatial exclusion operates at two separate levels: the individual and the group levels. First, the mentally disabled person is subject to a series of informal and formal exclusionary forces operating at the individual level. Informally, a mental disability often tends to make the individual distinguishable in a social setting. Moreover, individuals have been observed to make personal behavioral adjustments to exclude the offending individual. More formally, organizational exclusion can occur, as when an individual is disciplined for aberrant behavior in the workplace. Second, and more important for present purposes, is the set of mechanisms of group exclusion. This refers to the generic ability of communities to exclude undesirable or noxious objects and people from their neighborhoods. Several strategies may be used by communities to place 'social distance' between them and the mentally ill. These include formal strategies, for example, the use of legal (especially zoning) ordinances, and informal strategies, for instance, physical abuse of facility or client.

If it is true that a limited environment of social resources has a significant impact on one's life chances, then it is evident that the household has an enormous stake in the local environment. Hence the need becomes paramount to protect one's environment from any undesirable negative impact. It seems likely that the entrance of the mentally disabled into a community is perceived as a threat to the environmental resource base of the neighborhood, and hence of the market capacities contained within it. Accordingly, the community's power for spatial exclusion is often marshalled to protect its 'turf' from the incursion of the mentally ill.

3.5 Planners

Urban planners have responded to increasing community opposition by developing locational strategies which minimize conflict over facility siting decisions. Most of these conflict-minimizing strategies have tended to reinforce the trends toward isolation and exclusion evidenced in the behavior of the community, client, and health professional.

In broad terms, phase one of the planners' strategy was aimed at *containment of opposition.* The locational search was directed toward sites where opposition could be manipulated through one of two siting strategies. The first of these is the 'fly-by-night' approach, whereby a facility is opened by stealth, without informing the host neighborhood. The hope is that by the time the facility's presence is discovered, the community will realize that any fears it might have conjured up were groundless. A second strategy has been called the 'low-profile' approach, in which an attempt is made to educate and persuade the host community to accept the facility before it is opened. The low-profile approach may target community leaders, or could take the form of a more general public awareness campaign (through mailings, public meetings, and so on). Needless to say, both the fly-by-night and the low-profile approaches are not risk free; in fact, if such strategies are perceived as subterfuge by the host community, the potential for inciting a most vitriolic opposition is great.

It was because of the unpredictable outcomes of the containment strategies that a second phase of siting approaches was developed. These may be termed *risk aversion* strategies. These had, as their objective, the complete avoidance of any siting conflict. And, since such conflict typically arose around the need to apply for a zoning variance (mental health facilities usually breached strict land-use/zoning regulations when sited in residential areas), planners next sought out areas where such variances were not needed. Of course, such opposition-free sites proliferated in the mixed land-use/zoning districts typical of our inner cities. As a consequence, during this period, a large proportion of mental health facilities were sited in the core areas.

The most interesting recent developments in planning strategy have occurred in the third phase of policy formulation. This has seen the growth of a movement for *'fair-share zoning'*. Many host communities perceived themselves becoming 'saturated' with mental health facilities, with other neighborhoods having none. Thus, community opposition developed in neighborhoods which felt they were being asked to shoulder more than their 'fair share' of the caring burden. In many areas (for example, New York State), local zoning ordinances were passed to prevent further mental health facilities from opening in overburdened communities. It was then only a matter of time before the cry to 'open up the suburbs' to mental health facilities was heard, and the fair-share zoning or zoning 'as-of-right' movement was born.

So far, fair-share zoning has had only a small impact on siting strategies. Even if suburban properties were to be made available, they are typically beyond the pocket of, and have less access to core services for, the ex-psychiatric patient. Moreover, somewhat belatedly, planners are beginning to realize the positive aspects of the ghetto for ex-patients. For the moment, the future of the ghetto is on hold, although, already, some ghettos are being subjected to slow attrition (through gentrification, etc; compare Wolch and Gabriel, 1983).

3.6 Summary
The ghettoization of ex-psychiatric patients in the public city is a common sociospatial outcome of the complex interplay among four agents who are part of the mental health care system. Each of these agents uses space purposively to affect the required social structuring. The psychiatric professional uses state-sanctioned principles of isolation and exclusion for treatment. The client undergoes an informal spatial filtering in search of a social support mechanism and establishes a coping mechanism in the inner city. The community seeks to protect its turf through the processes of residential differentiation. And the planners use their state-sanctioned power to ensure conflict-free siting decisions. All four agents, taken together, act to create an inexorable force for ghettoization, thus resulting in a single empirical phenomenon which satisfies a host of sociospatial imperatives.

The public city ghetto, and other types of spatial manifestations of social process, are only temporary resolutions of the sociospatial dialectic. As social relations evolve, so do their spatial expressions (as in the example of gentrification of the ghetto). Equally importantly, the peculiar spatial structures which have evolved have a reflexive impact on the character of social relations. For instance, the development of the public city has had the effect of raising community awareness of the dilemmas of mental health care and of changing community attitudes; it has also had a major impact on the quality of life of the ex-psychiatric patient and has caused, in several jurisdictions, a significant reallocation of expenditures on welfare services.

4 Retrospect and prospect
The assessment of the discipline of health services planning presented in this paper has emphasized two major theoretical positions: first, that a social theoretic view stresses that population health is a function of the wider social context within which the health care system is embedded; and second, that specific health outcomes are determined by the way in which key actors impinge upon the technical problem of health service provision. A third conclusion is more substantive in its emphasis, and this refers to the role of space in the creation and perpetuation of the social relations of psychiatry.

In prospect, the implications of this assessment are profound. I am advocating a realignment of the discipline's traditional concern with three separate research themes (disease ecology, access and optimal system design, and administrative organization). I would replace these with a single integrated approach which emphasizes the origin and evolution of the health system, its organization and practice, and the politics of health care delivery. In the specific example of this paper, the following issues in the social theory of psychiatry were raised: the statization of the profession of psychiatry and the evolution of community mental health care as part of the restructuring of the welfare state; the inner city as a coping mechanism, the everyday experience of illness, and the effect of both on client health outcomes; the pattern of community acceptance and rejection and its impact on health outcomes; and the planning apparatus's role in residential differentiation and in the supply of health care (that is, the presence or absence of a facility in a neighborhood).

Many other significant research issues are raised by the social theoretic approach. For example, we have only briefly touched on the role of self-reproduction and iatrogenesis as determinants of the supply of health care, on the growth of medical corporatism, and on the impact of the state on the social relations of health care. (These issues have all received some attention in the literature: for example, see Doyal, 1980; Mohan, chapter 7 in this volume; Navarro, 1976; Starr, 1982.) In addition, the whole question of an appropriate social theory for health systems is relatively underdeveloped (see Giddens, 1981; Thrift, 1983). One can only hope that, in the future, more researchers can be persuaded to abandon the comfort of the well-defined well-illuminated mainstream research traditions to search in murkier areas for the key to health services planning.

References

Clark G L, Dear M, 1984 *State Apparatus: The Structures and Language of Legitimacy* (George Allen and Unwin, Hemel Hempstead, Herts) forthcoming

Dear M, 1981, "Social and spatial reproduction of the mentally ill" in *Urbanization and Urban Planning in Capitalist Society* Eds M Dear, A J Scott (Methuen, London) pp 481-497

Dear M, Bayne L, Boyd G, Callaghan E, Goldstein E, 1980 *Coping in the Community: The Needs of Ex-psychiatric Patients* (Canadian Mental Health Association, Hamilton, Ontario)

Dear M, Taylor S M, 1982 *Not on our Street: Community Attitudes to Mental Health Care* (Pion, London)

Donabedian A, 1973 *Aspects of Medical Care Administration: Specifying Requirements for Health Care* (Harvard University Press, Cambridge, MA)

Doyal L, 1980 *The Political Economy of Health* (Pluto Press, London)

Drury P, 1983, "Some spatial aspects of health service developments: the British experience" *Progress in Human Geography* 7 60-77

Foucault M, 1977 *Discipline and Punish: The Birth of the Prison* (Pantheon Books, New York)

Giddens A, 1981 *A Contemporary Critique of Historical Materialism* (Macmillan, London)

Mayer J D, 1982, "Relations between the traditions of medical geography: health systems planning and geographical epidemiology" *Progress in Human Geography* 6 216-230

Meade M S (Ed.), 1980 *Conceptual and Methodological Issues in Medical Geography* (University of North Carolina Press, Chapel Hill, NC)

Navarro V, 1976 *Medicine under Capitalism* (Prodist, New York)

Pyle G F, 1979 *Applied Medical Geography* (John Wiley, New York)

Rosenberg M, 1983, "Accessibility of health care: a North American perspective" *Progress in Human Geography* 7 78-87

Segal S P, Aviram U, 1978 *The Mentally Ill in Community-based Sheltered Care* (John Wiley, New York)

Siggins M, 1982, "Madness in South Parkdale" *Today Magazine* 6 March, pp 6-10

Starr P, 1982 *The Social Transformation of American Medicine* (Basic Books, New York)

Thrift N, 1983, "On the determination of social action in space and time" *Environment and Planning D: Society and Space* 1 23-58

Townsend P, Davidson N, 1982 *Inequalities in Health: The Black Report* (Penguin Books, Harmondsworth, Middx)

Wolch J R, Gabriel S A, 1983, "Development and decline of service-dependent population ghettos" research paper, School of Urban and Regional Planning, University of Southern California, Los Angeles, CA 90007, USA

Modelling for Health Services Planning: an Outline and an Example

M CLARKE, A G WILSON
University of Leeds

1 Introduction

Health services, at a broad level, have the same characteristics as most other services. There is a demand (or expression of need) from a population, facilities are supplied, and there is some matching or allocation of the demand to the facilities. Since demand and supply are spatially separated, the planning task can be seen as a location–allocation problem: the location of facilities and the allocation of people from residences to particular facilities. (For a valuable review of the range of location–allocation problems, see Leonardi, 1981; for a general framework for studying service sectors, see Wilson, 1983.) However, we wish to emphasise from the outset that the conventional regional science approach is inadequate. There are few possibilities for the relocation of infrastructure or developments on new sites, and so the policy focus often lies outside the conventional location–allocation approach.

Our task in this paper is to explore the range of modelling methods which can be brought to bear on the health services to provide an adequate analytical base for planning purposes. This will then help us to generate alternative plans and to test the impact of these plans. We need to produce evaluation indicators which will provide the basis for policymaking and monitoring. We will see that the full range of modelling techniques (for example, as described in Wilson, 1981) can be brought to bear, but that, as is usually the case, it is the particularities of the service being considered which provide much of the interest. We need to devote much preliminary attention, therefore, to the adequate description of the health service, rather than assuming that it takes some standard form.

The strategy for the paper will therefore be as follows. In section 2, we review the planning tasks (and associated problems) as they are perceived *at different scales* in the British health service (though we expect the ideas to be more widely applicable). We then examine (in section 3), in broad terms, the techniques which are available for modelling, and we include a review of model outputs which can provide a major contribution to *information systems* for planning. We also, briefly, review other applications of modelling ideas in the light of our own framework. In section 4, we present a more detailed example to illustrate our own ideas: the modelling and planning of hospital services within a district health authority. We offer some concluding comments, particularly about priorities for further research, in section 5.

One final point in this introductory section refers both to the *multi-*disciplinary nature of much health service planning research and to the need for an *inter*disciplinary approach. A brief checklist of disciplines that address planning problems in the health service would include *at least* the following: health economics, social policy, geography, operations research, community medicine, and accountancy. However, it is very rare that these disciplinary approaches are integrated into a unified framework. We would see this integration as a first step towards producing better planning frameworks and models and encouraging the wider collection, dissemination, and use of information in planning. We shall argue in this paper that through adopting a systems analytic approach we can draw on the contributions from different fields in a coherent manner.

2 Planning and problem solving in the health services
2.1 Introduction
As with many service sectors, the nature of the problem looks different at different spatial scales. We begin, therefore, by sketching the nature of the resource allocation and planning system as it now operates for the British health service (subsection 2.2). We then review some problems and associated planning tasks (subsection 2.3) and summarise the requirements to be sought from an associated analytical capability (subsection 2.4). Throughout the argument, we are conscious that health service policy-making is contentious and far from entirely a technical matter. We also need, therefore, as a background, to provide some understanding of the social processes involved and of the ways in which these are changing.

2.2 Resource allocation and planning at different scales
It is undoubtedly an important principle of resource allocation that it can be efficiently made only to a relatively small number of units, though what this number should be is a matter for speculation (and research?). In Britain, there are now three tiers of health service government, following a reorganisation which was implemented in April 1982, and we focus on this rather than the earlier history. For completeness, we should also note that there is an upper tier allocation from total government funds (represented by the Treasury) to the appropriate Ministry, in this case the Department of Health and Social Security (DHSS). The DHSS then allocates to regional health authorities (RHAs), and each region to district health authorities (DHAs). There are fourteen RHAs in England and varying numbers of districts within each region—in Yorkshire, for example, there are sixteen districts. There are 193 districts in England, with an average population of around 230000.

The allocations from the DHSS to regions is essentially financial and is formula-based (DHSS, 1976); this is also the case for the allocations from regions to districts (though there are some regionally supplied services— such as ambulance services—and some regional or subregional specialities, neither of which could be efficiently supported in particular districts).

The operational management and planning of health services is at the district level. There are then important scales within the district level—the creation of administrative units, for example, which are the basis of resource allocations within a district. According to district size, these may represent different kinds of services—for example, community and hospital—or groups of hospitals within subareas of the district.

For this system to work, there must be an adequate flow of information in both directions (compare, for example, the concept of Lange-Lerner planning described in Wilson, 1981, chapter 9). Part of the task of modelling, therefore, is to contribute to information systems at various scales which will improve this flow.

For the purposes of this paper, we focus mainly on planning tasks at the district scale because it is here that we need to establish indicators which also form the basis for those which can be used at regional and national scales.

2.3 Problems and associated planning tasks

We have seen that, between the major levels of the health service, the major planning tasks are associated with budget allocations. For many years, these allocations were made on the basis of adjustments to historical allocations and on the whole, there was enough growth to ensure that at least the most obvious new developments were implemented. In 1976, this changed at the upper tiers, as a result of proposals made by the Resource Allocation Working Party (RAWP) (DHSS, 1976). It has been recognised that earlier procedures were producing allocations which were obviously inequitable: the most powerful teaching hospitals, for example, were relatively overfunded. The RAWP Report proposed a formula basis, which was then implemented with a phased progression towards RAWP targets. It is also possible to use the RAWP formula for the allocations from regions to districts, though it is interesting that many regions are now finding this inadequate (NAHA, 1983).

At the lower levels, within a district, the process of adjusting historical budgets still predominates. There are a number of possible reasons for this. First, it may well be in the interest of the most powerful groups (hospital consultants in certain specialties?) for this to continue to be the case. Second, the moves in other public sectors towards corporate planning, and the explicit formulation of objectives which form the basis for budget changes, have had little impact in the health services. Third, and this may be a partial explanation for the second reason, there are inadequate indicators on which policy can be based. This may be seen as a conceptual problem: an inability to devise appropriate indicators. Fourth (and 'fuel' for the third reason), there is insufficient elementary data. This will emerge at a number of points in our discussion on modelling, but a particular example is the inadequacy of cost data, which obviously inhibits both policymaking and monitoring.

This situation is bound to change soon, for at least two reasons. First, even with relatively rough and ready indicators, the Black Report (Townsend and Davidson, 1982) found inequities and inadequacies, which will begin to force reappraisal. Second, there is no longer enough growth money to fund obvious new developments. Indeed, the budgets of some DHAs are now being cut in real terms. This means that the historical allocations have to be scrutinised, and resources clawed back for problem solving and the implementation of new developments. For this to be achieved, however, there must be a solution to some of the technical problems mentioned above: a better data base and better indicators, both integrated into an information system.

One of the most significant developments, in terms of management information systems in the NHS, will come with the implementation of the recommendations of the Körner Committee (DHSS, 1982). Amongst other things, Körner has proposed the setting up of a computerised patient administration system at the district level. This should provide district administrators with a much better picture of the way in which their care systems function. At the present time most information processing is undertaken by the region, and requests for special tabulations of information can often take a considerable period of time to be processed.

Within a district, the allocation of the budget between services and facilities can only be adequate if based on an intimate knowledge of the various modes of operation. In effect, it is necessary to know in detail the production functions of each element of the district system: the outputs which can be achieved for given (costed) resource inputs. This is necessary in the first place to demonstrate that each element is operating as efficiently as possible; and second, because this is the data out of which evaluation indicators can (in part) be constructed and used as the basis of policy appraisal. Against this background, typical planning problems can be identified at different scales within a district.

At the broadest scale, the budget has to be allocated between major sectors (units), say hospitals, on the one hand, and community services, on the other. For a number of years, government policy has been to try to improve the position of the community services, but this has been difficult because of the historically-based procedures. There are some interesting interdependencies too. If insufficient money is spent on services for the elderly in the community, there is likely to be an increase in the number of geriatric patients in hospitals. The cost of these alternatives need to be weighed against each other and set against the relevant benefits.

There are, potentially, some classic location problems. Where should a major new hospital go? What should be the spatial distribution of accident and emergency facilities? The first type of problem is relatively rare. The building of major new hospitals can not often be afforded and, when one is built, the choice of sites is usually restricted to land already owned by the health authority. Hence the use of classic location–allocation methods becomes redundant. The second illustrates a much more common type of problem: given the existing set of hospital buildings, how should specialities be distributed across them? For a given building, how should it be utilised; that is, what mix of specialities?

This may be viewed purely as a management problem with little spatial input. However, it can be shown that these types of decisions often have important spatial ramifications, in terms of who gets what and where and who does not (see Clarke and Williams, 1982). For example, the reduction of the number of beds available in a certain speciality may well lead to an increase in the waiting list. As a consequence, GPs (general practitioners) may respond by referring patients to other hospitals, perhaps outside the district. This may entail longer and more costly journeys for the individual involved.

At finer scales, there are other problems of a stochastic nature. A method of assigning beds to a speciality, for example, sometimes defines 'territory' which is not efficiently used. Careful planning of modes of operation is necessary to achieve an effective degree of flexibility.

We have already mentioned the need to be efficient within any particular element of the service. This means the effective planning of combinations of resource inputs in each case.

Finally, we note the problem of allocating patients to services. Quite often, there are alternative modes of care or treatment—as we saw in the case of the elderly, described already. These alternatives need to be articulated carefully, and the costs and benefits weighed. Typically, it will be appropriate to provide a mix in each case; 'variety' may be better than a simple view of the 'best'.

We also need to note that the nature of the strategic planning problems change, both with the changing needs of the population and with the alternative ways in which care may be provided. For example, the number of elderly persons (aged seventy-five years and over) in England is projected to increase from 2.348 millions in 1975 to 2.967 millions in 1991, an increase of over 26%, and the eighty-five years and over group is projected to increase by 33% (OPCS, 1978). This clearly implies an increase in demand for services for the elderly over the country as a whole. How this will reflect itself at the district level clearly depends on existing population distributions and future change. Hence districts need access to population forecasts produced at the appropriate spatial scale. Alternative forms of care and treatment may be considered for these elderly patients as policies and priorities change. We return to this question in section 4.

In section 4, we present the models which form the basis for tackling many of these problems within the context of a DHA. We should emphasise that it is important to generate a framework which is comprehensive and not simply designed to tackle particular and visible problems, the so-called disjointed incrementalist approach. In conclusion, we should also note that there are other problems that are regional or subregional (but multidistrict) which can be tackled using similar ideas to those we present at the district level. This is an issue to which we return in section 5.

Before proceeding to the examples in section 4, we now turn to a broad review of the techniques which are available for modelling.

3 Approaches to modelling

3.1 The main elements

The broad framework for a model system is shown in figure 1. The need or demand for health services is obtained by applying morbidity rates to a population model. The supply can be seen as the manipulation of resource inputs to generate outputs (such as bed-days) by speciality in a facility at a location. These are costed, and the three boxes in the top right-hand corner of the figure constitute a representation of production functions. The allocation involves two stages (which may be executed simultaneously): first, the assignment of an ill patient to a speciality (and possibly to one of several alternative modes of treatment within or between specialities), and second, to a particular facility at a location.

All approaches will contain these elements in some form or other. In the next subsection (3.2), we briefly review the range of techniques available, and then, in subsection 3.3, examine the range of approaches adopted in the literature. We outline our own approach in subsection 3.4, before presenting the model in detail in section 4.

3.2 The techniques available

At the outset we can note that there is a wide range of techniques that we can call upon to assist in the analysis and planning of health services. For convenience we can divide these into three groups: locational methods, management methods, and methods from systems analysis. There is a review of the basic techniques which can be used for modelling in locational analysis in Wilson (1981). All have some role to play here, but, as we shall see, there is also a substantial part for systems analysis in a broader sense.

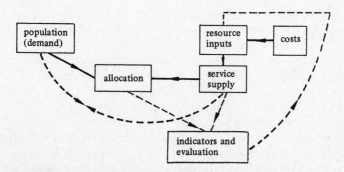

Figure 1. Framework for a model system.

It is likely that, in many cases, spatial interaction models will be useful, first to allocate users to services in at least some instances, and second, in association with embedding theorems, to help in the formulation of optimum plans. The concepts of accounting are also important, particularly in the building of a comprehensive model. This will enable us to keep track of all patients, resources, and money; will ensure consistency in the models; and will provide much of the basis for an information system. Optimisation methods are likely to be relevant in only a limited way in location problems, as noted earlier, at least in terms of the location of major facilities, because the resources for new buildings on new sites will not usually be available. There may be a possibility of formulating, as a mathematical programme, the problem of assigning specialities to existing buildings, but this depends on an in-depth understanding of the non-linearities of the cost functions involved. The techniques of network analysis will not usually be relevant except possibly for detailed planning of specific service sectors, like the ambulance service (although the methods have been applied, for example, to the allocation of specialities within a district by Duncan and Noble, 1979).

Finally, there is the possibility of using recently developed methods of dynamical analysis to analyse the structural stability of spatial configurations and to test this against likely future changes. It will also be of crucial importance to build a detailed dynamic population model to predict changing demand patterns, and one effective way of doing this is through the microsimulation methodology.

To implement any of the models implied by the availability of these methods, it will be necessary to put a lot of effort into conventional systems analysis. First, we will need a detailed understanding of the elements of the system, particularly, for example, the nature of the cost function. A second example, to which we shall return, is the detailed analysis of the process of allocation of patients to facilities. Of all the techniques discussed, therefore, it is likely that it is the concepts of accounting which will turn out to be the most important in this context.

3.3 Previous applications of modelling methods
In this section we discuss a range of existing modelling applications in health service planning. By necessity the review is selective, but, in any case, a number of extensive accounts are already available (for example, Boldy, 1976; 1980; Shigan, 1978). Here we take the opportunity to comment on some of the modelling applications, in relation to our earlier comments in section 2 of this chapter, and to identify areas for further research. The framework around which this section is organised is presented in table 1, which is focused on allocation problems at a number of different spatial and temporal scales. The examples and references quoted are each illustrative of a particular approach and are by no means exhaustive. We consider each of the different types of allocation problem in turn.

Table 1. Examples of different types of allocation problems in health services research.

Allocation: of/to	Spatial/ unit scale	Temporal scale	Example and reference
resources/regions	national-regional	annual	Resource Allocation Working Party (DHSS, 1976)
resources/specialities	administrative unit	annual	DRAM (Hughes and Wierzbian, 1980)
physical infrastructure, hospitals, ambulance stations)/locations	administrative unit	strategic	location-allocation (Mayhew and Leonardi, 1981)
groups of patients/ alternative types of service	administrative unit	annual	balance of care models (McDonald et al, 1974)
individuals/care types	administrative/ hospital unit	annual	list processing (Clarke and Prentice, 1982)
groups of patients by location/hospitals	administrative unit	annual	spatial interaction models (Riley, 1982)
costs/specialities	hospital	annual	statistical estimation (Ashford et al, 1981)

3.3.1 *Resources to regions*

As we have already noted, since the introduction of the RAWP method of allocating resources between regions, an attempt has been made towards reducing the gross inequities in the overall distribution of resources across the country. Although not strictly a modelling exercise in itself, the RAWP method is formula-based and represents an attempt to quantify the resources provided to regions in relation to their needs. This was to be achieved by comparing the age and sex distributions of regions and through the use of standard mortality ratios (SMRs). It was decided against using morbidity statistics relating to illness and to concentrate on the cause of death in regions. It can be argued, of course, that this decision is inadequate, but it largely stems from the lack of adequate data on morbidity, a topic to which we return in section 5. Rather than provide a detailed critique of the RAWP method (since we can refer the reader to the chapter by Bevan and Spencer in this volume), we consider two points only. First, for any revenue equalisation system to work, the necessary political and managerial desire for it to work must exist. Second, if it does work, the majority of complaints will come from those who lose relatively and they will be critical of the methodology used. This implies that, although the methodology for allocating vast sums of money must be relatively sophisticated, it must be well understood. (The same comment applies to the Rate Support Grant in the allocation of resources to local authorities in this country.) The crucial point remains, however, that there is a lack of information about the definition of, and specification of, need.

3.3.2 *Resources to specialities*

The problem of allocating resources to specialities within an administrative unit has attracted much attention (for a review, see Gibbs, 1977). Again, we find problems with defining need and with the relationship between demand and the supply of services. It has been pointed out by several authors (for example, Feldstein, 1967) that there is an intimate relationship between the amount of services provided and the apparent need for that service. As the amount of service provided increases, so, it is argued, does the demand, although clearly there is an upper limit at which saturation is achieved. Much research needs to be undertaken in this area to ascertain exactly what processes are at work.

Perhaps the most notable contribution to resource allocation at this scale has come from the International Institute for Applied Systems Analysis (IIASA) health care systems team (for example, Aspden, 1980; Gibbs, 1978; Hughes, 1978). Their set of models has addressed the allocation of resources to specialities at a number of levels. However, in the implementation of these models, a number of problems have been faced—in particular, the nature of the representation of the supply side. As we have already noted, the specification of an appropriate, more detailed, production function at this level would be a major advance.

3.3.3 *Physical infrastructure to locations*

This group of methods comes under the classic location–allocation umbrella, widely developed in regional science. These models developed out of management science methods, such as the warehouse location and travelling salesman problems. The appropriateness of public facility location methods has not often been called into question, perhaps because there are few real applications. Although the methodology has improved, and a greater deal of realism can be incorporated into the models (for example, Brotchie et al, 1980; Wilson et al, 1981), whether they are the best analytic tools for the practical problems encountered in facility location issues in the health service remains doubtful (as Leonardi, 1981, hinted in his review). One of the original reasons for developing location–allocation models was the so-called combinatorial problem—there was such a high variety of possible alternative locations and configurations, it was argued, that only a computerised search mechanism could find the best alternative. But this may have arisen because we have a particularly simplistic view of the nature of planning issues, as expressed in these models, and it is this that results in such combinatorially rich specifications. It is more likely that, because of the constraints inherent in the planning process (for example, in terms of sites available), very few alternative designs or system configurations ever become feasible options (see Clarke and Williams, 1982).

If location–allocation models are of use, it is probably in informing planners how the existing provision of services differs from an optimal one (suitably defined). Procedures for incremental change may then be adopted.

3.3.4 *Groups of patients to alternative forms of care*
As we noted earlier, one of the most pressing problems in the health
service is the provision of different packages of care to certain client
groups, particularly the elderly. For these groups of patients the problems
are often multifaceted, but require separate attention. For example, a
frail elderly person living at home may need a home help, a visiting nurse
and chiropodist, and meals on wheels. There is often the choice as to
whether the patient requires residential care (and all these services provided
at one location), hospital care (for some specific condition), or day care.
An added complication is that these services are not provided by a single
administrative authority, but usually by two or more. And typically the
amount of need in the community will always exceed available supply.
   Here we have a classic regional science problem, characterised by
complexity, spatial trade-offs, interdependence, and a large number of
constraints. As yet, however, little progress has been made in tackling it.
The 'balance of care' model developed by McDonald et al (1974) is a
notable exception and is now finding application within the health service
(for example, Mooney, 1978, along with Boldy and Howell, 1980).
Contributions from regional scientists would be useful additions to the
small number of developments in this area.

3.3.5 *Individuals to care types*
Assuming we have developed an overall strategy for allocating resources
at the macrolevel within a health authority, how do we decide which
individuals get particular forms of care? For many services this is a
straightforward issue (for instance, a patient with appendicitis is admitted
to general surgery), but for the sorts of care packages described above,
where the attributes of both the patient and the service need to be
considered, the matter is not so clear cut. One feature of the current
system is that many geriatric patients are occupying acute-care hospital
beds for long periods when they would be better located elsewhere.
   What is needed is an approach that relates the individuals' attributes to
care packages, and a method for achieving this has been outlined by
Clarke and Prentice (1982). This was based around defining an index of
need for individuals and relating this to the total need as a whole. The
derivation of the index was to be undertaken subjectively by medical and
administrative staff, and an allocation of need to supply performed. The
effects of defining different indices of need could then be explored and
different allocations derived. The planner could then assess the implications
of different outcomes and pick the one that was thought most desirable.

3.3.6 *Groups of patients to hospitals*
Under this heading we consider the use of spatial interaction models in
allocating patients to hospitals. Examples of the approach include Mayhew
and Leonardi (1981), Riley (1982), and Clarke (1983). In these studies
(and others), origin zones are defined on the basis of some administrative

units, and destination 'zones' are either individual hospitals or health authorities. Either distance, travel time, or cost is used as the 'cost matrix'. In the normal gravity model tradition, it is assumed there is a trade-off between the amount or quality of services offered at a location and the 'difficulty' in travelling to that destination in relation to other alternatives. Most applications of the models have produced good estimates of flow patterns compared with observed data. This, however, is to be expected. It is when the models are used in a forecasting role that their applicability may be less good. This is because these models do not recognise the fine structure of the patient admission and administration system. In Britain the majority of individuals arrive at hospital after first consulting their GP. It is almost always the case that the GP will make the decision as to where to refer the patient. Before the patient is admitted, he or she may visit a consultant's outpatient clinic one or more times. Direct inpatients are often taken by ambulance to the nearest facility at which treatment can be provided. To assume that a patient has some elasticity of travel demand in relation to many types of treatment seems inappropriate. However, at coarse levels of resolution, spatial interaction models may still give a reasonable description of these flows 'on average'. For a further and more detailed discussion of the use of spatial interaction models in health care planning, see Clarke (1983).

3.3.7 Costs to specialities
One area of health service planning that is attracting a great deal of attention is the determination, at a fairly detailed level, of the costs of providing certain forms of care. This is particularly the case for acute-care hospital services (for a bibliography, see Forte, 1982). Two approaches seem to have developed in this area: first, an accounting approach that attempts to identify the factor inputs into a service, and then cost them (for example, McGee and Osmolski, 1979); and second, a statistical approach that attempts to estimate speciality costs from available information using statistical methods (for instance, Ashford et al, 1981; Coverdale et al, 1980). There is no doubt that this area of research will grow in the future and that its output will serve as important inputs to other types of modelling approaches.

4 A simulation model of a district health authority
4.1 Introduction
In this section we present the details of a simulation model of the hospital services provided at the district level. The principal aim of the modelling exercise is to provide planners with a tool that will help explore the consequences of various policy proposals in relation to strategic planning issues. In this chapter we can briefly discuss the main features of the model only, and for further details we refer the reader to Clarke and Spowage (1982; 1983). Our philosophy in constructing the model outlined here has been to develop a tool of general applicability, both in a

spatial sense (it could be used in other districts, providing the appropriate information was available) and in a disciplinary sense (the output from the model would be of use to different groups of people within an authority (for example, the treasurer's department, unit administrators, the district management team, planners, and so on). The model has been designed, therefore, so that it can address a wide range of planning issues. This contrasts with some of the more specialised modelling exercises we reviewed in the previous section. We could also add a belief that interdependence has important effects in large complex systems; this is another advantage of a comprehensive approach.

The application we describe in this section has been constructed in cooperation, initially with the Kirkless Area Health Authority and more recently with the Dewsbury District Health Authority. To a large extent we have used data that are either published in official publications or are collected by the authority as a matter of course (for example, hospital activity analysis data). However, in certain cases data has not been available at the district level, and recourse to either national or regional data has been necessary.

The model consists of four main components. First, we have a model of population dynamics in which we annually update the characteristics of the district population. Second, a morbidity model converts these characteristics into demand or need for hospital care. Third, there is a model of the supply side, which represents the type and amount of care that can be provided at various locations for different conditions and client groups. Finally there is an allocation model which allocates need to supply and generates a set of indicators, in terms both of care provided and of resources consumed. We describe each of these in turn and present some early results from our work.

No attempt is made within the existing framework to embed any optimisation methods. We believe that it may be possible to construct a fairly crude mathematical programming model for the allocation of resources between important groups of services (for example, between acute and community care, or between hospitals). We also believe that operations research methods are an important tool for a number of management issues. Both these approaches could be built into our existing set of models (for details, see Clarke and Prentice, 1982, and Wilson and Clarke, 1982). However, we are also of the opinion that it is useful to construct models that allow planners to explore the consequences of their decisions in some detail. The approach outlined here allows for this possibility.

4.2 Population dynamics
The population component of the model consists of two parts. First, we generate synthetically a sample of individuals and households, together with their associated attributes that we consider to be of interest. Second, using microsimulation methods, we update successively the attributes of this sample for each year of the simulation exercise.

The reasons for specifying a population at the microlevel have been justified elsewhere (Clarke and Spowage, 1982; Williams and Clarke, 1983), but a brief summary of these points is useful at this stage. In considering the need for health care, a large number of individual factors may be relevant. Obviously, age and sex are prime contributors to morbidity differentials in the population, but factors such as marital status, location, occupation, household structure, and so on may also be of importance, as may be the interrelationship between these variables. In addition, in addressing the issue of population dynamics, we may wish to focus on the *variability* between individuals and households, in terms of the way in which this affects the various transitions between states. All these factors imply that the representation of the factors in our model will be an important issue. A microlevel representation is a highly efficient method for handling variability and interdependence, particularly because, in most cases, only a sample of the population is required to represent the full range of information about the population, and, because, compared with the traditional occupancy matrix, it contains no zero entries.

A microlevel representation of the population involves generating lists of individual and household attributes for a sample of the population. An example of this is given in table 2. Two methods for deriving these lists can be considered. First, we could sample from the population in an authority, but this would usually prove expensive in time and resources. An alternative is to use statistical synthesising techniques to generate a joint probability distribution of household and individual attributes from which a population can be sampled using Monte Carlo methods. The method involves generating this joint distribution in such a way as to be consistent with any available information on the conditional and marginal distributions of attributes. These may be obtained from sources, such as the Census, The Family Expenditure Survey, the General Household Survey, and so on. For a full description of the theory of the method, see Clarke and Williams (1983) or McFadden et al (1977).

In our application we employed this synthetic sampling approach, making considerable use of the 1981 Census, in addition to other sources. A list of attributes generated is given in table 3. In tables 4, 5, and 6, we present some comparative results between the model outputs and known distributions for Kirklees in 1981. These were generated using a sample size of 5000 households, representing about 13000 individuals. Table 4 contains the observed and predicted age and sex distributions, and, considering that some data used in generating this distribution was for 1971 (the 10% household data from the 1981 Census was not available at the time of writing), the distribution is reasonable. Tenure split, shown in table 5, is almost exactly right, and the spatial distribution of population (table 6) also shows a close matching. None of the 'actual' distributions in these tables were direct inputs to the model structure.

Table 2. Example of microlevel specification.

Number of households in previous list	Label	Age cohort	Age	Sex	Marital status	Race	Educational status and occupational class	Number of weeks worked in previous year	Annual wage	Wage trajectory	Full-time (1) or part-time (0) job
1	1058.1	4	30	male	divorced	white	3, 11	52	5110.11	1.40	1
2	2069.1	2	21	male	single	white	2, 19	0	0.00	0.00	0
3	2187.1	3	25	male	married	white	4, 16	52	4842.06	1.27	1
3	2187.2	2	23	female	married	white	4, 3	52	3635.18	1.11	1
4	2206.1	8	54	male	married	white	4, 3	52	8914.73	1.25	1
4	2206.2	9	55	female	married	white	2, 3	52	7567.65	1.05	1
4	2206.3	3	28	female	single	white	2, 21	52	0.00	0.00	0
4	2206.4	4	33	male	single	white	2, 16	52	4069.80	0.98	1
4	2206.5	1	20	male	single	white	2, 21	0	0.00	0.00	0
5	2728.1	7	46	male	married	white	4, 11	52	3461.27	0.91	1
5	2728.2	6	41	female	married	white	2, 18	52	4225.86	1.24	1
5	2728.3	2	21	female	single	white	2, 6	52	3875.89	1.22	1
6	3031.1	11	69	male	married	white	4, 20	0	0.00	0.00	0
6	3031.2	10	60	female	married	white	4, 21	0	0.00	0.00	0
7	3039.1	7	46	male	married	white	2, 14	52	6804.96	1.34	1
7	3039.2	6	42	female	married	white	3, 7	52	5142.55	1.28	1
7	3039.3	1	12	female	single	white	1, 0	0	0.00	0.00	0
8	4092.1	6	44	male	divorced	white	3, 9	52	7495.00	1.33	1
9	4107.1	4	34	female	divorced	black	4, 20	0	0.00	0.00	0
9	4107.2	1	7	male	single	black	1, 0	0	0.00	0.00	0
10	4521.1	7	45	male	married	white	3, 15	52	3693.00	0.91	1
10	4521.2	6	42	female	married	white	3, 20	—	—	—	—
10	4521.3	1	11	female	single	white	1, 0	—	—	—	—
10	4521.4	1	7	female	single	white	1, 0	—	—	—	—

Given an initial population, one of our modelling tasks is to update its characteristics each year of a (say) ten-year period. We have already noted some key demographic trends, and, with the next census not scheduled until 1991, it is essential that we attempt to model demographic change during this period. To achieve this we employ a microsimulation model; we test whether each individual or household is eligible for certain demographic transitions and then determine whether they occur, again using Monte Carlo sampling. To run the model, we require information on the conditional probability of an event (birth or death, whatever) taking place as a function of certain individual or household attributes, such as age, sex, marital status, race, and so on. Much of this is obtainable from published data, though often not at the appropriate spatial scale.

Given that we can obtain these conditional probabilities in one form or another, we can process each individual and household on our list through a series of events. The following events are considered for each eligible household and individual: birth, death, marriage, divorce, net out-migration, leaving home, residential relocation, labour market transitions (retirement, redundancy, school leaving, job change, reentering labour market). For a full discussion of the model used, see Clarke and Spowage (1982).

Table 3. Initial population attributes and classification.

Attributes	Classification
Household	
Label	Not applicable
Sex of head of household	Male, female
Marital status of head of household	Single, married, widowed, divorced
Household size	1–10
Number of children	1–8
Tenure	Owner-occupied, public-sector or privately rented
Location	Twenty-four Kirklees wards
Socioeconomic group of head of household	I–IV
Household income	Sum of individuals' income plus benefits
Individual	
Label	Not applicable
Age	Absolute age
Age cohort	Fifteen age cohorts
Sex	Male, female
Marital status	Single, married, widowed, divorced
Country of birth	UK, Irish Republic, India, Pakistan, Carribean, Rest of the World
Occupation	1–18 occupation groups, unemployed and not in the labour force, retired
Educational status	1–4, based on age at leaving full-time education (15, 16, 18, 21 plus)
Annual income	Derived from wage model and based on age, occupation, sex

Table 4. Age and sex distribution for Kirklees, 1981 (sample size = 13 000).

Age range	Values for males		Values for females	
	observed	predicted	observed	predicted
0–19	32.04	30.47	28.44	27.57
20–24	7.34	6.80	6.84	7.46
25–29	7.04	6.62	6.39	6.65
30–34	7.86	7.91	7.40	7.74
35–39	6.56	6.70	5.99	6.27
40–44	5.96	6.64	5.43	5.68
45–49	5.47	5.88	5.09	5.22
50–54	5.57	6.03	5.38	5.53
55–59	5.82	5.62	5.60	4.94
60–64	4.90	5.16	5.14	5.28
65–69	4.42	4.42	5.29	5.11
70–74	3.44	3.20	4.83	4.18
75 plus	3.56	4.55	7.68	8.37

Table 5. Tenure distribution for Kirklees, 1981: observed and predicted values (sample size = 13 000).

Type of tenure	Observed values	Predicted values
Owner-occupier	63.96	63.72
Council rented	26.23	26.33
Other	9.81	9.95

Table 6. Distribution of population between census wards in Kirklees, 1981 (sample size = 13 000).

Ward	Values		Ward	Values	
	observed	predicted		observed	predicted
1	4.41	4.33	13	2.94	2.70
2	4.25	4.23	14	4.91	4.79
3	4.57	4.42	15	5.09	5.08
4	3.66	3.42	16	3.77	3.83
5	3.32	3.47	17	5.40	5.62
6	3.44	3.37	18	3.50	3.82
7	3.76	3.80	19	2.35	2.56
8	4.46	4.59	20	3.64	3.82
9	4.74	4.99	21	4.29	4.42
10	5.18	4.82	22	3.60	3.61
11	4.60	4.25	23	5.74	5.84
12	3.33	3.03	24	5.03	5.19

4.3 Health care demand: a morbidity model

We have outlined in the previous section how we deal with generating a sample population and ageing it over time. We now turn to discuss how we model the demand for health care, restricting ourselves to hospital services at this stage, and, in particular, to inpatient treatment. This discussion follows Clarke and Spowage (1983). Agreeing upon what is meant by 'the demand for health care' is extremely problematic, not to mention attempting to construct a model of it. A range of studies have attempted to identify the factors that influence the variations in demand for health care between different groups of individuals, between and within different regions of a country and so on. One very important distinction to make is between revealed demand and latent demand. Revealed demand is a measure of the number of people who received treatment for a particular condition: latent demand can be defined as the number of people with a certain condition, identified as such by the health system *or not*, who require treatment according to some predetermined criteria. The problem is that, in using revealed demand as a measure of need, we ignore those requiring treatment but not being diagnosed. Many studies (notably Feldstein, 1967) have commented on the relationship between demand for treatment and the supply of care facilities. They note that, as the level of supply increases, as measured say by the number of beds provided, there is an almost inexorable rise in demand. However, the demand they are considering is revealed demand, not latent demand. Without entering into a medical debate, it may be argued that latent demand for treatment is fairly constant[1], especially over the sort of time scales we are considering, and the important factor to investigate is the way in which this latent demand is transformed through diagnosis, new forms of treatment, and so on, into revealed demand. This is clearly a complex phenomenon outside the scope of this paper.

There is a diverse number of ways by which an individual may arrive at a hospital for treatment. In figure 2, we outline the main flows under consideration. We distinguish between these various flows for the following reasons. First, there are clear differences between many of them. The referral system, by which an individual originally consults his GP and, depending on the outcome, is referred to one of several medical channels of treatment, is a very different process than say the accident and emergency system. When it comes to examining policy options and identifying controllable variables, this distinction becomes important. A second factor relates to data availability. The Hospital Inpatient Inquiry[2], a major source of information on health care, provides information only on revealed demand—that is, individuals who receive treatment in hospitals.

---

[1] For example, just as many individuals may have been deemed suitable for a heart transplant twenty years ago as today.

[2] This is an annual one-in-ten sample of all hospital inpatients in England and Wales.

However, we are more interested in the general morbidity characteristics
of the population, together with information on the referral system. This
then allows policy options, such as alternative treatment types, to be
examined. The only comprehensive morbidity data available for England
and Wales is contained in two publications—*Morbidity Statistics from
General Practice, 1970-71* and *1971-72* (DHSS, 1978; 1979). These
include data on all visits to a small sample of GPs in the respective years.
From these data it is possible to generate conditions and outcomes (in terms
of referrals) for individuals on the basis of age and sex, but only at a
national level. We supplement this data with local data where appropriate.
More specifically, the morbidity data give us two useful types of information:
(1) The number of episodes, consultations, and persons for each of twenty-
six diagnostic groups by age and sex (shown in table 7). Episodes are the
medical events—from first consultation to 'discharge'. Consultations are the
number of visits by a patient to a GP, and persons are the number of
individuals involved. This information allows us to introduce multiple
events into our model—this acknowledges that a person may be ill with
the same condition more than once in a year.
(2) The outcomes of visits to GPs, by condition. The following rates are
identified for each condition:
(a) referral rate—percentage of all patients referred for a given condition;
(b) inpatient rate;
(c) outpatient rate;
(d) investigation rate;

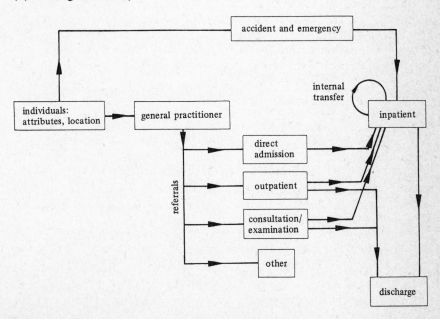

Figure 2. Examples of flows in the patient-hospital interface.

(e) local authority informed rate; and

(f) other.

Thus we can sample for each individual the outcome of a visit to a GP. The nature of the condition and the outcome would then become extra individual attributes. In the present model we allow for up to three conditions being identified in any year.

However, these morbidity data provide us with information on only a subset, albeit a large one, of all the demand for hospital services. As can be seen from figure 2, not all patients arrive via the referral system: accident and emergencies typically form a significant proportion of inpatient flows. For these flows we must return to health district data, where information on accident and emergency admissions is available. The additional flows in figure 2, such as transfers, we also obtain from local data.

It can be seen from figure 2 that not all of the possible flows in this system have been identified. For example, inpatients who become out-patients are ignored. This is because at this stage of model development we restrict ourselves to inpatient care. In addition, in the first simulation period, we will have to account for the existing waiting list, which we obtain from the health authority, by speciality.

The full morbidity model is outlined in figure 3. One important aspect of this framework is transferring morbidity conditions into demand for treatment in a speciality. Clearly, an individual with a certain condition

Table 7. Diagnostic conditions (ICD classification).

DG [a]	Description	DG [a]	Description
1	Infective and parasitic diseases	16	Male genital disorders
2	Neoplasms (malignant)	17	Diseases of breast and of female
3	Neoplasms of lymphatic		genital system
4	Benign neoplasms	18	Conditions of pregnancy,
5	Endocrine, nutritional,		childbirth, and puerperium
	and metabolic diseases	19	Diseases of skin and of
6	Diseases of blood		subcutaneous tissue
	and of blood-forming organs	20	Diseases of musculoskeletal
7	Mental disorders		system and of connective tissue
8	Diseases of nervous system	21	Congenital anomalies
9	Diseases of eye	22	Certain causes of perinatal
10	Diseases of ear and mastoid		morbidity
	processes	23	Symptoms and ill-defined
11	Rheumatic fever, hypertensive		conditions
	disease, and heart disease	24	Fractures, dislocations,
12	Diseases of peripheral circulatory		sprains
	system	25	Other injuries and reactions
13	Diseases of respiratory system	26	Persons without current
14	Diseases of digestive system		complaint or sickness
15	Diseases of urinary system		

[a] Diagnostic group.

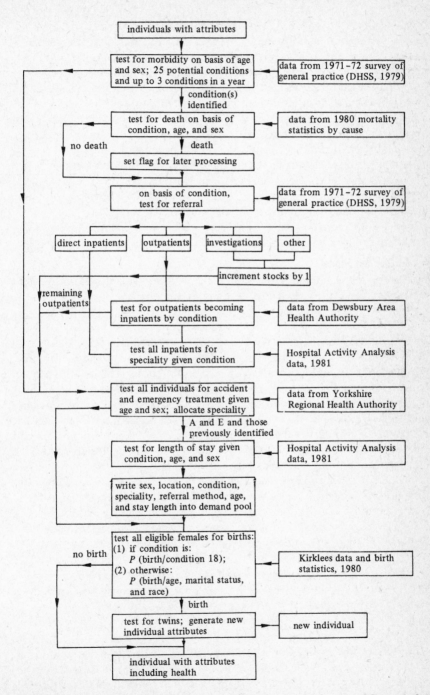

Figure 3. Morbidity model (P is the probability of giving birth; A and E stands for accident and emergency).

(say a malignant neoplasm) could be treated in either general medicine, general surgery, or radiotherapy. Also, in some districts where a certain speciality may not exist, people, who in other areas may get treated within that speciality, may get treatment in general medicine or surgery. The data for performing this transformation from condition to speciality is obtainable at a district level from hospital activity analysis.

Of course, an extra component of demand arises from those individuals living outside the area but receiving treatment within the area. These cross-boundary flows may form a significant proportion of demand for certain specialities (for example, in Kirklees, 17.3% of adult patients treated for mental illness at Storthes Hall Hospital came from outside the area) when a regional speciality is located in an area. With reorganisation in April 1982 and the scrapping of the area health authorities, the proportion of cross-boundary flows between the new authorities can be expected to increase, just as their size has decreased.

4.4 Supply-side model

In constructing a model of the supply side of the hospital system, we are faced with the complicated task of determining how the various inputs into a hospital, in terms of manpower and resources of different types, are transformed into the provision of medical care of various forms. Many direct analogies can be seen with an input–output framework. The 'final demand' may be the provision of bed-days for a given speciality. In effect, we have to articulate a complex production function. This relationship between supply and inputs is clearly not linear: sometimes a marginal increase in supply can be provided with few resources implications (when there is some slack in the system), but on other occasions a small increase in supply may imply a substantial increase in inputs (for example, if a new consultant had to be appointed). In addition, in certain situations an increase in one input (say beds provided) will only allow more care to be provided if the appropriate range of other inputs is increased (say operating theatre time available). This is why we often find in summary statistics specialities with low bed-occupancy rates, yet long waiting lists.

The costings of resource inputs, in terms of say the inpatient costs per bed-day, by speciality and by hospital, is an important task. As we noted in section 3, much work has been undertaken in recent years to develop methods for achieving costings. For our own purposes we have developed an accounting framework that utilises all published information on district costings to derive bed-day costs (the method is fully described in Forte and Wilson, 1983). For each inpatient we are then able to determine the total cost of inpatient treatment.

In our current model we have not, as yet, built in a full representation of the supply side: we focus on bed-days, supplied by speciality and by hospital, and we trace the underlying accounts linking these to resource inputs and costs. We regard the extension of this side of the modelling effort as the next major task.

4.5 The demand–supply interface

In allocating demand to supply at the area or district level, extensive use has been made of hospital activity analysis (HAA) data. In particular, the mapping of patients' conditions (and speciality) into a particular facility will depend very much on local factors. The demand component of the allocation procedure consists of the following main groups:

(a) Direct inpatients: we assume that all patients in this category have their demand satisfied.

(b) Accident and emergency patients: once again, we assume that patients in this category are directly admitted.

(c) Outpatients who become inpatients: the majority of patients in this category are either placed on the waiting list or become 'booked and planned' patients.

(d) Waiting list: this consists of two separate components—the beginning of year list and those who get added to it during the year. We assume that those who have been waiting the longest with a given condition, assigned to a speciality, get treated first.

(e) Inflows from outside districts: as the figures on these are an expression of revealed demand, we assume that all patients get treated.

(f) Internal transfers: the probability of an inpatient being transferred once admitted is taken from HAA data.

The allocation procedure is outlined in figure 4 (and discussed in greater detail in Clarke and Spowage, 1983). Once a patient has been assigned a

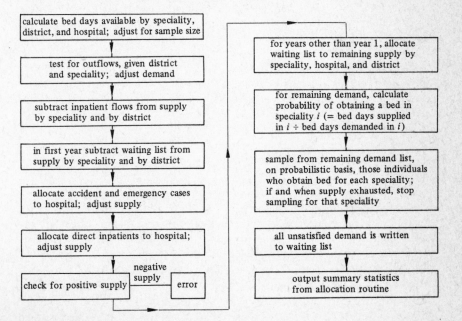

Figure 4. Allocation model.

bed the probability of being admitted to a certain hospital is derived (from HAA data) and the length of stay determined on the basis of condition, age, and sex. That number of bed days is subtracted from the total available supply. If no supply is available, the patient is admitted to an alternative location, if available, or if not, put on the waiting list. For each inpatient, the cost of treatment is calculated from our speciality costing data. When all potential demand has been processed a variety of summary statistics are output.

We can recall from our earlier discussion of the microsimulation approach that the information stored within the list processing representation could be cross classified in any way required. This allows for a large number of

Table 8. Inpatient demand by condition.

DG[a]	Age range: from/to										Total
	0/1	2/4	5/14	15/24	25/34	35/44	45/54	55/64	65/74	75 plus	
Males											
1	20	20	20	30	30	10	0	0	0	0	132
2	10	0	0	0	0	30	30	0	10	20	101
3	0	0	0	0	0	0	0	0	0	0	0
4	0	10	0	0	10	30	0	10	0	0	61
5	10	0	0	0	10	10	0	10	30	10	81
6	0	10	0	0	0	30	0	20	0	0	61
7	0	30	20	41	20	10	30	20	0	20	193
8	0	0	20	20	10	0	20	0	0	10	81
9	0	20	10	30	10	10	20	10	20	20	152
10	0	10	0	10	0	0	0	0	0	0	20
11	0	0	0	10	30	10	112	112	101	122	497
12	0	0	20	20	0	20	51	81	20	71	284
13	41	91	101	61	51	71	41	61	61	20	599
14	20	51	112	142	173	101	71	71	0	51	792
15	0	0	20	10	0	51	0	20	41	20	162
16	20	30	10	20	0	10	10	20	10	0	132
17	0	0	0	0	0	0	0	0	0	0	0
18	0	0	0	0	0	0	0	0	0	0	0
19	0	10	0	20	41	41	10	10	0	10	142
20	0	0	0	61	41	81	61	112	20	41	416
21	10	0	20	10	10	0	0	10	0	0	61
22	254	0	0	0	0	0	0	0	0	0	254
23	30	20	112	51	71	61	91	51	20	30	538
24	0	20	20	20	0	10	0	0	20	0	91
25	10	10	51	142	152	91	10	91	10	0	568
26	10	0	0	10	0	20	10	0	0	0	51

[a] For diagnostic group descriptions, see table 7.

indicators to be produced, and we discuss the implications for their use in
planning in section 5. A number of examples of these are presented in
tables 8, 9, 10, 11, and 12. In table 8, we present the number of
inpatients by condition, age, and sex for the first simulation period.
Table 9 is the cross-classification of conditions by speciality, again for the
first year, and table 10 contains the types of operation for each of twelve
specialities. Turning now to resource implications, in table 11 we present
the cost by hospital and by speciality in the first year, and in table 12 the
distribution of costs by age and sex for the same period. We emphasise
that these are only illustrative at this stage as further model development
is in progress.

Table 8 (continued)

DG[a]	Age range: from/to										Total
	0/1	2/4	5/14	15/24	25/34	35/44	45/54	55/64	65/74	75 plus	
Females											
1	20	51	30	10	10	20	20	20	10	10	203
2	0	0	0	10	51	41	41	41	20	41	244
3	0	0	0	0	0	0	0	0	0	10	10
4	0	10	0	10	20	61	20	10	10	10	152
5	10	0	0	10	30	0	10	30	0	10	101
6	0	10	0	30	30	0	71	41	41	51	274
7	10	10	10	20	71	0	41	0	30	30	223
8	10	20	0	10	0	10	20	10	10	10	101
9	10	20	0	0	10	20	10	0	0	20	91
10	0	10	10	0	0	0	0	0	0	0	20
11	0	0	0	10	0	0	30	61	91	244	436
12	10	0	10	20	71	61	10	30	71	152	436
13	20	41	51	30	20	51	20	101	51	91	477
14	41	20	30	61	152	112	101	41	30	61	649
15	10	20	0	0	10	20	30	20	10	20	142
16	0	0	0	0	0	0	0	0	0	0	0
17	0	0	20	274	213	173	142	142	10	10	984
18	0	0	0	101	81	41	0	0	0	0	223
19	10	0	10	41	10	20	10	10	41	20	173
20	0	0	0	51	61	91	112	71	71	81	538
21	10	0	0	10	0	0	0	0	0	0	20
22	304	0	0	0	0	0	0	0	0	0	304
23	20	30	61	71	112	101	71	30	10	81	589
24	0	0	0	0	0	0	0	10	30	81	122
25	0	30	81	152	51	61	61	20	10	91	558
26	0	10	0	51	30	41	10	0	0	0	142

[a] For diagnostic group descriptions, see table 7.

Table 9. Speciality by condition (excluding obstetrics).

DG [a]	Speciality [b]										
	1	2	3	4	5	6	7	8	9	10	11
1	101	132	0	0	61	0	0	10	10	20	0
2	51	10	0	20	213	0	0	0	51	0	0
3	0	0	0	0	0	0	10	0	0	0	0
4	0	0	0	0	152	0	20	0	41	0	0
5	61	20	0	30	30	0	10	0	20	0	10
6	122	20	0	41	91	0	0	0	61	0	0
7	233	61	0	81	10	0	10	0	0	0	20
8	71	51	0	20	0	0	41	0	0	0	0
9	0	0	0	0	0	0	0	244	0	0	0
10	10	30	0	0	0	0	0	0	0	0	0
11	426	0	0	233	0	0	0	0	0	0	274
12	183	20	0	213	254	20	0	10	10	0	10
13	507	355	0	122	10	71	0	0	0	0	10
14	81	30	0	20	1248	0	0	0	41	0	20
15	10	30	0	0	233	0	0	0	30	0	0
16	0	0	0	0	132	0	0	0	0	0	0
17	0	0	0	0	183	0	0	0	802	0	0
18	0	0	0	0	0	0	0	0	223	0	0
19	0	10	142	0	61	0	101	0	0	0	0
20	10	0	0	91	10	0	842	0	0	0	0
21	0	0	0	0	41	0	20	0	0	20	0
22	0	41	0	0	0	0	0	0	0	518	0
23	162	61	0	10	680	0	30	20	112	30	20
24	0	0	0	0	0	0	213	0	0	0	0
25	375	41	10	10	375	30	203	71	10	0	0
26	0	20	0	0	30	0	10	0	132	0	0

[a] For diagnostic group descriptions, see table 7.

[b] 1, general medicine; 2, paediatrics; 3, dermatology; 4, geriatrics; 5, general surgery; 6, ear, nose, and throat; 7, orthopaedic surgery; 8, ophthalmology; 9, gynaecology; 10, special care; 11, coronary care.

Table 10. Types of operation by speciality (excluding obstetrics).

Surgical operation [a]	Speciality [b]										
	1	2	3	4	5	6	7	8	9	10	11
1	0	0	0	0	0	0	41	0	0	0	0
2	0	0	0	0	20	0	0	0	0	0	0
3	0	0	0	0	0	0	0	254	0	0	0
4	0	0	0	0	0	122	0	0	0	0	0
5	0	0	0	0	10	0	0	0	0	0	0
6	0	0	0	0	0	0	0	0	0	0	0
7	0	0	0	0	112	0	0	0	0	0	0
8	20	0	0	0	1116	0	0	0	71	0	0
9	0	0	0	0	213	0	0	0	71	0	0
10	0	0	0	0	213	0	0	0	0	0	0
11	0	0	0	0	41	0	0	0	964	0	0
12	0	0	0	0	10	0	0	0	284	0	0
13	0	0	0	0	10	0	741	0	0	0	0
14	0	0	0	0	122	0	0	0	0	0	0
15	0	0	0	0	20	0	132	0	0	0	0
16	30	10	0	0	183	0	10	0	0	0	0
17	0	0	0	0	51	0	203	0	61	0	0
Total	51	10	0	0	2121	122	1126	254	1451	0	0

[a] 1, nervous system; 2, endocrine system; 3, eye; 4, ear, nose, and throat; 5, upper alimentary tract; 6, thorax (with heart and lungs); 7, breast; 8, abdomen; 9, urinary system; 10, male genital organs; 11, female genital organs; 12, obstetrics; 13, orthopaedic; 14, peripheral vessels; 15, skin and subcutaneous tissue; 16, other surgical procedures; 17, nonoperative procedures.
[b] For speciality descriptions, see table 9.

Table 11. Cost, in thousands of pounds, by hospital and speciality (excluding obstetrics).

Speciality [a]	Hospital [b]					
	1	2	3	4	5	6
1	1111.1	1241.9	0.0	0.0	0.0	0.0
2	0.0	425.2	0.0	0.0	0.0	0.0
3	158.8	0.0	0.0	0.0	0.0	0.0
4	0.0	924.4	60.6	0.0	526.5	185.0
5	521.0	1071.5	0.0	0.0	0.0	0.0
6	0.0	0.0	0.0	31.5	0.0	0.0
7	0.0	0.0	123.4	1652.1	0.0	0.0
8	102.7	0.0	0.0	0.0	0.0	0.0
9	185.9	430.2	0.0	0.0	0.0	0.0
10	0.0	290.2	0.0	0.0	0.0	0.0
11	0.0	242.5	0.0	0.0	0.0	0.0
Total	2079.5	4625.9	183.9	1683.7	526.5	185.0

[a] For speciality descriptions, see table 9.
[b] For reasons of confidentiality, hospitals are not identified by name.

Table 12. Cost, in thousands of pounds, by age group, sex, and speciality (excluding obstetrics).

Speciality (defined in table 9)	Age range										Total
	0–1	2–4	5–14	15–24	25–34	35–44	45–54	55–64	65–74	75 plus	
Males											
1	0.0	0.0	1.3	266.1	100.0	110.4	63.7	179.9	430.7	175.1	
2	63.9	108.6	59.9	10.1	0.0	0.0	0.0	0.0	0.0	0.0	
3	0.0	0.0	0.0	3.9	8.4	41.3	16.1	24.5	0.0	9.0	
4	0.0	0.0	0.0	0.0	0.0	0.0	0.0	32.0	42.7	321.8	
5	10.7	13.6	41.3	105.7	106.1	139.4	38.5	123.5	34.0	94.6	
6	0.0	0.0	3.8	5.7	1.0	4.8	0.0	0.0	0.0	0.0	
7	0.0	36.2	31.7	53.1	46.9	77.8	99.1	158.9	85.6	63.6	
8	0.0	2.2	1.1	7.1	4.9	16.5	4.9	5.5	9.3	14.3	
9	0.0	0.0	0.0	0.0	0.0	0.0	0.0	0.0	0.0	0.0	
10	216.1	0.0	0.0	0.0	0.0	0.0	0.0	0.0	0.0	0.0	
11	0.0	0.0	0.0	0.0	27.4	9.1	49.7	26.4	30.4	0.0	
Total	290.8	160.5	139.1	451.8	294.6	399.3	272.1	550.7	632.9	678.4	3870.1
Females											
1	0.0	0.0	0.0	42.9	49.4	93.3	125.6	207.8	92.1	414.6	
2	41.6	75.1	66.0	0.0	0.0	0.0	0.0	0.0	0.0	0.0	
3	5.2	0.0	7.1	0.0	0.0	13.6	0.0	0.0	4.5	25.2	
4	0.0	0.0	0.0	0.0	0.0	0.0	0.0	194.2	148.8	956.9	
5	4.3	13.5	25.9	121.9	153.2	119.0	107.0	107.4	81.6	151.3	
6	0.0	0.0	1.0	0.0	3.8	7.6	0.0	3.8	0.0	0.0	
7	0.0	8.0	0.7	43.7	49.5	69.7	86.3	128.3	217.2	519.3	
8	1.6	2.2	0.0	0.0	0.5	4.4	3.8	0.0	0.0	24.2	
9	0.0	0.0	3.0	222.2	130.8	119.3	52.3	57.8	0.0	17.1	
10	74.1	0.0	0.0	0.0	0.0	0.0	0.0	0.0	0.0	0.0	
11	0.0	0.0	0.0	7.1	5.1	11.2	47.7	10.1	18.3	0.0	
Total	126.8	98.7	103.7	437.8	392.4	438.1	422.8	709.5	576.1	2108.6	5414.4

4.6 Summary
We have briefly outlined an approach to modelling inpatient care in a DHA. The model could certainly be extended to other forms of care, perhaps most importantly to look at joint-care issues where the relevance of alternative packages of care is most noticeable. The fact that many assumptions had to be made concerning the way in which the inpatient system operates reflects the lack of information available about the health care system. It is often argued that if more information was made available there would be no use for it. This is certainly not the case, but there is something of a chicken and egg situation operating here. Effective planning models have not been widely disseminated, and often the reason for this is the lack of adequate information. It is then argued that because there is little *use* for systematic information processing, there is therefore little incentive to devote resources towards producing it. We show in the next section that, given adequate data and model outputs, we can construct an interesting range of indicators which have substantial uses in planning.

5 The operation of a model system for planning: conclusions and directions for further research

5.1 Information and planning: an overview
In this section we examine the use of information in health service planning and management, once again, mainly concentrating on acute care. This is done in the context of the current concern with the generation and use of information and indicators in the NHS, and we aim to show how model development can make a major contribution. As we have already mentioned, in recent years we have witnessed the evolution of the RAWP system for allocation of resources to regions and the Black Report on inequalities within the NHS. Both these reports were heavily reliant on the use of indicators as expressions of need, inequity, overprovision, and so on. At the district level, waiting lists and overall budgets have traditionally been the main general policy indicators which have been used. There is now pressure for authorities to use a much wider range. This arises from the annual review each district has with its region; from the scrutiny of DHSS auditors, who develop their own indicators—for example, on operating theatre costs; and from other national pressure— for example, the list of indicators suggested in the recent government paper entitled *Health Care and Its Costs* (DHSS, 1983). In the short run, indicators have to be obtained from available data; in the longer run, we have the report of the Körner Committee (DHSS, 1982), which has set out to examine what range of information should be collected by the NHS for different components of the overall care system, and, as we will see later, this will improve data bases for the construction of indicators.

All these developments have occurred in parallel with the rapid growth of information technology—the development of capacity to handle information—together with the changing foci of concern, outlined in section 2, within the health service planning system.

At the outset, it is useful to distinguish between the collection and generation of data and information and the use of that information in planning. For some time now a vast amount of information has been collected on hospital inpatients, their conditions, their treatment, and their outcomes, both through the HAA surveys and through the one-in-ten sample collected for the Hospital Inpatient Inquiry.

However, relatively little use of this information is made by decision-makers at the district level. Some important indicators are derived, such as waiting lists, average lengths of stay, occupancy rates, and so on, and these are (usefully) compared with previous years' figures, those of other districts, and regional averages. What has only recently begun to emerge is a move towards performance indicators which more explicitly relate the care provided to the level of resource inputs and the needs of the community. *Health Care and Its Costs* (DHSS, 1983) represents a step towards this, but only a preliminary one.

What is clearly a first requirement for an information system is a framework into which it can be embedded. Figure 5 provides a useful starting point in this respect.

The objectives that an authority adopts will relate to the existing provision of services, the perceived level of current and future need, and the resources at its disposal. These objectives will be translated into resource allocations to various sectors of the health care system. Resources are then used to provide various types of care. This utilisation will take the form both of capital and of revenue expenditure. The resources provided through this process (buildings and equipment, staff, and medical supplies, for example) are translated into a care system to meet identified need. The combination of inputs, and the way in which they are managed, will determine precisely how the demand for care is met and the outcomes produced. These can then be compared with the objectives set out at the beginning of this cycle.

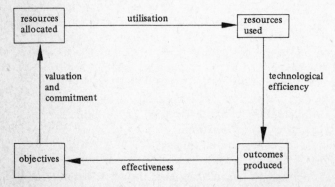

Figure 5. A planning framework (source: Calvert, 1980).

There are two uses of this framework. First, it demonstrates how a modelling approach can be useful in determining how far policies (resource allocations) meet objectives. Second, it demonstrates how different types of information are required at various stages in this process. For example, if we wish to improve throughput in a particular speciality, we need to know how a marginal increase in resources will manifest itself in increased levels of service supply. As we have emphasised throughout this chapter unless we have detailed knowledge of the production functions of the specialties concerned, this will be a difficult goal to achieve. This level of detail is still not achieved in *Health Care and Its Costs*. Another important point is that indicators of outcomes will have to be derived in the same language or form as the objectives that are set—or vice versa—for obvious comparative reasons.

This has at least two implications for planners. Objectives must be stated in terms that are susceptible to assessment, rather than bland statements of intent. Second, more thought must be put into the design of indicators that allow an objective assessment of success or failure in this respect, as opposed to crude indicators such as waiting lists by speciality.

We now argue that these general problems can be tackled more effectively using the kind of model we sketched in section 4; we turn to this topic in the next subsection.

5.2 Models and information systems for health services planning

The first point to note is that the use of a model system such as that outlined in section 4 is compatible with the scheme sketched in figure 5. Objectives are formulated in the light of outcomes—as represented by a set of indicators; resources are allocated and deployed by a set of management decisions (the y variables of our earlier paper—Wilson and Clarke, 1982); the outcomes of this deployment of resources can be calculated in the model. In effect, the model adds a lot of detail to figure 5, and it is to this that we now turn.

The deployment of resources in all forms constitutes a detailed specification of the state of the supply side of the health care system. This, together with some parts of the model, adds up to a specification of a set of production functions: given the resource inputs, what can each speciality (or whatever) offer—in terms of inpatient bed-days per annum? The demand side of the model represents a set of needs to be allocated to this supply. The allocation submodel matches demand to supply, estimates waiting lists or surplus bed-days, and so on.

The simplest use of the model is therefore to compute, for a set of resource inputs, a set of indicators which describes the outcomes—the matching of demand and supply. The policymakers of an authority can then use the model to explore the effects of changing the pattern of resource inputs. Really, it should be possible to do this in an interactive mode with the computer. We should also add that, in some cases (perhaps particularly at the interdistrict scale), it should be possible to embed this system within an optimising framework, so that it is possible to offer—at least as guidance—a 'best' disposition of resources.

It is misleading, however, to imply that this kind of model-based planning system is simple to build or necessarily simple to use. We therefore structure the rest of this discussion in this subsection as follows: first, we examine and emphasise the increased detail of a model-based indicator set relative to more conventional alternatives; second, we discuss some of the complexities of these procedures in practice; third, we discuss the liaison aspects of this kind of planning; and fourth, we summarise the discussion in terms of the kind of planning framework implied.

5.2.1 Indicators as the basis for an information system

The first point to emphasise is that on the one hand, the resource inputs are all costed—at least with the appropriate unit or average costs—and, on the other, the demand side is represented by a realistic population of individuals. And there is a detailed connection from each side of the model to the other. No information is lost and so summary indicators can be much more detailed than is the case if raw data is used. We can illustrate this by comparing what is possible with our particular model-based system with the kinds of indicators listed in *Health Care and Its Costs* (DHSS, 1983). We restrict ourselves to acute hospital services. In *Health Care and Its Costs*, these indicators are broken down into three categories: activity, financial, and manpower. The activity indicators are by very broad speciality groups (medicine, surgical, etc), and we would hope to have much more detail. Then there are numbers of admissions, average length of stay, measures of bed occupancy, and waiting lists, among others. We could break these down by residential location, social class, occupation, or whatever for finer speciality groups and we could connect these activity measures explicitly to the supply side and hence give unit costs. The financial indicators are obtained by hospital category: costs per day, per case by hospital, etc. Again, we aim to produce speciality costs and to be able to relate these to the unit of resource inputs and the unit costs of these in each case. This gives a better basis for judging likely direction of change. The manpower indicators are to a major extent concerned with nursing staff per inpatient day and so on. We would hope to be able to cover all categories of staff, because we use this information as part of our costs model. So again, everything connects: we can give nursing requirements by speciality by hospital and cost them and say which patients (by *their* characteristics) they are working for.

In effect, we have a comprehensive and detailed accounting system which keeps track of resources, money, supply units, and allocations to demand, and retains all the connections between them.

5.2.2 *Some complications*

The scheme sketched out above represents a kind of cost-effectiveness analysis—with the evaluation of effectiveness ultimately left to judgement when the indicator sets are appraised. This would represent a considerable improvement on present practices. However, we should recognise that we need to pursue notions of marginal or opportunity cost where relevant, instead of simply average costs worked out from annual budgets or whatever. In some cases, it might be possible to tackle more explicitly the task of benefit measurement.

The model in its present form will often build in apparent indivisibilities—like the assignment of a ward of so many beds to a particular speciality—which should be considered to be variable. In other words, for instance in the allocation of beds to specialities, there may be a need for more flexibility to achieve efficiency, but more detail needs to be built into the model for us to be able to represent this.

Finally, we are also aware that relatively simple-minded assumptions are made in the allocation of patients with certain conditions to modes of care. At present, we use allocations which are based on the proportions of current practice. In some cases we need to recognise higher degrees of interdependence which are important for policy. For example, an additional consultant geriatrician may improve assessment procedures in such a way that a number of geriatric-ward beds can be vacated; these, in turn, may then be filled by long-stay patients who are 'blocking' beds in medical wards. This would be a new resource input and a policy change which would then alter the proportions of the elderly flowing into different modes of care.

5.2.3 *Liaison*

It should be explicitly recognised that there will be many conflicts of interest in the planning system implied by the ideas presented here—or, indeed, in any other planning system. There will not be enough resources to satisfy all demands; it will be very difficult to make changes unless senior medical staff can be part of any agreement to do so. For this reason, the notions of planning teams and planning agreements taking in the different parties involved, as representing a continuing interaction, are very important. The information system described here should provide an effective basis for such arrangements.

5.2.4 *A planning framework*

It is convenient to summarise the argument so far in terms of the kind of shift implied from the present position. At the core of the planning framework is an information system, a set of regularly updated indicators which provide the basis both for management and for strategic planning. In the latter context, these indicators provide the basis for the development of explicit objectives. The effects of changes in resource allocation can then be explicitly explored on the computer (and the real consequences

monitored and the model adjusted if need be). The information generated
can be the basis of planning agreements between the different interests
involved and can provide foci for negotiation. It is also useful to add that
machinery will often be needed to ensure that the usual practice of
proceeding with very minor adjustments to historical allocations is changed.
For example, it may be necessary to have groups which review all posts
as they become vacant. A case would have to be made explicitly for
refilling. Decisions would be taken in the light of planning agreements,
but would also add a finer scale of scrutiny to planning teams.

Finally, we note that this part of the discussion has been mainly
couched, at least implicitly, in terms of district-level planning. The
information system could be amended to be useful both at a broader
scale (regions or small systems of districts) and at a finer one (district
units or single hospitals).

5.3 Directions for future research
It is important to recognise that both short-run and long-run strategies are
needed. In the long run, we can look forward to the implementation of
the Körner Committee recommendations, and hence have better data
bases. It will be increasingly possible to take advantage of advances in
information technology.

We can also look beyond Körner: there is a need to link the GP patient
administration system with that of hospital in' and outpatient systems.
This must be the next step forward if we are to progress, in terms of
overall management of health care, and also to achieve an understanding
of how the system actually operates—particularly with respect to allocation.
In the short run, we have to make the best of what is available to us.
This means finding effective ways of combining data from different sources
and being able to make reasonable estimates when direct data is not
available. An example of the latter is our approach to speciality costs.
There is also an advantage in trying to develop a comprehensive framework,
because this provides an overall accounting basis and some missing quantities
can be estimated as residuals. It will also be necessary within this, of course,
to carry out detailed cost-effectiveness analyses of particular projects.

Thus the research strategy implied by the present position is as follows.
Develop a comprehensive information system which is regularly updated,
and continually seek to improve the data and the modelling techniques
which form the basis of its validity. And perhaps most importantly of all:
embed this information system in planning and policy frameworks which
are used. It is pressures from this use which will force an adequate
information system to emerge in time.

References

Ashford J R, Butts M S, Bailey T C, 1981, "Is there still a place for independent research into issues of public policy in England and Wales in the 1980's?" *Journal of the Operational Research Society* **32** 851-864

Aspden P, 1980, "The IIASA health care resources allocation submodel: DRAM calibration for data from the SW health region, UK" WP-80-115, International Institute for Applied Systems Analysis, Laxenburg, Austria

Boldy D, 1976, "A review of the application of mathematical programming to tactical and strategic health and social service problems" *Operational Research Quarterly* **27** 439-448

Boldy D, (Ed.), 1980 *Operational Research Applied to the Health Services* (Croom Helm, Beckenham, Kent)

Brotchie J F, Dickey J W, Sharpe R, 1980 *TOPAZ—General Planning Technique and Its Applications at the Regional, Urban and Facility Planning Levels. Lecture Notes in Economics and Mathematical Systems, 180* (Springer, Berlin)

Calvert J R, 1980, "Relative performance" in *Indicators of Performance* Ed. D Billing; Surrey Society for Research into Higher Education, University of Surrey, Guildford, Surrey, England, pp 65-72

Clarke M, 1983, "A critique of the use of spatial interaction models in health care planning and analysis" working paper, School of Geography, University of Leeds, Leeds, England

Clarke M, Prentice R, 1982, "Exploring decisions in public policymaking: strategic allocation, individual allocation, and simulation" *Environment and Planning A* **14** 499-524

Clarke M, Spowage M, 1982, "Specification of a microsimulation model of a District Health Authority" WP-338, School of Geography, University of Leeds, Leeds, England

Clarke M, Spowage M, 1983, "A District Health Authority simulation model: the in-patient sub-model, specification and first results" working paper, School of Geography, University of Leeds, Leeds, England

Clarke M, Williams H C W L, 1982, "Spatial organisation of activities and the location of public facilities" paper presented at the workshop on 'Spatial Choice Models in Housing, Transport and Land Use Analysis', International Institute for Applied Systems Analysis, Laxenburg, March; copy available from M Clarke

Clarke M, Williams H C W L, 1983, "Synthetic sampling methods and the generation of initial populations" working paper, School of Geography, University of Leeds, Leeds, England

Coverdale I, Gibbs R, Nurse K, 1980, "A hospital cost model for policy analysis" *Journal of the Operational Research Society* **31** 801-811

DHSS, 1976 *Sharing Resources for Health: The Report of the Resource Allocation Working Party* Department of Health and Social Security (HMSO, London)

DHSS, 1978 *Morbidity Statistics from General Practice 1970-71* Department of Health and Social Security (HMSO, London)

DHSS, 1979 *Morbidity Statistics from General Practice 1971-72* Department of Health and Social Security (HMSO, London)

DHSS, 1982 *Steering Group on Health Services Information. A Report on the Ecollection and Use of Information about Hospital Clinical Activity in the NHS* Department of Health and Social Security (HMSO, London)

DHSS, 1983 *Health Care and Its Costs* Department of Health and Social Security (HMSO, London)

Duncan I B, Noble B M, 1979, "The allocation of specialties to hospitals in a health district" *Journal of the Operational Research Society* **30** 953-964

Feldstein M S, 1967 *Contributions to Economic Analysis, 51: Economic Analysis for Health Service Efficiency* (North-Holland, Amsterdam)

Forte P, 1982, "Cost and modelling in health services: a bibliography" WP-337, School of Geography, University of Leeds, Leeds, England

Forte P, Wilson A G, 1983, "Models of hospital costs" working paper, School of Geography, University of Leeds, Leeds, England

Gibbs R J, 1977, "Health care resource allocation models—a critical review" RM-77-55, International Institute for Applied Systems Analysis, Laxenburg, Austria

Gibbs R J, 1978, "The IIASA health care resource allocation model: Mark I", RM-78-8, International Institute for Applied Systems Analysis, Laxenburg, Austria

Hughes D J, 1978, "The IIASA health care resource allocation sub-model Mark 2—the allocation of many different resources" RM-78-50, International Institute for Applied Systems Analysis, Laxenburg, Austria

Hughes D J, Wierzbian .., 1980, "DRAM: a model for health care resource allocation" RR-80-23, International Institute for Applied Systems Analysis, Laxenburg, Austria

Leonardi G, 1981, "A unifying framework for public facility location problems—part 1: A critical overview and some unsolved problems" *Environment and Planning A* 13 1001–1028

Macdonald A G, Cuddeford G C, Beale E M L, 1974, "Balance of care: some mathematical models of the NHS" *British Medical Bulletin* 30 262–270

McFadden D, Cosslett S, Duguay G, Jung W, 1977, "Demographic data for policy analysis" *The Urban Travel Demand Forecasting Project, Phase 1. Final Report Series* volume 8; Institute of Transportation Studies, University of California, Berkeley, CA, USA

Magee C C, Osmolski R, 1979 *Manual of Procedures for Specialty Costing* University of Wales, Cardiff, Wales

Mayhew L D, Leonardi G, 1981, "Equity, efficiency and accessibility in urban and regional health care systems" WP-81-102, International Institute for Applied Systems Analysis, Laxenburg, Austria

Mooney G H, 1978, "Planning for balance of care of the elderly" *Scottish Journal of Political Economy* 25 149–165

NAHA, 1983 *National Association of Health Authorities News* number 63, July

OPCS, 1978 *Population Projections 1976–2016* (Office of Population Censuses and Surveys (HMSO, London)

Riley M, 1982, "Accessibility to hospitals: a practical application" *Environment and Planning A* 14 1107–1111

Shigan E N (Ed.), 1978, "Systems modelling in health care: proceedings of an IIASA conference, 1977" CP-78-12, International Institute for Applied Systems Analysis, Laxenburg, Austria

Townsend P, Davidson N, 1982 *Inequalities in Health: The Black Report* (Penguin Books, Harmondsworth, Middx)

Williams H C W L, Clarke M, 1984 *Micro-analysis and Simulation in Urban and Regional Analysis* (Cambridge University Press, Cambridge)

Wilson A G, 1981 *Geography and the Environment. Systems Analytical Methods* (John Wiley, Chichester, Sussex)

Wilson A G, 1983, "A generalised and unified approach to the modelling of service-supply structures" WP-352, School of Geography, University of Leeds, Leeds, England

Wilson A G, Clarke M, 1982, "Frameworks for modelling in relation to strategic planning in a health service" WP-334, School of Geography, University of Leeds, Leeds, England

Wilson A G, Coelho J D, Macgill S M, Williams H C W L, 1981 *Optimization in Locational and Transport Analysis* (John Wiley, Chichester, Sussex)

Health Care in London: Planning Issues and the Contribution of Local Morbidity Surveys

S E CURTIS, K J WOODS
Queen Mary College, University of London

1 Introduction

One of the most pressing problems facing the National Health Service (NHS) is the poor quality of primary health care services in London. Since the Royal Commission on the NHS reported that "in parts of London ... the NHS is failing dismally to provide an adequate primary care service to its patients" (Great Britain, 1979, page 89), attention has been focused on the deficiencies of the existing services and on ways in which they can be improved. Variations in the quality and quantity of London's primary health care services have been comprehensively documented in a survey prepared for the Royal College of General Practitioners (RCGP) (Jarman, 1981), and in May 1981 a report published by the London Health Planning Consortium (Acheson, 1981) emphasised the need for urgent action, making 115 separate recommendations for improvement.

A common theme of these reports is the absence of data on morbidity and on the use of primary health care services to assist in planning. The RCGP's report (or, as it is better known, the Jarman report, after its author) commented, "we found it very difficult to obtain the satisfactory data on morbidity which might affect the demand for general practitioner services and we recognise that this is a gap in the survey" (Jarman, 1981, page 1). Likewise the Acheson (1981) report on health and social conditions in inner London is notable for its absence of morbidity information.

The principal reasons for the omission of such data are the practical problems of collecting them, but it is clear that studies of morbidity and service utilisation in local areas do have the potential to provide inputs to health services planning in a number of ways. First, they can provide information about the prevalence of illness and the performance of local health services in meeting the health care needs of the local population. In so doing they provide a basis for the definition of local priority groups and may suggest how particular local services can be improved in quite specific ways. Goldacre (1981) suggests, for instance, that morbidity patterns are especially relevant to the planning of services such as outpatients clinics.

Second, local morbidity studies can contribute to the development of resource allocation policies by focusing on the relationship between morbidity and other social indicators in particular places. Fox and Goldblatt (1982) have presented results from the OPCS (Office of Population Censuses and Surveys) *Longitudinal Study* which demonstrates an association between housing tenure, car ownership, and mortality. Council residents with low rates of car ownership had the highest mortality rates (as measured by the standardised mortality ratio). Morbidity studies can test whether the relationships at a national level for mortality persist when morbidity is considered at the local level. If the associations are consistent, then widely available social indicators, for example, from the census, may provide a basis for resource allocation between areas that reflects need in terms of predicted mortality and morbidity. However, if the relationships are shown to vary from one area to another, then the argument for more locally based criteria of need assessment is enhanced. It was essentially this kind of study that Sir Douglas Black's Report advocated when it recommended "the development of area social condition indicators for use in resource allocation" and the "study of the interaction of the social factors implicated in ill health over time, and within small areas" (Townsend and Davidson, 1982, page 137).

Undoubtedly there are considerable practical difficulties to be overcome in undertaking such studies. In the latter part of the paper we review some of them and describe our own experiences in northeast London. First, however, we outline the planning context which gives rise to the need for such studies, the changing structure both of London's population and of its health services.

2 Population and health-service changes in London

The results of the 1981 Census show that the postwar decline in the size of London's population has continued since 1971 at an even faster rate than in the preceding decade. Inner London boroughs experienced the largest proportional decline, though, significantly, the population in outer London boroughs also fell by 5.1% overall. Indeed, between 1971 and 1981 every borough in Greater London experienced a decline in its population, ranging from −28.9% in Kensington and Chelsea to −0.2% in Sutton. These changes reflect the steady movement of the population into the areas surrounding London. Thus the population in the southeast outer metropolitan area increased by 4.81% and in the outer southeast metropolitan area by 8.24% (OPCS, 1982a).

These gross changes in the size of London's population have considerable implications for the delivery of health care services within the Thames Regional Health Authorities (RHAs) which serve the southeast metropolitan area. Authorities are faced with the problems of developing services in areas of growing population at a time when the overall resource constraint on the NHS is extremely tight and when growth monies have to be found from within existing budgets. Along the lines of the principles established by the report of the Resource Allocation Working Party (RAWP) (DHSS, 1976), the redistribution of existing resources between the inner and outer parts of the southeast metropolitan area has become an important element in the plans of the Thames RHAs (see Eyles et al, 1982). In practice this means reducing levels of service provision in the central parts of London, and particularly cutting back the level of hospital provision for acute cases because the majority of NHS expenditure is concentrated in this sector. To guide planning in this respect the DHSS, together with the Thames RHAs, the postgraduate hospitals, the University Grants Committee, and the University of London established the London Health Planning Consortium (LHPC) in 1977. With respect to hospitals, the LHPC has produced two reports (LHPC, 1979; 1980) which advocate an overall cutback of nearly 5000 acute-case hospital beds between 1977 and 1988, equivalent to 11% of the 1977 level of provision. These projections were accepted by the special London Advisory Group set up by the Secretary of State in 1980 and later endorsed by him (DHSS, 1981).

The majority of the predicted reductions are heavily concentrated in the inner-city teaching health authorities, but, in the outer metropolitan area, some authorities, like Essex, Surrey, and West Sussex, were predicted to require modest increases in their bed numbers to cope with growing populations. We do not intend to review the methods employed by the LHPC to determine the predicted pattern of acute-case beds in 1988, save to say that, in taking account of morbidity differentials to modify hospitalisation rates (a key element in determining the required level of bed provision), the overall level of mortality, as measured by the standardised mortality ratio, was employed because no suitable data on morbidity exist. In this respect the LHPC followed the assumptions made by the earlier RAWP report (DHSS, 1976) that statistics of morbidity, if identified, would mirror the pattern of mortality, an assumption which has generated a good deal of debate (see Avery Jones, 1976; Buxton and Klein, 1978; Eyles et al, 1982).

As a nonexecutive body the LHPC cannot implement the proposals resulting from its analysis, but the RHAs and the new district health authorities, established in April 1982, will almost certainly produce strategic and operational plans which will have, in practice, the same effect. The concentration of acute-case hospital services in fewer (often teaching) hospitals will be a common theme as health authorities attempt to release financial resources for geographical redistribution and for the development of nonacute-case health services in their districts. The need for the latter is especially urgent, for, although the populations of inner London health authorities are relatively well provided in terms of acute-case hospitals, the same is not true of primary health care services, nor of community services for the elderly, the mentally handicapped, and the mentally ill. The LHPC, through the Acheson (1981) report, have considered ways in which primary health care can be improved. Significantly, part of the impetus of the Acheson inquiry was the realisation that a reduction of acute-case hospital services would throw a greater burden onto the hard-pressed services outside the hospital. Thus the chairman of the LHPC noted "that changes in hospital provision which we believe to be needed over the next ten years will not have the desired effect unless solutions are, within the same time scale, found to the major problems providing effective primary care services in London" (Acheson, 1981, annex 2). The proposals of the Acheson report have been reviewed elsewhere (Woods, 1982) and it is not the intention to discuss them here. However, the urgency for action stems not only from the planned changes in the NHS mix of services but also from the social and health characteristics of London and especially of inner London's population.

Easily hidden by the general downward trend of population totals are changes occurring in London's population structure. These have not been the same throughout London, but, as far as health and social services are concerned, they have usually resulted in disproportionate numbers of people, who are recognised as having above-average needs for welfare services, residing in inner London. Jarman (1981) identified three high-need zones—a westend zone (Kensington and Chelsea, Westminster, Camden, and Hammersmith) with a highly mobile young female population, often living in bed-sits, supplemented during the working day by an invasion of commuters and especially in the summer by visitors and tourists; an eastend zone (Hackney, Tower Hamlets, Newham, and Southwark) with working-class populations, usually living in council accommodation, experiencing high unemployment rates, and having significant immigrant communities, like the Bengalis in Spitalfields; and a nonwhite immigrant zone (Brent, Ealing, and Haringey) with high proportions of new common-wealth immigrants. The remaining London boroughs form an outer zone characterised by populations with smaller proportions of high-need groups. Almost certainly the pattern of morbidity and hence the nature of health-care services required to meet it will be different in each zone. It is easy to anticipate (on the basis of age and sex only) that the needs of residents in the eastend zone are somewhat different from those of residents in the westend zone, and both sets of needs are different from the needs of recent immigrants. The limited evidence quoted in Jarman (1981) supports this. Using data related to payments made to general practitioners (GPs) and NHS dispensing records, Jarman found that GPs in the westend zone claimed fewer payments for services like vaccination, immunisation, cervical cytology, night visits, and maternity medical services, but prescribed more central nervous system stimulants, appetite suppressants, vitamins, and hypnotics than in the eastend zone, where there was a high proportion of dispensed prescriptions for minor analgesics, expectorants, and cough suppressants.

The extent to which these differences are due to differences in morbidity, as opposed to differences in action in relation to morbidity, is debatable, since the interpretation of symptoms is mediated amongst other things by experience and expectation. As with morbidity, these are socially variable and spatially variable phenomena. Recent research by Cornwell (1983) in working-class Bethnal Green has emphasised the significance of family and social networks in the understanding of health and illness and in the process of seeking medical advice. In the context of London's changing population, sensitivity to particular needs and customs is becoming a central issue as far as ethnic minorities are concerned. Some health authorities have established interpreter services to facilitate easier communication between medical staff and patients, but, as Donovan (1983) indicates, there has been little research attempting to link the health of black people with the social conditions in which they live. Research of this nature will require careful analysis of health care services needs and attitudes to services, and these analyses will have to be sensitive to customs and values if they are to be of any use. For potential health surveyors this creates a challenge, in the sense that the validity of established methods of collecting morbidity data have not been extensively tested in a population as socially and ethnically diverse as that of inner London. In responding to this challenge we now turn to the complex methodological problems of measuring morbidity in the dynamic context of London's changing population and health services.

3 Approaches to the measurement of morbidity
3.1 *Introduction*
The measurement of morbidity using standard instruments to permit comparisons between individuals and populations is difficult because of the wide spectrum of conditions, from severe to minor illnesses, with effects which may be long- or short-term. Furthermore, a number of different dimensions or interpretations of morbidity, and various criteria for measurement, can be identified. It is possible, for example, to make distinctions between mental and physical illnesses, or between illnesses which are the concern of particular medical specialisms, or between acute and chronic conditions. Morbidity may be assessed in terms of clinically diagnosed illnesses with medical 'labels', in terms of reported symptoms, or in terms of the impact of the illnesses on the subjects' activities.

Whichever way morbidity is assessed, it is often employed as a surrogate for the more difficult concept of health. Morbidity is frequently used to indicate the degree to which the health of individuals or populations departs from a 'normal' or 'optimal' state of health which they may expect to experience. Although it is possible to identify some consensus between cultural and social groups about what constitutes 'normal health' or 'illness', these definitions are not value free, differences exist at the level of the group and the individual, and the definitions may change through time.

Thus the choice of an instrument to survey morbidity levels will depend upon which arbitor is chosen to assess the subject's state of health and upon which dimension of illness is of particular interest. Surveys of sickness have employed various data sources and methods of measurement, including medical records of use of health care services and of clinical examinations, self-reported morbidity recorded in interviews or in self-completion questionnaires and proxy reporting by nonmedical respondents. The range of techniques of measurement available have been comprehensively reviewed elsewhere (by, for example, Berg, 1973; Jazairi, 1976; Chen and Bush, 1979; Holland et al, 1979; Hunt and McEwen, 1980; CHHI, 1981).

Of particular interest here are methods employing questionnaires which can be used to obtain information about self-reported illnesses directly from respondents. These methods are the most appropriate for surveying morbidity, in its widest sense, in the community, including mental and physical illnesses and undiagnosed or untreated morbidity as well as that which comes to the attention of medical services and receives treatment.

For this type of community study of general morbidity the choice of appropriate instruments will mainly depend upon the following considerations:

(a) The information is often required in a *standardised form.* Studies of this type are commonly designed to permit comparisons between individuals or groups in terms of the prevalence of illness and its severity. Such comparisons may be sought within the particular community under study or between one community or locality and another. Thus it may be necessary to use *systematic measurement* for all the subjects surveyed, and a degree of *comparability* with other morbidity surveys conducted elsewhere may be desirable.

(b) The measure chosen must usually be appropriate for a range of *different types of respondent* with varying demographic, social, and health characteristics.

(c) *Ease of administration and acceptability to respondents* of the measure may be particularly important for morbidity studies based on household surveys.

The researcher may select from a number of survey instruments which have been developed and tested for morbidity surveys. These differ, in terms of their orientation, between those which:

(1) emphasise the incidence of symptoms or complaints;

(2) concentrate on the functional impact of morbidity; and

(3) assess perception of more general dimensions of health.

Some examples of those which have been applied to populations in Britain, and particularly in London, are considered in the following subsections.

3.2 *Symptoms and complaints*

Information on symptoms experienced by respondents or on diagnosed complaints may correspond to specific medical conditions, so may be readily related to the need for particular forms of medical care. However, these data may suffer from inaccuracies in diagnoses of conditions or from lack of complete information on symptoms. Furthermore, when making general morbidity assessments it is difficult to compare different conditions in terms of their relative severity.

Instruments to record experience of physical symptoms typically consist of checklists of ailments. Wadsworth et al (1971) used checklists of symptoms in their survey of residents in Bermondsey and Southwark.

In 1977 and 1978, checklists of acute and chronic conditions were employed in the health section of the General Household Survey (GHS) (OPCS, 1979). However, respondents may experience difficulty in distinguishing between acute and chronic illnesses, and the checklists have also been criticised for combining items relating to *symptoms* and *conditions.*

A more satisfactory basis for symptom checklists is offered by Hannay (1978) in his comprehensive list of items describing symptoms only, which was originally developed for a morbidity survey in Glasgow.

An alternative approach to the recording of medical conditions is to ask more open questions about any illnesses the respondent has experienced. This is the type of question employed, for example, in the GHS prior to 1977 and from 1979 onwards. The responses may be coded using classification systems such as the *International Classification of Diseases* (WHO, 1980a), but there may be difficulties in standardising the responses when a wide range of different illnesses are reported.

Another group of techniques which employ data on the experience of symptoms by respondents are those used for the detection of mental illness. Goldberg and Huxley (1980) review studies of prevalence of psychiatric illness in British communities using measures such as the Present State Examination and the General Health Questionnaire (GHQ). (The use of some of these measures is restricted to interviewers with psychiatric training.) The GHQ is available in various different versions, from the complete test with 140 items to a shortened instrument with twelve questions. The twelve-item version was found to produce a 14.5% level of misclassification of respondents. This measure is most effective in identifying the *existence* of mental illness, rather than its *severity* (Tennant, 1977). Other similar measures include Rutter et al's (1970, appendix 7, page 422) Malaise Inventory, designed to assess anxiety and depression in women from their reported experience of certain symptoms.

Though techniques of the types described can be used to measure the *prevalence* of physical and mental morbidity, the problem remains of how to compare illnesses in terms of their *severity* or impact on the individual. Some methods have been suggested that are based, for example, on assessments by medical practitioners of normative rates of service use (Anderson, 1978), or that are based on prognosis and duration of the illness, and on threat to life, degree of disability, and discomfort caused by the illness (Wyler et al, 1968). The alternative approach is to measure ill health directly in terms of its effects on the subject's functioning, using measures of incapacity discussed in the next subsection.

3.3 *Measures of disability/incapacity*
Measures of the degree of disability or incapacity resulting from an illness, rather than the number and type of illnesses experienced, can be used to assess the impact of a range of illnesses on different types of patients and do not rely on clinical examination. However, the problems with these

methods include the difficulty of prognosis, the disparity between ability and performance, and the question of weighting the various forms of disability (Chen and Bush, 1979).

At the simplest level, questionnaires may be used to elicit information on prevalence of different types of incapacity. The World Health Organisation (WHO, 1980b) has published schemes for categorisation of different forms of impairment, disability, or handicap.

Measures of functional incapacity have commonly been developed with severely disabled or handicapped respondents in mind. One such instrument is the Activities for Daily Living Measure (Katz et al, 1963). This assesses patients' capacities for bathing, dressing, toileting, transfer, continence, and feeding, and therefore gives an indication of nursing dependency. The GHS (OPCS, 1979) included a section for elderly respondents, comprising items on ability to carry out daily activities, developed from an earlier OPCS survey of the elderly at home (Hunt, 1978). A series of filters were used to ensure that the questions were not addressed to healthier respondents for which they were unsuitable.

Another approach to measuring the impact of illness is to assess the 'opportunity' or 'economic' costs of morbidity for individuals or society; for example, in terms of disability days or working days lost. Studies attempting to cost the effects of illness are most common in the North American literature (for example, Muskin and Dunlop, 1979), but British surveys have also recorded disability days [for instance, the GHS (OPCS, 1979) inquires into days of acute sickness in the preceding fortnight].

A second measure, the Sickness Impact Profile, is a 235-item instrument collecting information which can produce weighted additive scales on fourteen aspects of functional incapacity: social interaction, locomotion, sleep and rest, nutrition, daily work, household management, mobility, body movement, communication, leisure activities, intellectual functioning, interaction with family members, emotions, and personal hygiene. The weightings for items were derived using panel assessments. This measure therefore offers a very comprehensive assessment of functional incapacity and has been validated in comparison with other disability indicators (Bergner et al, 1976). A modified version of this measure, the Functional Limitation Profile, has been developed in the Department of Community Medicine at St Thomas's Hospital for a study of the disabled in Lambeth (Patrick et al, 1981). An alternative approach to scaling disability has also been applied in Lambeth, using Guttmen scaling to rank different aspects of physical incapacity in the elderly (Williams et al, 1976). Two scales were produced, one applying to women and one to men, which comprise series of ranked items.

The measures discussed so far have mainly been developed for use with the disabled and are not appropriate for populations in more average health. However, one instrument designed for less specialised use is the Nottingham Health Profile (NHP) intended for large survey populations and validated for a number of different types of respondents (Hunt and McEwen, 1980; Hunt et al, 1980; Backett et al, 1981). The NHP comprises two sections: one of thirty-eight items relating to six different dimensions of ill health (physical mobility, pain experienced, sleep disturbance, social isolation, emotional reactions, and energy level), and a second schedule of seven items concerning impact of sickness on particular types of activity. Items in the first section of the NHP have been weighted using Thurstone's (1927) Method of Paired Comparisons, so that six independent additive scales can be derived corresponding to the six dimensions of morbidity. This measure has been applied in surveys of populations served by GPs in Nottingham (Hunt et al, 1981), and in Manchester (Leavey, 1982). The instrument takes the form of a self-completion questionnaire suitable for use in mailed surveys, household interviews, and clinical settings.

3.4 Questions on perception of general health

A final group of instruments for morbidity surveys consists of questions designed to elicit overall assessments of state of health and attitudes to health. Techniques for obtaining general health ratings are reviewed by Ware et al (1978). Many of these are single-item semantic differential questions of the type used in the GHS, which inquired: "Over the last 12 months, would you say that your health has on the whole been good, fairly good or not good?" (OPCS, 1979, page 185).

Ware et al (1978) have developed a rather different instrument in the North American context which elicits respondents' reactions to a series of items reflecting different aspects of their health perceptions. These dimensions may be summarised as current and prior health, health outlook, and propensity to adopt the sick role.

This work has been paralleled in Britain by studies of health perception among particular population groups. Working-class people have been most extensively studied by, for example, Locker, 1978; Blaxter and Paterson, 1982; Pill and Stott, 1982; Cornwell, 1983), and women have received particular attention. This work has been largely descriptive and though it is revealing and valuable in the context of health education and health promotion, it has not yet produced more sophisticated instruments for measurement and comparison of health perceptions and attitudes to health.

4 Local morbidity surveys in London

There have been relatively few surveys conducted in London which have been concerned with morbidity in a general sense and that have been designed to represent the population of local communities as a whole. Few studies carried out in specific localities allow for comparison to be made with other areas.

Several studies which have collected morbidity data have concentrated on particular demographic or social groups. The elderly populations of inner London have received attention by, for example, Williams et al (1976) in Lambeth and by Jackson and Bartley (1982) in Newham. Surveys have also been made of the health of children living in London. Methods for assessing child health have not been reviewed in this paper. However, one example of a measure developed and applied in a London setting is provided by Richman (1977), who found that certain aspects of inner-city living, such as high-rise housing, are associated with behaviour problems. Studies of young children have often employed the birth register as a sampling frame (for example, Cullinan and Treuherz, 1981; 1982; Coupland, 1982; Watson, 1982). Several have recorded the health status of the mother as well as that of the child. Coupland (1982) reports that mothers interviewed in inner London were slightly more likely than respondents from outer London to report experience of both chronic and acute illness (see table 1).

Other morbidity surveys of London populations have been rather specific in terms of the type of illnesses studied. For example, Holland and Waller (1971) investigated the prevalence in Lambeth of four chronic conditions (cardiorespiratory disease, functional disability, skin disease, and duodenal ulceration). Studies of mental illness in London are among those reviewed by Goldberg and Huxley (1980, chapter 2). These include the study by Brown and Harris (1978) of depressive illness among women in Camberwell, from which it was concluded that inner-city stress might be associated with relatively high rates of depression. Studies of psychiatric illness occurring in populations served by GPs may also provide evidence of morbidity rates, although these are based mainly on use of services (for instance, Shepherd et al, 1966; Wing et al, 1972). Wing et al (1972) found rates of reported psychiatric illness to be similar in GP-served populations in Camberwell and Nottingham.

Table 1. Data on women's self-reported health in inner and outer London. [Source: a survey by Coupland (1982) of women aged 16–45 with young children living in two health districts in east London (Tower Hamlets and East Roding). The instrument used was based on the GHS questionnaire for 1977 and 1978, which collected data on morbidity using checklists of complaints (OPCS, 1979).]

Self-reported state of health	Percentage of women living in	
	inner-London health district [a]	outer-London health district [a]
No chronic or acute health complaints	9	13
Acute health complaints only	20	19
Chronic health complaints only	13	14
Chronic and acute health complaints	57	54

[a] The sample size is 150 (= 100%); percentages have been rounded up or down to the nearest whole number.

Another group of studies providing information relevant to London's populations are those which concentrate on rather severe impairment resulting in physical disability. The survey reported by Knight and Warren (1978) included part of London as one of its study areas, and comparisons were made between the different localities sampled. These authors reported a relatively low incidence of physical disability in London compared with urban populations in the industrial north. By contrast, Skinner (1969) reported a higher incidence of physical disability, indicated by registration figures for the handicapped, in Tower Hamlets than in England and Wales as a whole. A screening questionnaire showed that the registered proportion handicapped (0.96%) underestimated the proportion with handicap (4.4%). Disability in the community in inner London is also being investigated in the Longitudinal Disability Survey in Lambeth by the Department of Community Medicine at St Thomas's Hospital. The results of their initial screening study suggested a rate of incidence of disability of 15.4% among the local population. They compared this result with findings from an earlier study in Lambeth (Bennett et al, 1970) and with the national study by Harris and Buckle (1971), and concluded that differences in question wording may have affected the rates of prevalence recorded (Patrick et al, 1981).

Surveys employing wider definitions of morbidity, with data specific to London, include a household survey in Bermondsey and Southwark (Wadsworth et al, 1971). This demonstrated that the prevalence of illness recorded seemed higher than that recorded in earlier studies in different parts of Britain, but was unable to make direct comparisons because an original instrument was used, which cross-checked data on symptoms, medication, and health services use. There are, however, some examples of surveys of London populations which have incorporated standard OPCS health-status questions, addressed to respondents in a range of social and demographic groups. For example, the recent OPCS survey of access to GPs in London (OPCS, forthcoming) also included measures of respondents' state of health similar to those used in previous OPCS household surveys, which may provide some indication of variations between different parts of the city.

Another study, carried out to assess the effects of aircraft noise on populations in west London, also recorded responses to standard OPCS questions on chronic and acute illnesses and compared the results with information from the GHS for Greater London (Tarnopolsky and Morton-Williams, 1980). The authors found that the prevalence of acute and long-standing illnesses in the study area was generally similar to that for Greater London as a whole. However, the authors also gave a breakdown of the results by age and sex, which suggested some differences in the rates of long-standing illnesses and recent restricting illnesses. In particular, long-standing illnesses appear to be less prevalent among those aged over sixty-five, and recent restricting illnesses are more prevalent among those aged 45–64 (table 2). A comparative study by Skrimshire (1976) of populations in Newham and Oxfordshire demonstrated that the east London respondents reported higher rates of respiratory diseases and of multiple illnesses than for England and Wales generally (table 3).

Table 2. Data on chronic and acute illnesses from the west London survey compared with GHS results for Greater London.

Self-reported illness, and age group	Percentage of respondents in	
	west London survey, 1977 [a]	Greater London survey, 1976 [b]
Long-standing illness		
aged 16–44 years	16	16
aged 45–64 years	31	33
aged 65 plus years	44	59
total	26	25
Recent restricting illness		
aged 16–44 years	9	10
aged 45–64 years	12	10
aged 65 plus years	10	11
total	10	10

[a] Data from Tarnopolsky and Morton-Williams, 1980, table 2.6. [b] Data from 1976 GHS for Greater London (quoted in Tarnopolsky and Morton-Williams, 1980, table 2.6).

Table 3. Prevalence of self-reported illnesses in Newham compared with England and Wales (source: Skrimshire, 1976, table 3).

Self-reported illness, and age group	Percentage of respondents in	
	Newham sample, Spring 1976	England and Wales sample, Spring 1973
Long-standing illness		
aged 0–14 years	15.9	6.9
aged 15–44 years	19.9	13.9
aged 45–64 years	26.5	31.0
aged 65 plus years	53.1	49.4
Limiting long-standing illness		
aged 0–14 years	8.7	2.8
aged 15–44 years	11.8	6.1
aged 45–64 years	19.1	18.6
aged 65 plus years	38.8	35.0
Recent restricting illness		
aged 0–14 years	14.5	9.8
aged 15–44 years	15.4	12.3
aged 45–64 years	10.3	13.1
aged 65 plus years	12.2	16.7

Skrimshire's (1976) study was unusual in that the comparison of morbidity
levels between the two areas was a major objective rather than an incidental
possibility with the results.   In the next section a project is described
which also seeks to make interarea comparisons within London.

5 The Comparative Need for Health Care Project

This research, on the comparative need for health care, follows on from
the studies of morbidity in London already reviewed and seeks to
investigate the issue of local variations more fully in the context of two
boroughs in east London.   The Project is funded by the King Edward VII
Hospital Fund for London and the Northeast Thames RHA.   It was designed
to compare the prevalence of self-reported morbidity in these two areas
and to study the relationships between morbidity, demographic and socioeconomic characteristics of respondents, and their use of medical services.

5.1 *The survey design*

The survey is based on a random sample of households in the boroughs of
Tower Hamlets and Redbridge.   All adults in these households were
interviewed.   The sampling frames selected for this study were the borough
rating lists for the two areas.   These were chosen in preference to the
electoral roll because it was thought that certain groups, especially in
London's inner city, were likely to be underrepresented in the electoral
register (especially students, recent migrants, and ethnic minorities).   The
disadvantage of this sampling frame in practice was the fact that some of
the entries were out of date, especially for those council rented properties
in Tower Hamlets managed by the Greater London Council rather than by
the Local Authority.   Thus a number of the addresses selected were either
vacant or had been demolished, so that the number of eligible addresses in
the sample was reduced.   This problem, combined with a slightly higher
refusal rate amongst Tower Hamlets respondents, resulted in a rather
smaller inner-city sample than originally planned.   It appears that elderly
women were particularly underrepresented in Tower Hamlets.   This group
may be particularly reluctant to permit access to interviewers in spite of
efforts made to establish the bona fide nature of the survey by use of
interviewer identification cards and letters of introduction.

The instruments used to assess health status include OPCS questions
used in the General Household Survey since 1979 on general perceptions
of health, long-standing illnesses, restricting illnesses over the preceding
two weeks, and items on sight and hearing difficulties.   Also, section one
of the Nottingham Health Profile (NHP) and a self-completion checklist of
common complaints comprising the most frequently reported items from
Hannay's (1978) list of symptoms have been incorporated in the study.
Thus the health section of this questionnaire provides data on a wide range
of self-reported morbidity for an almost (although not completely)
representative sample of the local populations in the two areas.

The question of interviewer effects on responses to health questionnaires may be important (Brorsson, 1980; O'Muircheartaigh and Wiggins, 1981). In this study, an effort was made to minimise the influence of interviewer bias on area differences by allocating addresses to interviewers randomly within each borough and, where possible, deploying interviewers to work in both boroughs. This design permits some analysis of the extent of interviewer effects. However, this system involved additional costs, especially for travel, and would not have been possible for a more widely dispersed sample.

A further problem, occurring most often in the inner-city populations, is that of language difficulties among immigrants who do not speak English. In terms of numbers, the most significant of these groups in Tower Hamlets comprises Bengalis. A Bengali translation of the health profile was provided and in some cases an interpreter accompanied the interviewer. The question arises of how those from the ethnic minority groups react to questions on morbidity and whether their response patterns can be expected to differ from those of the indigenous population. These issues, of choice of sample frame, problems of nonresponse, interviewer effects, and language barriers, are common to all morbidity surveys, and are perhaps especially relevant in studies of inner-city areas, such as in London. They invite further work on the development of survey methodology in this field.

5.2 *Initial results from the survey*
Preliminary results from the survey have provided the summary statistics shown in table 4. These data illustrate the differing social and economic complexions of the two boroughs, Tower Hamlets being typical of inner London's eastend and Redbridge representing outer London.

Initial findings on self-reported morbidity are shown in tables 5 and 6. Because the instruments used have been previously employed in surveys of other areas, including the GHS, it is possible to make comparisons, not only between the two study areas but also with findings at the national level. Table 5 shows the reported prevalence of long-standing and recent restricting illnesses in the two study areas. These results show that, within broad demographic groups, the levels of chronic sickness appear to be high in the Tower Hamlets population (45% reported illness) compared with that of Redbridge (35%). Furthermore, the inner-city populations recorded a relatively high prevalence of chronic morbidity compared with 1980 data from the GHS (36% reported chronic sickness in Great Britain generally). In Tower Hamlets, there is a higher level of acute sickness reported, most particularly among women aged 45–64 years. In the Redbridge population, overall prevalence of acute sickness (8.4%) is lower than in Tower Hamlets (16.5%) and in the OPCS data (13%). Evidence from the NHP also indicates relatively high morbidity levels in Tower Hamlets, with the mean scores on all dimensions being higher for Tower Hamlets than for Redbridge (table 6). The scores are also higher for corresponding demographic groups in the inner-city sample, except in the case of the sleep dimension for elderly women.

At the time of writing, the analysis of these data is still in progress and further work remains to be carried out on the associations between the morbidity levels measured and the social and economic characteristics of the survey populations. However, the preliminary results reported here do appear to indicate a difference in the prevalence of self-reported illness along a number of dimensions of morbidity. The implications of these findings and those of previous studies are considered in the concluding section.

Table 4. The Comparative Need for Health Care Project: characteristics of survey respondents in Tower Hamlets and Redbridge, 1982.

Characteristics	Percentage of respondents living in	
	Tower Hamlets	Redbridge
Demographic characteristics of individual respondents [a]		
Males		
aged 16–44 years	29.3	23.9
aged 45–64 years	14.8	16.0
aged 65 plus years	6.9	7.5
Females		
aged 16–44 years	25.9	25.7
aged 45–64 years	15.0	15.4
aged 65 plus years	8.1	11.6
Socioeconomic group of head of household [b]		
Professional (3, 4)	2.0	7.8
Employers and managers (1, 2, 13)	9.5	20.7
Intermediate and junior nonmanual (5, 6)	12.0	15.6
Skilled manual (8, 9, 12, 14)	22.6	23.8
Semiskilled manual (7, 10, 15)	17.6	3.0
Unskilled	3.0	0.4
Unclassified (retired and other economically inactive)	33.1	28.5
Housing tenure [c]		
Owner-occupied	0.5	74.8
Rented from the local authority	87.8	15.4
Privately rented, unfurnished	7.1	7.3
Privately rented, furnished	0.5	1.3
Rented from a housing association	1.5	–
Other	2.5	1.2

[a] N ($\equiv$ total number of respondents for whom data were available) was 406 for Tower Hamlets and 482 for Redbridge.
[b] N was 199 for Tower Hamlets and 231 for Redbridge. Numbers in brackets refer to Registrar General's Standard Economic Groupings (see OPCS, 1980).
[c] N was 196 for Tower Hamlets and 234 for Redbridge.

Table 5. The Comparative Need for Health Care Project: self-reported health characteristics of survey respondents in Tower Hamlets and Redbridge, 1982. The data for Great Britain are taken from the 1980 GHS (OPCS, 1982b, tables 7.2, 7.6, and 7.9).

Self-reported illness, and age group	Percentage of respondents living in		
	Tower Hamlets[a]	Redbridge[a]	Great Britain
Long-standing illness			
aged 16–44 years	37 (196)	23 (226)	23
aged 45–64 years	48 (107)	37 (144)	43
aged 65 plus years	70 (54)	67 (84)	60
all aged 16 plus years	45 (357)	35 (454)	36
Limiting long-standing illness			
aged 16–44 years	14 (194)	8 (226)	12
aged 45–64 years	27 (107)	16 (142)	27
aged 65 plus years	45 (51)	36 (84)	44
all aged 16 plus years	22 (352)	15 (452)	23
Recent restricting illness			
aged 16–44 years	13 (201)	6 (229)	12
aged 45–64 years	22 (110)	12 (147)	14
aged 65 plus years	19 (59)	10 (86)	17
all aged 16 plus years	16 (370)	8 (462)	13

[a] Numbers in brackets represent the total number of respondents for whom data were available.

Table 6. The Comparative Need for Health Care Project: Nottingham Health Profile (NHP) scores for survey respondents in Tower Hamlets and Redbridge.

NHP dimension of morbidity	Mean scores for respondents living in	
	Tower Hamlets[a]	Redbridge[a]
Energy level	16 (369)	11 (465)
Pain experienced	8 (365)	4 (465)
Sleep disturbance	18 (367)	15 (462)
Emotional reactions	14 (362)	7 (462)
Social isolation	9 (367)	5 (465)
Physical mobility	8 (366)	6 (463)

[a] Number in brackets represent number of respondents for whom mean scores were calculated. Mean scores are mean values over the entire population, rounded to the nearest whole unit. The scores have not been age adjusted. However, higher scores were obtained, on average, in the inner city for respondents within all age groups and for all dimensions except sleep disturbance (see text).

6 Implications of local morbidity surveys for provision of primary health care

The data by which to compare general morbidity levels in London's populations are rather limited and must be drawn largely from studies not specifically designed for the purpose, although there are exceptions, including The Comparative Need for Health Care Project in which questions are addressed directly to this issue. The information available does seem to suggest that similar demographic groups report differing morbidity experiences in different geographical areas. Though the evidence is somewhat equivocal, it does seem to suggest, for example, that urban living in London may increase the prevalence of stress-related disorders, such as mental illness, and of illnesses connected with respiratory disorders. The Comparative Need for Health Care Project suggests a higher prevalence of self-reported illness in the inner city compared both with outer London and with the population of Great Britain in general.

As we have noted already, to some extent these findings can be anticipated on the basis of alternative indicators of ill health, such as mortality data for different areas. For example, data for inner and outer London reviewed in the Jarman report (Jarman, 1981, table 11.1) indicated higher death rates from mental disorders and respiratory diseases in inner London than in outer London. Planning methods reviewed in section 2, which have proceeded on the assumption of an association between sickness and death rates, might be enhanced and modified on the basis of morbidity studies, which illustrates how far area patterns of illness in the community in fact correspond with prevalence measured by mortality or by health services utilisation.

Measures of morbidity are also a useful source of data on those conditions which may have a serious impact on the quality of life of the sick person without being life-threatening and for which mortality rates are particularly inappropriate as surrogate indicators. Arthritic and rheumatic diseases; influenza and other infectious diseases; symptoms of tiredness; and stress complaints, such as ulcers, headaches, and back pains, are examples of these illnesses. They may have considerable significance in terms of resource needs, particularly for primary and community health care or for nonacute-case and outpatient hospital services.

The importance for resource planning of the link between morbidity and other surrogate indicators of need has already been mentioned. The existence of variation between areas of London, and between London and other parts of the country, which cannot be explained solely in terms of demographic differences, underlines the need to investigate the relationship between illness and social and economic factors. These socioeconomic indicators may prove relevant to the assessment of local health-care needs and feasible as surrogate need indicators. More research is necessary in this respect, not only by empirical study of the links between indicators, but also by development and application of theoretical models which will help us to understand better the social factors determining health experience. Models of this type are pertinent to planning for health promotion and illness prevention, as well as for curative health care.

In view of this potential of data from morbidity surveys, it is also necessary to improve the scope for incorporating such surveys into the health planning process. Research in this field should seek to make more clear to health care planners and administrators the nature, value, and possible applications of self-reported morbidity data relating to local areas, particularly in cities such as London where health needs are so diverse and pressing.

References

Acheson D, 1981 *Primary Health Care in Inner London: Report of a Study Group* Chairman: Professor Donald Acheson; copy available from the Department of Health and Social Security, Alexander Fleming House, Elephant and Castle, London SE1 6BY

Anderson R, 1978, "Health status. Indices and access to medical care" *American Journal of Public Health* 68 458-463

Avery Jones F, 1976, "The London hospitals scene" *British Medical Journal* 2 1046-1049

Backett E M, McEwen J, Hunt S M, 1981 *Health and Quality of Life* inhouse research report, Social Science Research Council, Hamilton House, Temple Avenue, London EC4

Bennett A E, Garrad J, Halit T, 1970, "Chronic disease and disability in the community: a prevalence study" *British Medical Journal* 3 762-764

Berg R L, 1973 *Health Status Indexes* (Hospital Research and Educational Trust, Chicago, IL)

Bergner M, Bobbitt R, Pollard W, Gilson B, 1976, "The sickness impact profile: validation of a health status measure" *Medical Care* 14 57-67

Blaxter M, Paterson E, 1982 *Mothers and Daughters: A Three Generational Study of Health Attitudes and Behaviour* (Heinemann Educational Books, London)

Brorsson B, 1980, "Measurement of health and of health service use in the community: a review of methodology and studies of interviewer variability in a Swedish health survey" *Acta University Uppsala Abstracts* number 350, Faculty of Medicine, University of Uppsala, Uppsala, Sweden

Brown G, Harris T, 1978 *Social Origins of Depression* (Tavistock Publications, Andover, Hants)

Buxton M J, Klein R E, 1978, "Allocating health resources: a commentary on the report of the Resource Allocation Working Party" research paper 3, Royal Commission on the National Health Service; available from The Government Bookshop, PO Box 569, London SE1 9NH

Chen M, Bush J, 1979, "Health status measures, policy and biomedical research" in *Health: What is Worth? Measures of Health Benefits* Eds S Muskin, D Dunlop (Pergamon Press, Elmsford, NY) pp 15-41

CHHI, 1981 *Health Indexes 1978-1981* Clearing House on Health Indexes (National Center for Health Statistics, US Department of Health and Human Services, Washington, DC)

Cornwell J, 1983 *Health—a Coincidence? Accounts of Health and Illness in a Working Class Community: The Case of Bethnal Green* PhD thesis, Department of Geography, Queen Mary College, University of London, London (in preparation)

Coupland V, 1982, personal communication, March 1982

Cullinan T, Treuherz J, 1981, "Born in East London 1979-1980" report prepared for the City and East London Area Health Authority; copy available from the Department of the Environment, 2 Marsham Street, London SW1

Cullinan T, Treuherz J, 1982, "Ill in East London 1979-1981" report available from the Department of Environmental and Preventive Medicine, St Bartholomews Hospital, London and Medical College, St Leonards Hospital, Nuttal Street, London W1

DHSS, 1976 *Sharing Resources for Health: The Report of the Resource Allocation Working Party* Department of Health and Social Security (HMSO, London)

DHSS, 1981, "Acute hospital services in London" report of the London Advisory Group to the Secretary of State for Social Services; copy available from Department of Health and Social Security, London

Donovan J, 1983, "Ethnicity and health" working paper in geography number 4, Department of Geography, Queen Mary College, University of London, Mile End Road, London E1 4NS

Eyles J, Smith D M, Woods K J, 1982, "Spatial resource allocation and State practice: the case of health services in London" *Regional Studies* **16** 239-253

Fox J, Goldblatt P O, 1982 *Longitudinal Study 1971-75* OPCS Series L5 No 1 (HMSO, London)

Goldacre M, 1981, "Mortality statistics as measures of need for outpatient services" *British Medical Journal* **283** 26 September issue, pp 870-871

Goldberg D, Huxley P, 1980 *Mental Illness in the Community. The Pathway to Psychiatric Care* (Tavistock Publications, Andover, Hants)

Hannay D R, 1978, "Symptom prevalence in the community" *Journal of the Royal College of General Practitioners* **28** 492-499

Harris A, Buckle J, 1971 *Handicapped and Impaired in Great Britain* part 1 of report M418 of the Social Survey Division of the Office of Population Censuses and Surveys (HMSO, London)

Holland W, Ipsen J, Kostrzewksi H (Eds), 1979 *Measurement of Levels of Health* (World Health Organization, Copenhagen, Denmark)

Holland W, Waller J, 1971, "Population studies in the London Borough of Lambeth" *Community Medicine* **10** September issue, pp 153-157

Hunt A, 1978 *The Elderly at Home: A Survey of People Aged Sixty-five and Over Living in the Community in England in 1976* Department of Health and Social Security (HMSO, London)

Hunt S, McEwen J, 1980, "The development of a subjective health indicator" *Sociology of Health and Illness* **2** 231-246

Hunt S, McKenna S, McEwen J, Williams J, Popp E, 1981, "The Nottingham Health Profile: subjective health status and medical consultations" *Social Science and Medicine* **15A** issue 3, part 1, pp 221-229

Jackson J, Bartley C, 1982, seminar, Health Research Group, 24 May; details from the Department of Geography, Queen Mary College, Mile End Road, London E1

Jarman B, 1981, "A survey of primary care in London" OP-16, Royal College of General Practitioners, 14 Princes Gate, London SW7

Jazairi N T, 1976 *Approaches to the Development of Health Indicators* (OECD, Paris)

Katz S, Ford A, Moskowitz R, Jackson B, Jaffe M, Cleveland M, 1963, "Studies of illness in the aged. The index of ADL. A standard measure of biological and psychosocial functions" *Journal of the American Medical Association* **185** 914-919

Knight R, Warren M, 1978 *Physically Disabled People Living at Home: A Study of Numbers and Needs* Report on Health and Social Subjects number 13, Department of Health and Social Security (HMSO, London)

Leavey R, 1982 *Inequalities in Urban Primary Care: Use and Acceptability of GP Services* Department of General Practice, Department of Health and Social Security Research Unit, The University, Manchester, England

LHPC, 1979 *Acute Hospital Services in London: A Profile* London Health Planning Consortium (HMSO, London)

LHPC, 1980 *Towards a Balance: A Framework for Acute Hospital Services in London: Reconciling Service with Teaching Needs* London Health Planning Consortium (DHSS, London)

Locker D, 1981 *Symptoms and Illness: The Cognitive Organisation of Disorder* (Tavistock Publications, Andover, Hants)

Merrison, 1979 *Royal Commission on the National Health Service* Chairman: Sir Alexander Walter Merrison (FRS, DL), Cmnd 7615 (HMSO, London)

Muskin S, Dunlop D (Eds), 1979 *Health: What is it Worth? Measures of Health Benefits* (Pergamon Press, Elmsford, NY)

O'Muircheartaigh C A, Wiggins R D, 1981, "The impact of interviewer variability in an epidemiological survey" *Psychological Medicine* **11** 817-824

OPCS, 1979 *The General Household Survey 1978* Office of Population Censuses and Surveys (HMSO, London)

OPCS, 1980 *Classification of Occupations and Coding Index* Office of Population Censuses and Surveys (HMSO, London)

OPCS, 1982a *County Moniters for Inner and Outer London* CEN 81 CM 17/1 and 17/2 (Office of Population Censuses and Surveys, London)

OPCS, 1982b *The General Household Survey 1980* Office of Population Censuses and Surveys (HMSO, London)

Patrick D L, 1981 *Health and Care of the Physically Disabled in Lambeth. The Longitudinal Disability Interviewer Survey. Phase 1 Report* Department of Community Medicine, St Thomas's Hospital Medical School, London

Patrick D L, Darby S C, Green S, Horton G, Locker D, Wiggins D, 1981, "Screening for disability in the inner city" *Journal of Epidemiology and Community Health* **35** 65-70

Pill R, Stott N C, 1982, "Concepts of illness causation and responsibility, some preliminary data from a sample of working class mothers" *Social Science and Medicine* **16** 43-52

Richman N, 1977, "Behaviour problems in preschool children: family and social factors" *British Journal of Psychiatry* **131** 523-527

Rutter M, Tizard J, Whitmore K (Eds), 1970 *Education, Health and Behaviour* (Longman, Harlow, Essex)

Shepherd M, Cooper B, Brown A C, Kalton G W, 1966 *Psychiatric Illness in General Practice* (Oxford University Press, London)

Skinner F, 1969 *Physical Disability and Community Care. A Study of Prevalence and Nature of Disability in Relation to Environmental Characteristics and Social Services in a London Borough* (Bedford Square Press, National Council of Social Service, London)

Skrimshire A, 1976 *A Deprived Health District in a Prosperous Region. A Study of Reported Sickness in a Part of Newham* Department of Social and Administrative Studies, Oxford University, Oxford, England

Tarnopolsky A, Morton-Williams J, 1980 "Aircraft noise and prevalence of psychiatric disorders" research report, SCPR, London

Tennant C, 1977, "The general health questionnaire: a valid index of psychological impairment in Australian populations" *Medical Journal of Australia* **2** 392-394

Thurstone L, 1927, "A law of comparative judgement" *Psychological Review* **34** 273-286

Townsend P, Davidson N, 1982 *Inequalities in Health: The Black Report* (Penguin Books, Harmondsworth, Middx)

Wadsworth M, Butterfield W, Blaney R, 1971 *Health and Sickness: The Choice of Treatment* (Tavistock Publications, Andover, Hants)

Ware J E, Davis-Avery A, Donald C, 1978 *Conceptualization and Measurement of Health for Adults in the Health Insurance Study. Volume V: General Health Perceptions* Department of Health Education and Welfare, Rand Corporation, Main Street, Santa Monica, CA

Watson E, 1982, "Progress on the study of use of child health services by mothers in Tower Hamlets" seminar, 11 November 1982, Department of Clinical Epidemiology, The London Hospital, Mile End Road, London E1

WHO, 1980a *International Classification of Diseases. Basic Tabulation List with Alphabetical Index* ninth edition (World Health Organisation, Geneva)

WHO, 1980b *International Classification of Impairments, Disabilities and Handicaps* (World Health Organisation, Geneva)

Williams R, Johnston L, Willis L, Bennett A, 1976, "Disability: a model and measurement technique" *British Journal of Preventative Social Medicine* **30** 71-78

Wing J, Hailey A, Bransby E, Fryers T, 1972, "Reported prevalence" in *Evaluating a Community Psychiatric Service* Eds J Wing, A Hailey (Oxford University Press, London) pp 78-85

Woods K J, 1982, "The Acheson Report" *London Journal* **8** 108-110

Wyler A, Masuda M, Holmes T, 1968, "The seriousness of illness rating scale" *Journal of Psychosomatic Research* **11** 363-374

The Use of Primary Medical Facilities:
The Complex Case of Measles Vaccinations
in the USA and the UK

A M KIRBY
University of Colorado at Boulder

Introduction

In this paper, a theme already addressed by the author is elaborated, namely the interrelationships between health and health care at the local and national scales (Kirby, 1982a). These interrelationships are summarised in figure 1. It can be seen that there exists a relationship between the overall level of expenditure upon health services within a state and the local distributive levels of that expenditure. Similarly, there is a relationship between local patterns of expenditure and local patterns of morbidity and mortality, although the degree of causality is always open to doubt. What is most interesting is the lack of relationship between national health expenditure and national health outcomes: a study of eighteen developed countries, in which medical expenditure varied as a proportion of gross national product from 4.7% to 7.1%, notes that "health service factors are relatively unimportant in explaining the differences in mortality between our 18 countries" (Cochrane et al, 1978, page 204). The reason for this apparent discrepancy relates to the interplay of local and national issues. Local (environmental) conditions will dictate particular demands for health care; if, however, these are not met, or if the spatial distribution of expenditure is simply inadequate, it is clear that the national health picture will become distorted.

The remainder of this discussion will focus upon a particular expression of this national/local question, namely the attempt to eradicate measles in the USA and the UK.

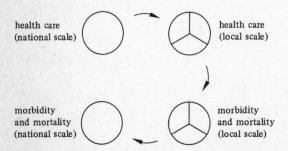

Figure 1. Notional relationships between health and health care at the national and local scales: note that there is no relationship between national levels of expenditure and national patterns of health.

The national picture: the USA

As indicated in figure 2, a major change has occurred in the incidence of measles in the USA since the Korean war. Up to 1962, the prevaccination era, something like half-a-million cases per annum were usual. In 1981, in contrast, there were only 3032 cases reported, a 99.4% reduction.

The Measles Education Program has operated in a legal context to ensure that students entering school at kindergarten or first grade should have measles immunity, which is then enforced until twelfth grade. Thirty-nine states have such comprehensive checks; eleven require documentation of immunisation only on school entrance.

The localised concentration of remaining measles outbreaks is shown in figure 3, where it can be seen that only Texas and Pennsylvania had in excess of five cases per 100000 population in 1981. Pennsylvania is one of those states that does not require comprehensive immunity, and statistical analyses show that outbreaks are significantly higher in such states (Robbins et al, 1981, pages 270–274). Texas and Florida do not fall into the same category, but the existence of relatively numerous illegal immigrants must pose some problems for immunity control.

Figure 2. The incidence of reported measles outbreaks in the USA, 1950–1981.

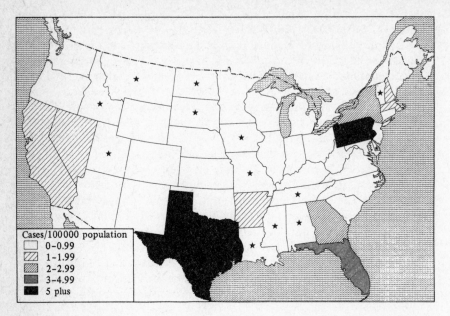

Figure 3. Incidence of reported measles outbreaks by state, 1981. A ★ represents cases arising from out-of-state introductions. (Source: US Department of Health, 1982.)

The national picture: the UK

The situation in the UK is rather different. Data for England and Wales, for example, indicate that the number of reported cases of measles has not slipped below the half-million mark since the Second World War, despite the introduction of vaccination in 1967. The numbers of immunisations have declined more steeply than births in recent years, which is a national characteristic: the virtual collapse of whooping cough immunisation has produced a major increase in reported cases. The essentially voluntary nature of the vaccination programme in the UK means that its success is highly limited (figure 4): only 50% of any birth cohort is ever vaccinated.

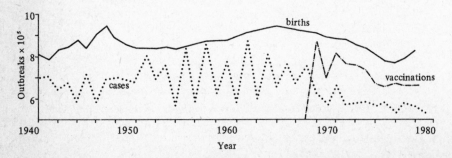

Figure 4. Incidence of reported measles outbreaks in England and Wales, 1940–1980.

The contrast between the epidemiological position in the USA and the UK is therefore quite marked. The US emphasis upon school registration being contingent upon health requirements has almost removed the individual's right to 'choose' the disease (although local variations—at state level—do still exist). In the UK, the onus of vaccination is placed upon the parent, and, in consequence, the presence of measles remains far more apparent. This means, of course, that the geographic factor is likely to be different too. As the UK does not possess internal organisational variations of the sort witnessed in the USA, it is unlikely that we would find gross differences in terms of measles outbreaks, between, for example, individual regional health authorities (RHAs). Instead, it is far more likely that vaccination histories are influenced by highly localised factors, relating to individual primary medical practitioners, neighbourhood attitudes, and clinic accessibility. It is therefore at this scale that the analysis within the next section of the paper is presented.

Local vaccination practice

Analysis of vaccination records was undertaken in 1981, drawing upon a full enumeration of children born between 1975 and 1979 within the Berkshire Area Health Authority (AHA). Children are vaccinated at one of twenty-one centres, which are administered either by individual practitioners or by groups thereof. There exists a choice of vaccination programmes, and the parent decides upon which the child is to receive, if any, and the location at which the treatment will be administered. All vaccination programmes, including the diphtheria/tetanus/polio/measles variant discussed here, involve a series of separate treatments.

The data file was separated into two groups: a 1975–1978 birth cohort, which by 1981 had completed its projected treatment; and a 1979 birth cohort, which in 1981 was commencing its programme of vaccination. Results are presented below for each cohort.

Initial investigations indicate two things. First, that the numbers of children commencing vaccination programmes varied quite markedly over the five-year period. As indicated in figures 5, 6, and 7, median smoothing of the data reveals a pattern of continual change, without regard for, say, seasonal factors (for discussions of the technique, see the appendix). More importantly, the three plots—each for an individual clinic—show little congruence. In other words, temporal fluctuations exist between clinics. Of course, this may simply reflect random variations in birth rates between small areas within the Berkshire AHA, although this interpretation is undermined if we examine figures 8, 9, and 10, which illustrate the *failure* rate for vaccination programmes: these are expressed as ratios of the number of children failing to complete a course of vaccinations vis-à-vis the number of children registered. Once again, variations exist both between clinics and over time, although seasonal fluctuations are not apparent.

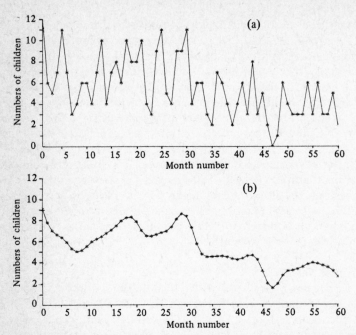

Figure 5. Clinic 775, Reading: numbers of children registering for measles vaccinations over a sixty-month period between 1975 and 1979. (a) Raw data; (b) median smoothing.

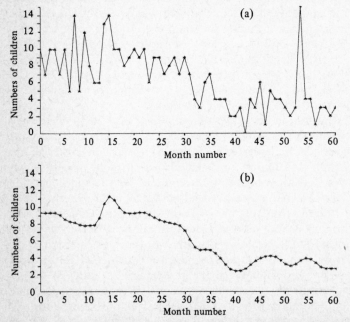

Figure 6. Clinic 776, Reading: numbers of children registering for measles vaccinations over a sixty-month period between 1975 and 1979. (a) Raw data; (b) median smoothing.

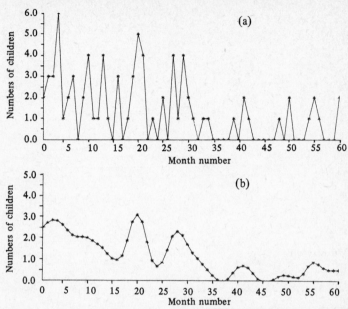

Figure 7. Clinic 777, Reading: numbers of children registering for measles vaccinations over a sixty-month period between 1975 and 1979. (a) Raw data; (b) median smoothing.

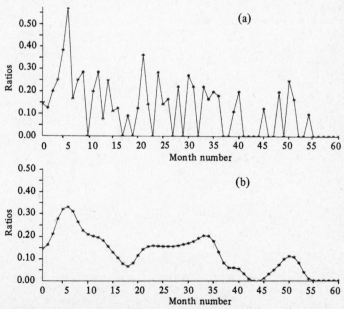

Figure 8. Clinic 775, Reading: ratios of children failing to complete vaccination programmes and total registrations over a sixty-month period between 1975 and 1979. (a) Ratios; (b) smoothed ratios.

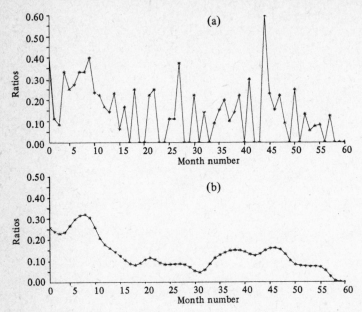

Figure 9. Clinic 776, Reading: ratios of children failing to complete vaccination programmes and total registrations over a sixty-month period between 1975 and 1979. (a) Ratios; (b) smoothed ratios.

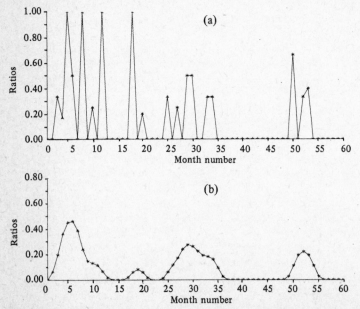

Figure 10. Clinic 777, Reading: ratios of children failing to complete vaccination programmes and total registrations over a sixty-month period between 1975 and 1979. (a) Ratios; (b) smoothed ratios.

Exploratory data analysis

These initial investigations emphasise the validity of examining the individual clinics to unravel variations in vaccination success. Stem and leaf plots (see the appendix for a discussion of the method), shown in figure 11, indicate that the failure rate varies markedly between clinics (Erickson and Nosanchuk, 1977). For the 1975–1978 cohort, none of the clinics had a failure rate below 10%, but two approached 40%. Far less variation was evident for the 1979 cohort, which indicates that recidivism increases over time, as would be expected.

1975–1978 cohort									1979 cohort												
(35)	9	7																			
30									30												
(25)	8	8							(25)												
20	4	0							20												
(15)	8	7	5	5	5	5			(15)												
10	4	4	2	2	2	1	1		10												
(5)	9	9							(5)	8	8	7	7	6	6	6	6	5	5	5	
0									0	4	3	2	2	1	0	0	0	0	0		

Figure 11. Stem and leaf plots of failure rates in individual clinics: data for birth cohorts in percentages.

Multiple regression analysis

What explanations can be derived to account for these large variations? Three introductory hypotheses were proposed, namely that variations in the rates of failure are a function of:

(1) The number of children registered at a clinic. This independent variable may be seen in two contexts, either in terms of an administrative burden, which will allow patients to slip through the net of indifference, or in terms of spatial constraints—a large clinic is likely to have a geographically extended catchment area.

(2) The number of patient transfers. Although data on transfers away from the area exist, it is likely that some failure statistics are really transfers. It is possible that some centres are inefficient in keeping records, in which case we might hypothesise a negative relationship between transfers and failures.

(3) The type of service. A general practitioner may be more attractive to patients and parents than a child health clinic, leading to lower failure rates.

These relationships were tested using as dependent variables the numbers of patients failing to complete treatment; and as independent variables the numbers of children registered, the numbers of transfers, and the type of clinic (a dummy variable). These results are presented in table 1.

Similar results may be noted for both cohorts, with the exception that the second equation (for the far-smaller 1979 cohort) had a far lower r^2 value (45%, as compared with 80%). The results may be summarised as follows:

(a) there exists a strong positive correlation between the numbers of children registered and the numbers failing to attend: this is a linear relationship;

(b) the number of failures and the number of transfers are negatively related;
(c) the number of failures is higher for child health clinics than for doctors' surgeries.

Table 1. Regression coefficients for 1975–1978 cohort failure data and for 1979 cohort failure data.

Independent variables	Regression coefficient	Standard error	t
1975–1978 cohort failure data			
Number of children	0.27	0.05	6.14
Number of transfers	−1.39	0.40	−3.47
Type of clinic	2.97	5.09	0.58
1979 cohort failure data			
Number of children	0.06	0.02	3.47
Number of transfers	−0.50	0.29	−1.72
Type of clinic	1.56	0.95	1.64

Interpretation of results

The results outlined above can be interpreted as follows. In the first instance, it is clear that failures are consistent with the numbers of enrolled patients. This means that very small catchments (spatially accessible) or very large practices (with high levels of organisation) have no influence upon failure rates. Conversely, the type of practice has some effect, although the average increase in failure rates for clinics (vis-à-vis general practitioners) is very small. The third relationship, namely that between transfers and failures, may imply that some of the very high failure rates exhibited by some clinics are in fact spurious and involve a confusion of failures and transfers.

With the caveat that some of the highest values for failure are inflated, the regression results still leave us to explain the (large) variations between individual clinics; this is attempted in the next section.

The use of primary facilities

The range of issues which can affect the use of primary facilities is very large. As Pritchard (1978) shows, for example, *accessibility* and *acceptability* appear to be relatively simple goals for a practitioner to observe, but, in fact, the layers of issues involved are numerous. For instance, in his study he shows that clinic design and ancillary personnel attitudes are both factors which appear trivial, but which can have a deterrent impact upon the client.

In addition to organisational questions, factors such as class and race overlay nearly all issues of health care usage. Waddington (1977), for example, shows the way in which working-class and middle-class clients respond in different ways to what is, in the UK, essentially a service for the middle class. Thus the notion of providing treatment via an appointment system "is tidier for those who have to administer it, but does not always fit the facts of working-class life ... . A number of studies have indicated the difficulties that working-class people have in coping with highly bureaucratized and indeed highly professionalised settings, and any attempts to de-bureaucratize medical settings may well pay dividends in terms of attracting working-class people to use those services more fully" (Waddington, 1977, page 615).

Clearly, class background is important in the understanding of the ability or willingness of the patient to complete a course of treatment, such as a vaccination programme, although such social data were not available in this study.

Using the informal method of evaluating client surnames, I made an attempt to consider racial backgrounds. This produced the expected finding that Asian patients tend to use Asian practitioners wherever possible, and that indigenous patients apparently try to use other clinics, even if relatively long journeys are involved (Kirby, 1983). Clearly, such factors must also place a strain on the likelihood of completing a treatment cycle.

These factors represent ways in which the *demand* for a service may be diminished. Of course, we must also introduce the importance of *supply*. Although this discussion has touched upon aspects of practice, it must again be stressed that broad variations exist, have existed, and will continue to exist, in terms of levels of provision between different geographical units. This applies particularly at the scale of RHAs, but can consistently be traced down to neighbourhoods within individual urban areas (Kirby, 1982b; Knox, 1982). In this context, then, failure rates are to be understood in terms of the list sizes within a particular area (now district) health authority, the case loads of individual practitioners within that framework, and the overall quality of care on offer by any particular practitioner.

Conclusions

In their discussions, the Working Group on Inequalities in Health stated that "the decline in recourse to vaccination and immunization is worrying" (Townsend and Davidson, 1982, page 171). As they rightly argue, inequalities in health are the result of an interplay of many factors: some are international (the amounts spent upon health care overall, a function of a nation's place within the world economy); some are national (such as the barriers between physician and client created by class or racial antagonisms). In addition, however, many of these factors manifest themselves at the *local* scale. As this preliminary analysis indicates— perhaps only by default—an understanding of why localised variations in vaccination rates occur is not readily achieved.

The Working Group suggests, a little lamely, that "doctors and others in the NHS [National Health Service] must be encouraged to convince members of the public of the importance of preventative measures" (Townsend and Davidson, 1982, page 171). This is not enough. As the US example shows very clearly, success in the removal of epidemic disease from a country must begin at the local scale, through an increase in immunisation rates: as this example also demonstrates, that increase is probably best effected via a mild form of compulsion, rather than through attempts to account for low participation rates.

Acknowledgements. This paper is based, in large measure, upon research funded by the Social Science Research Council (HR 6634), and that assistance is gratefully acknowledged. Thanks also go to Kelvyn Jones, for his research assistance; the Berkshire Area Health Authority, for great cooperation in making data available; and the Public Health Department of the University of California at Berkeley.

References
Cochrane A L, St Leger A J, Moore F, 1978, "Health service input and mortality output in developed countries" *Journal of Epidemiology and Community Health* **32** 200–205
Cox N J, Jones K, 1981, "Exploratory data analysis" in *Quantitative Geography* Eds N Wrigley, R J Bennett (Routledge and Kegan Paul, Henley-on-Thames, Oxon) pp 135–143
Erickson B H, Nosanchuk T A, 1977 *Understanding Data* (McGraw-Hill, New York)
Kirby A M, 1982a, "Health-care and the state: Britain and the United States" WP-387, Institute for Urban and Regional Development, University of California, Berkeley, CA 94720, USA
Kirby A M, 1982b *The Politics of Location* (Methuen, London)
Kirby A M, 1983, "Neglected factors in public services research" *Annals of the Association of American Geographers* **73** 289–295
Knox P L, 1982 *Urban Social Geography* (Longman, Harlow, Essex)
Pritchard P, 1978 *Manual of Primary Health-care: Its Nature and Organisation* (Oxford University Press, London)
Robbins K B, Brandling-Bennett A D, Hinman A R, 1981, "Low measles incidence: association with enforcement of school immigration laws" *American Journal of Public Health* **71** 270–274
Townsend P, Davidson N, 1982 *Inequalities in Health: The Black Report* (Penguin Books, Harmondsworth, Middx)
US Department of Health, 1982, "Measles—United States, 1981" in *Morbidity and Mortality Weekly Report* 5 February issue; US Department of Health and Human Services, Atlanta, GA (US Government Printing Office, Washington, DC)
Waddington I, 1977, "The relationship between social class and the use of health services in Britain" *Journal of Advanced Nursing* **2** 609–619

In this chapter, two techniques are employed which may be relatively unfamiliar: these are stem and leaf plots and data smoothing. In both cases, the emphasis is upon basic description, as opposed to inferential analysis.

Stem and leaf plots are one of a series of simple display procedures which permit the maximum amount of information to be extracted from the data. The stem represents the coarse ordering of the data values, and the leaves can be equated with the class frequency of a histogram (for a full example, see Cox and Jones, 1981, pages 136–137). Visual examination indicates quickly the modal and median values within the data set, yet preserves the visibility of individual values. In consequence, such plots are quicker than a histogram to produce and more informative.

Smoothing procedures are valuable in the evaluation of spatial or time series data, and overcome once again the complexity implicit in standard time series analysis or in trend surfaces. An assumption is made that the series is composed as follows: data = smooth + rough, where the 'rough' element is measurement error, short-term fluctuation, or local effects. Smoothing—which usually involves taking running medians by groups of three or five data values—removes scattered points (rough data), and leaves a smoothed curve: linear methods (such as trend surface analysis) will tend to mix these outliers into the smoothed curve. Of course, data can be smoothed and resmoothed, but an initial pass (as undertaken in this chapter) will present a simple curve which can be compared with other time series data and the location of major 'noise' elements. Once again, the reader is directed to Cox and Jones (1981, pages 140–141) for a fuller account and examples of the technique.

Models of Resource Policy of Regional Health Authorities

R G BEVAN
University of Warwick
A H SPENCER
National University of Singapore

1 Introduction

In his recent survey of spending on health care, Maxwell (1981, pages 101–102) clearly sets out why this has become a subject of such concern in developed countries:

"By the early 1970s it was clear that a crisis would soon arise in health-care spending .... For at least twenty years, throughout the developed world, annual increases in health-care expenditures had consistently outstripped increases in national income. The factors that had fuelled this increase had not spent their force, and one could safely predict that health-care expenditures would not quickly reach a natural plateau, either in money terms or as a percentage of GNP. On the other hand, governments, which had been the principal paymasters for increased health-care spending, would be more sensitive to further increases now that health care had become a very substantial component of public expenditure. The clash was bound to come eventually. It came earlier than it would otherwise have done because of the worsening macro-economic position facing governments in the developed world in the 1970s, particularly after the oil crisis of late 1973. Moreover, the sharp reduction in economic growth coincided in many of the Western developed countries with a widespread disillusionment with government in general and with welfare programs in particular."

In 1977 the Organisation for Economic Cooperation and Development (OECD) published the report of a study on public expenditure on health which described the problems of controlling health care as immediate and urgent for its member countries (OECD, 1977). If control alone mattered, then there would be little scope for regional scientists to contribute to the crisis of managing expenditure on health care. Maxwell, however, in his survey, which is more recent and comprehensive than that undertaken by the OECD (in particular, as far as statistics allow, it examines both public and private expenditures), argues that, although the spotlight of the mid- and late-1970s was on health care expenditures, with financial control receiving attention almost to the exclusion of everything else, financial control will soon be yesterday's problem. He sees the challenge as "not merely to limit, but also to choose in an informed way where to set the limits, and to obtain the best results one can within those limits" (Maxwell, 1981, page 105).

The OECD report saw the problems of choosing where to set limits on expenditure on health care as particularly difficult because of the prevalent fear of governments of the member countries that "the demand for health is insatiable on the basis of any pricing system that is socially and ethically acceptable" (OECD, 1977). The setting of such acceptable limits on the total of health care spending is likely to be achieved only if it is accompanied by policies aimed at distributing that total fairly.

The distribution of resources to health services will be judged to be fair against two kinds of criteria. One criterion is equity in access: this was put in an English official report, known as the RAWP (Resource Allocation Working Party) Report, from the Department of Health and Social Security (DHSS), as "equal opportunity of access to health care for people at equal risk" (DHSS, 1976c, page 7). A second criterion attempts to secure acceptable standards in those kinds of health services which tend to be neglected: in general, services for long-stay patients and, in particular, services for the mentally handicapped. (For a discussion of these problems in the United Kingdom, see Bevan et al, 1980.)

The UK Government has interpreted the policy of moving towards equal access to health services in terms of geography: a recent report (see Townsend and Davidson, 1982) on inequalities in health by social class, as measured by available statistics (which are mainly mortality data), was given a cool reception by the Secretary of State then responsible for health services. The problem of attempting to frame a policy to move towards equal geographical access is one to which regional scientists can naturally expect to make a contribution. Hodgart (1978) analyses the assumptions behind models which have been developed to solve problems of locating central facilities to optimise access to public services.

Central facilities for health services could be either hospital- or community-based. In this paper we are primarily concerned with the former. Our reason for so doing is illustrated by a point made by Saul Miller, Health Minister of Manitoba, namely that, when governments seek financial controls on health services, they concentrate on hospitals in accordance with the Willy Sutton principle: Willy, an expert thief, was asked why he concentrated his attention on banks; "Because," he replied, "that's where the money is" (quoted in Maxwell, 1981, page 104).

The problem of optimising access to hospital services requires distinctions to be made between the hospital specialities[1] on the basis of the size of catchment populations necessary to generate sufficient work load for each speciality to be provided. The common hospital specialities can be provided on the basis of a catchment population of about 100000–150000: this formed the basis for *A Hospital Plan for England and Wales* (MoH, 1962). But that plan recognised that "there are a small number of specialities, such as radiotherapy, neurosurgery, plastic surgery and thoracic surgery which need a larger catchment population and could only be provided

[1] See editor's note, page 6.

at certain hospitals" (page 6). The most recent guidance from the DHSS on radiotherapy services, for example, recommends that: "Normally a population of one million is considered to be the smallest to produce a sufficient caseload for a radiotherapy centre. In populous areas, centres serving 2 million or more people are preferable" (DHSS, 1978b, page 2).

Mayhew and Leonardi (see chapter 9 in this volume), taking into account the different sizes of catchment populations necessary for different specialities, have derived theoretical optimal arrangements for different kinds of hospital services. They have also shown (Mayhew and Leonardi, 1982) how theoretical arrangements vary according to changes in the criteria used to define optimality.

In this paper we look at the problem of formulating policies for hospital services through the processes of resource allocation and planning in the United Kingdom. We focus upon that problem as faced by a region, because this is the smallest scale at which an administrative authority could expect to be self-sufficient for health services; that is, to aim to provide most of the services which its residents need. This is one reason why UK health services have always been organised through a regional tier.

In the second section of the paper, we outline the national contexts within which policies have been developed: changes in finance, organisation, and planning. In the third section, we discuss the methods used nationally which are intended to secure equitable allocations of resources between the regions in England. In sections four and five, we discuss modifications made by regional working parties in the national methods to attempt to achieve the same objective subregionally, and how these methods are used in practice. In the final section, we suggest work that regional scientists might do that relates to how decisions are actually made and which would help regions move towards optimal arrangements of the different kinds of hospital-based services.

2 The changing contexts of policymaking
2.1 Finance
The National Health Service (NHS) was launched in 1948 on the fundamental misconception that its expenditure would probably decline, because once people were able to have free access to its services they would become healthier and have less need of them (see Bevan et al, 1980, for a review of changes in NHS finance from 1948 to 1979). Attempts were made to control expenditure through the imposition of annual cash ceilings, but expenditure continued to increase. This experience did not lead to rejection of the belief that spending ought not to increase, but to allegations of extravagance and inefficiency. In 1953 the Guillebaud Committee was asked to enquire into the cost of the NHS and to investigate those allegations. Its report (MoH, 1956) saw no scope for savings: it pointed out that the increases in cost had been accompanied by greater proportionate increases in services. Indeed, the report recommended that

new hospitals be built, recognising that, when these were completed, they would result in further increases in the cost of the NHS.

After the Guillebaud Report, attempts to constrain spending were replaced by a policy of commitment to real growth: for nearly twenty years from 1957, allocations of revenue increased in real terms by 4% per annum. This was generally allocated incrementally, with generous additional funding of the running costs of new hospitals (this was known as the Revenue Consequences of Capital Scheme—RCCS).

This phase of stable, sustained, real growth ended in the mid- to late-1970s (as part of the general crisis described by Maxwell), and from 1976 the annual rate of real growth of the NHS was reduced from 4% to between 1% and 2%, and there were year-to-year fluctuations in this growth because of the varying impact of cash limits (also introduced in 1976).

From 1982 the whole concept of what constitutes 'real growth' becomes problematic, since the Government has chosen to abandon the planning of public expenditure in constant prices. The methods of cash planning are supposed to set in cash what the NHS will receive for the next three years, on the assumption of annual rates of inflation of 6% for 1983–1984, 5% for 1984–1985, and 4% for 1985–1986 (HM Treasury, 1983). The Government has not fully financed the consequences of pay settlements made in 1982–1983: these were above the level assumed in making the cash allocations for that year. But those effects may be offset by lower-than-planned rates of inflation in 1983–1984. This picture is further confused by the way the Government refers to growth which is to be financed by 'efficiency savings'. These savings are not defined in terms of efficient (or inefficient) resource use. In practice they impose cuts on those regional health authorities (RHAs), which, according to the national methods of resource allocation (see section 3), are relatively overprovided, to provide growth money for the relatively deprived RHAs.

The general prospect for the NHS seem to be little or no growth in the purchasing power of the cash it receives for buying goods and paying its staff (pay accounts for over 70% of NHS expenditure). This is against an increasing need for its services from the growing proportion of elderly in the population: this demographic change is estimated to require about a 1% growth in services per annum to maintain existing standards. And there are various kinds of improvements in diagnosis and treatment, which means that the best kinds of care tend to increase in cost. The NHS is back to a similar position to its early years of having to provide services within a cash ceiling.

2.2 Organisational structure

Health services in England were organised initially by thirteen (later fourteen) regional hospital boards (RHBs). In the 1974 NHS reorganisation, these were replaced by fourteen RHAs (see table 1). Scotland, Wales, and Northern Ireland constitute regions for this purpose, with their respective government departments (the Scottish Home and Health Department, the Welsh Office, the Department of Health and Social Services) also having regional responsibilities. Before the 1974 reorganisation, 'NHS' was pejoratively said to represent 'National Hospitals Service'. This was because most of the money allocated to the NHS was administered by RHBs and hospital management committees (HMCs), both of which were only concerned with hospitals: RHBs saw their planning responsibility as being about deciding where new hospitals should be built, and within the RHBs each hospital was administered by an HMC.

The major weakness of the original structure of the NHS was said to be the fragmentation of health services into three parts: hospitals, general practices, and local authority services. Furthermore, teaching hospitals were outside the regional structure, each being separately administered by its own board of governors—a particular problem for the metropolitan boards given the concentration of teaching hospitals in London. The objective of the 1974 reorganisation was to move the focus from concern with hospitals to the needs of population and to provide a structure to enable these needs to be coherently organised. In England, ninety area health authorities (AHAs) were created, to be coterminous with the new local authorities serving in the main populations of 0.25–0.5 million. Family practitioner committees were established to cover the same boundaries as AHAs. An AHA consisted of one (or more) district(s) managed by teams which included a general practitioner. Undergraduate teaching hospitals were brought within the regional structure.

The 1974 reorganisation was hurriedly put into effect to coincide with the reorganisation of local government. It was criticised for having too many tiers, and in 1982 was restructured (DHSS, 1980a) with, effectively, the area tier being removed and the district tier being granted authority status. Previously districts were only managerially autonomous, having no statutory existence. [Data on the new district health authorities (DHAs) are given in table 1.] Each local authority responsible for social services is exceptionally coterminous only with one DHA. The administration of family practitioner

Table 1. NHS organisation in England.

Type of health authority	Number	Mean size of authority		Range of sizes of authorities' populations
		population (millions)	expenditure (£m at current prices)	
Regional (from April 1974)	14	3	500	2–5 millions
District (from April 1982)[a]	192	0.25	35	90000–840000

[a] From April 1974 to March 1982, area health authorities existed, the mean sizes of which were approximately double those of district health authorities.

services is not related to the new DHAs. The organisational links introduced
in 1974 and intended to promote coordination between hospitals, local
authority services, and family practitioner services have therefore been
weakened, and the 1982 reforms are intended to strengthen the management
of hospitals.

There are two important differences between the original and the 1982
organisations of the NHS. First, each authority (RHA and DHA) is now
responsible for services for a defined residential population and not only
for the hospitals within its boundary; in particular, each DHA has much
wider concerns than that of an HMC, which was solely responsible for one
hospital. Second, undergraduate teaching hospitals are now administered
by DHAs (and there is at least one teaching hospital in each RHA).

2.3 Hospital planning

In the 1960s, health service planning was dominated by the concept of the
district general hospital (DGH), which was set out in detail in a building
note (MoH, 1961). The concept involved the concentration of ordinary
specialities on one site and was used in a plan of hospital building for
England and Wales (MoH, 1962). The plan justified that concentration
because of the trend of greater interdependence between the various
branches of medicine and the need to bring together a wide range of the
facilities required for diagnosis and treatment. The plan stated that
"The district general hospital offers the most practicable method of
placing the full range of hospital facilities at the disposal of patients and
this consideration far outweighs the disadvantage of longer travel for some
patients and their visitors" (MoH, 1962, page 6).

The original concept of the DGH was based on an optimal size of
600-800 beds serving catchment populations of 100 000-150 000. That
concept was reviewed by the Bonham-Carter Report (MoH, 1969), which
advanced three arguments for much larger hospitals.

First, the Report saw substantial advantages in basing all hospital
services for the mentally ill and elderly at a DGH, and favoured services
for the mentally handicapped being provided from within, or on the same
site as, a DGH. The 1962 Hospital Plan (MoH, 1962) implied only partial
integration of services for the mentally ill and elderly, and recommended
separate provision of services for the mentally handicapped.

Second, the Report examined in detail the specialities (and subspecialities
within general medicine and general surgery) that ought normally to be
provided on one site and the minimal requirements for consultant staffing
in each speciality (and subspeciality). The recommended minimum cover in
each speciality was two consultants, except for general medicine and
general surgery for which the desired minimum was six consultants for
each. The requirements could only be justified by larger catchment
populations than those recommended by the 1962 Hospital Plan: the
Report recommended an increase in the range of 100 000-150 000 to a
range of 200 000-300 000.

Third, the Report favoured larger hospitals on grounds of increased efficiency in the organisation and staffing of supporting technical and other services: it was suggested that these services could be optimally provided in one large DGH serving a catchment population of 200 000 or more.

The implications of these arguments for locating a wider range of services for a larger catchment population at a DGH on one site were for hospitals of 1000–1750 beds. This recommendation is said by Watkin (1975) to have had a 'lukewarm' reception by the Government, and the most recent statement on hospital size (DHSS, 1980b) recommends a policy similar to that of the 1962 Hospital Plan: a preferred size of 450–600 beds; only partial integration of services for the elderly and mentally ill; and no services for the mentally handicapped at DGHs. That recent statement of policy referred to the balance to be struck between advantages of concentration and the resulting requirements arising from longer travel distances for some patients and their visitors. It asserted that reports subsequent to the 1962 Hospital Plan, "in particular the Bonham-Carter Report of 1969, implied even greater concentration and made no reference to the convenience of patients" (DHSS, 1980b, page 3).

It is untrue, however, to say that the Bonham-Carter Report did not consider the convenience of patients. It specifically discussed the problems of accessibility:

"... if a larger population is to be served some patients and their visitors will have to travel longer distances to hospitals; moreover, a high proportion of hospital patients, and of their visitors, are elderly and many of them cannot afford to travel by private car or taxi, but must rely on public or ambulance transport" (MoH, 1969, page 8).

To cope with the problems of access, the Report recommended coordinated planning of hospital, ambulance, and public services; a sympathetic review of arrangements for giving financial assistance to those who cannot otherwise afford to visit relatives in hospital; and arrangements to be made for overnight accommodation for relatives of dangerously ill patients and for patients who may have to attend the hospital for prolonged investigation or treatment, but who do not require to be nursed in bed.

However, the Report had little constructive to say about the problems of managing the large hospitals proposed. Later research suggested that diseconomies of scale set in for hospitals of more than 600 beds (see Coverdale et al, 1980). This is one of the reasons why the preferred size of hospitals is now within the range of 450–600 beds. That range seems to be optimal on grounds of cost and does provide easier access for treatment of common conditions. But the most recent statement on hospital policy (DHSS, 1980b) does not provide a framework for coordinated planning of the full range of acute specialities.

This outline of changes in policy on hospital planning is sufficient to indicate that a coherent strategy for the provision of acute services will not emerge from treating that provision as if it were a problem in the location of a central facility. Regarding the problem in that way focuses discussion on what should or should not normally be provided at a DGH. But the search for a uniform concept of a DGH encounters difficulties with those specialities (and subspecialities) requiring large catchment populations: these specialities cannot be provided in every DGH without resulting in either unmanageably large hospitals or underutilisation. What is needed is a method of analysis that enables authorities to determine how these specialities should be arranged: the rudimentary elements of such a method are discussed in the final section of this paper.

2.4 Service planning

The 1974 reorganisation was intended to alter the emphasis on hospitals, and the proposals for reorganisation emphasised a new planning system (DHSS, 1972). This system was intended to enable policymaking to be better integrated and to focus upon developing services (which were not to be exclusively hospital-based) to meet the needs of communities served by the new authorities and districts.

It was intended that policy should be integrated in three different ways: *vertically*—to enable a dialogue on priorities to take place between the different tiers of the NHS and the DHSS; *horizontally*—to enable health authorities, local authorities, and family practitioners to coordinate services; and *corporately*—to enable the different disciplines and professions involved in providing care to agree policies.

The planning system was structured by client (or care) groups. These groups are defined in three different ways. Three groups are defined for patients by condition: the mentally ill, the mentally handicapped, and those requiring maternity services. Two groups are defined by age: the elderly and children. And there are two residual groups: acute services, (that is, hospital-based) and community services.

The broad framework of client groups is a major advance on what was available previously, and it is designed to give structure to what were seen as major problems for the new authorities: there had been (for example, see Bevan et al, 1980), and continue to be (for example, see Hencke, 1983), scandals about standards in hospitals for the mentally handicapped. The intention was to run down large hospitals for the mentally ill and the mentally handicapped and to develop community-based care; caring for the elderly is a growing problem because those over the age of sixty-five, and especially those over seventy-five, put heavy demands on health services, and the numbers of elderly were forecast to increase, and of the over-seventy-fives to increase dramatically.

Nevertheless, the care-group structure has a major weakness. The acute-care block accounts for nearly half of total spending by health authorities, and the planning system gives no framework for planning the different kinds of acute specialities. Furthermore, the services defined to fall within the elderly care group exclude acute services, if these are not administered by a geriatrician. Yet about half of the acute beds are occupied by people over the age of sixty-five. Similar problems of overlap arise with services for children and in the planning of community services.

The care-group structure and the principles behind the planning system were promulgated in the proposals setting out the planned reorganisation of the NHS (DHSS, 1972). At that time, the NHS was receiving generous annual increases of growth money. The planning system was actually launched in 1976 and coincided with the beginnings of retrenchment (DHSS, 1976a). The reduction in the expected rate of growth of NHS resources meant that, if the priority services for the mentally handicapped, the mentally ill, and the elderly were to be improved, the money would have to come from cuts in other services.

The Government initially proposed rationalisation of maternity services (given a falling birth rate) and of acute services (DHSS, 1976b; 1977; 1978a). However, concern about the relatively high rates of perinatal mortality meant that after a few years the Government decided that total expenditure on maternity services ought not to be reduced (DHSS, 1979c). This meant that the priority services could only be improved by rationalisation of acute care. This is difficult to achieve, given that there is no framework to plan these services; and there was understandable confusion about what was meant by making cuts in acute services and improving care of the elderly (given that the elderly are such heavy users of acute services).

A recent circular (DHSS, 1982a) has suggested changes which are intended to simplify the planning system and to make it less bureaucratic. Although these changes may make the production of plans easier for authorities, the system requires to become considerably more sophisticated if it is to provide a sound basis for regions and districts in their planning of the different kinds of acute services for the populations for which they are responsible.

3 Resource allocation to regions

The 1974 NHS reorganisation and the planning system were not designed to cope with problems arising from reductions in the growth of resources received by the NHS. The Resource Allocation Working Party (RAWP) was appointed in May 1975 in response to those problems. Its terms of reference were:

"To review the arrangements for distributing NHS capital and revenue to RHAs, AHAs and Districts respectively with a view to establishing a method of securing, as soon as practicable, a pattern of distribution responsive objectively, equitably and efficiently to relative need and to make recommendations" (DHSS, 1976c, page 5).

The RAWP produced an interim report in August 1975, and a final report the following year (DHSS, 1976c) known as the RAWP Report—

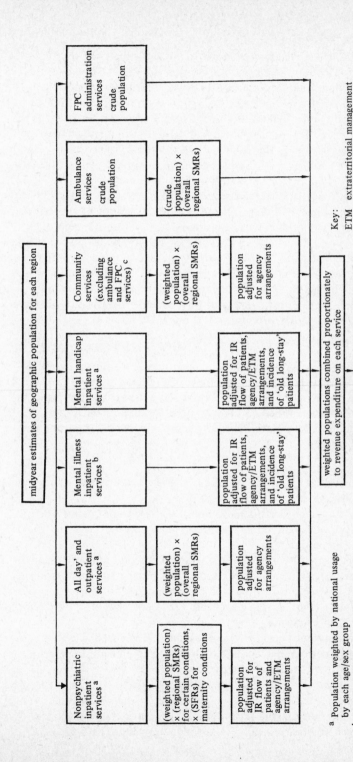

midyear estimates of geographic population for each region

Nonpsychiatric inpatient services [a]

(weighted population) × (regional SMRs) for certain conditions, × (SFRs) for maternity conditions

population adjusted for IR flow of patients and agency/ETM arrangements

All day' and outpatient services [a]

(weighted population) × (overall regional SMRs)

population adjusted for agency arrangements

Mental illness inpatient services [b]

population adjusted for IR flow of patients, agency/ETM arrangements, and incidence of 'old long-stay' patients

Mental handicap inpatient services [a]

population adjusted for IR flow of patients, agency/ETM arrangements, and incidence of 'old long-stay' patients

Community services (excluding ambulance and FPC services) [c]

(weighted population) × (overall regional SMRs)

population adjusted for agency arrangements

Ambulance services crude population

(crude population) × (overall regional SMRs)

FPC administration services crude population

weighted populations combined proportionately to revenue expenditure on each service

if appropriate to region, population adjusted for London weighting

revenue available nationally for services distributed in proportion to each region's weighted population

Key:
ETM   extraterritorial management
FPC   family practitioner committee
IR   interregional
SFR   standardised fertility ratio
SMR   standardised mortality ratio
×   multiplied by

[a] Population weighted by national usage by each age/sex group
[b] Population weighted by national usage by each age/sex group for marrieds and unmarrieds
[c] Population weighted by broad cost of national usage by each age group

Figure 1. The buildup of a revenue target (source: DHSS, 1976c).

which has been of seminal importance. Its methods are used by the DHSS to determine allocations of capital and revenue to RHAs. Regional working parties generally produce methods for allocating revenue that broadly follow the RAWP methods. (Capital, because of the problems of valuing stock—discussed below, is a different matter.) Any method that alters the way resources are distributed will naturally stimulate controversy, but the striking feature of the RAWP Report is the broad consensus about its principles and methods—a sharp contrast to recent changes in calculating the Rate Support Grant for local authorities (for example, see Kay, 1982).

A consequence of the RAWP Report has been the creation of a subculture of experts able to marshall criticisms of its methods. Much of this criticism has shown that the methods work well in deciding the entitlement of regions, and become (as the RAWP itself recognised) less secure the smaller the unit to which they apply: that is, they are not so good for AHAs as for RHAs, and not so good for DHAs as for AHAs. And though the weaknesses of the methods have been spelt out for use subregionally, it is exceptional for critics also to suggest a way which is significantly different from and better than that proposed by the RAWP.

The RAWP methods work by calculating resource targets for authorities (and districts). The core of each target is derived from the residential population of each authority and the expenditure it would receive if it were providing services at the national average. Figure 1 shows the way a revenue target for a region is built up from the national average provision for different services, applied to its residential population, with adjustments made for cross-boundary flows (arising when people who live in one region are treated in another).

3.1 The calculation of the components of a revenue target
The main principles behind the calculation of each component of a revenue target are outlined below.

Ambulance and family practitioner committee (FPC) administration services: the product of national average expenditure per head and the region's total population.

Mental handicap inpatient services: the sum of the products of national average expenditure by each age/sex group and numbers in each group in the region. Adjustments are made for cross-boundary flows and for 'old long-stay' patients (that is, those for whom it is not possible to know from which region they originally came).

Mental illness inpatient services: this is calculated in a similar way to the mental handicap component, except that allowance is made for marital status (which affects the incidence of mental illness).

Day' and outpatient and community services: the first element is the sum of the products of national average expenditure by each age/sex group and numbers in each group in the region. This element is then multiplied by the standardised mortality ratio (SMR) for the region. The SMR is a surrogate measure of morbidity (the incidence of sickness). It is the ratio of the number of deaths actually occurring in the region and the expected number of deaths in the region (calculated by applying national mortality ratios to the numbers in each age/sex group of the region). The effect of using SMRs is that, if the region's deaths are, for example 10% higher than would be expected from those national statistics, then the component for these services would be increased by 10%.

(No compensation is made for any of the above services for cross-boundary flows. It makes no sense to do this for community services. The reason for such compensation not being made for day' and outpatient services is that the necessary data on patients are not available.)

Nonpsychiatric inpatient services: this component is calculated in a similar manner as for those described already, except that SMRs are applied by conditions (where appropriate, conditions being defined by the International Classification of Diseases), with standardised fertility ratios (SFRs) being used for maternity services. The component is built up from the products of estimated national average expenditure on each age/sex group by condition and numbers in each age/sex group in the region. Compensation is made for these services for cross-boundary flows.

3.2 Protection of the extra costs of clinical training

Those hospitals which provide clinical training for medical and dental students on a significant scale are more expensive than comparable acute hospitals: teaching hospitals training medical students cost some 20% more than comparable hospitals. These extra costs are due not only to teaching but also to the joint activities of teaching, research, and advanced medicine commonly found in teaching hospitals. It is extraordinarily difficult to disentangle the separate cost implications of these different activities, and a recent study has concluded that it makes little sense to attempt to do so in England (Perrin and Magee, 1983). The DHSS, in making its allocations to regions, makes a notional separation of a sum, known as the service increment for teaching (SIFT), intended to give protection solely for the extra costs of providing facilities for the clinical teaching of medical and dental students.

The SIFT allocation is separate from the calculation of a region's target. The DHSS uses an estimate of a SIFT rate per (whole-time equivalent) student for medical and dental students in clinical training at hospitals. Each region is allocated the product of the SIFT rate and the estimated total student numbers (whole-time equivalents) two years on from the year of allocation in the region. The SIFT rate per student is derived from estimates of the excess costs of teaching hospitals per student associated with each medical school over estimated national average costs of treating the work load of those hospitals (see Bevan, 1982, for a detailed exposition and critique).

3.3 The calculation of capital targets

Estimation of each region's target for the allocation of capital is similar to that used for the allocation of revenue, but to estimate fair shares of capital requires an assessment of the value and distribution of existing stock, which is difficult to make because there is no regular national survey of NHS capital stock. The RAWP Report (DHSS, 1976c) used a 1972 survey, which showed that for most regions more than half their stock was built before 1918 (and for three regions the proportion was more than 70%). The RAWP used broad depreciation methods (for example, stock built before 1918 was depreciated by 70%) which could not allow for the location and state of the stock (an important potential weakness given the age of much of the stock). The RAWP methods provided estimates of capital stock for each region and total stock for England. Each region's target is derived by dividing total stock plus future total allocations of capital by the region's population, making allowance (as in the revenue method) for the need for capital of different services and for the population characteristics of each region (age, sex, and SMRs).

3.4 Criticisms of the RAWP methods

Of particular interest here are criticisms made of the RAWP methods for calculating revenue targets. This is because discussion about the allocation of revenue in the NHS now takes place with those methods providing the starting point for development or, exceptionally, a point of departure. The methods of allowing for the costs of clinical training of medical and dental students and of calculating capital targets have not been so thoroughly examined by regional working parties and are not criticised here. The main criticisms made of the RAWP approach to revenue are: the choice of years for the population base; the use made of SMRs; the method of compensating for cross-boundary flows; and the method of adjusting for old long-stay patients who are either mentally ill or mentally handicapped. These criticisms are briefly summarised in the following paragraphs.

The year of the population base: The RAWP recommended that the year chosen "should be the estimate of the mid-year population of each Region nearest to the year for which allocations are made. In practice, for each allocation year this would probably be the mid-year estimate for the year two years earlier" (DHSS, 1976c, page 14). This necessarily introduces a lag in the making of allocations for those regions undergoing changes, relative to England as a whole, in the size and structure of their populations. Winyard (1981) gave details of the impact of that lag and drew attention to the way the method penalises regions with rapidly increasing populations. The Oxford Region, for example, had been penalised because its expenditure was above its estimated target, whereas, had its target been calculated from more recent data, its actual spending would have been seen to be below its target and it would have been entitled to more money. In the

East Anglia Region the growth in population resulted in the movement of its target exceeding the rate of movement towards its target. This meant that for this region, if that trend continued, it would have taken more than 500 years for it to receive its target allocation! The DHSS announced, following these criticisms, that revenue allocations would be based on population projections to appropriate years and that changes would be made to accommodate problems faced by regions with rapid population growth (DHSS, 1982b).

The use of SMRs: The argument about the use of SMRs is inevitably inconclusive. This is because morbidity cannot be measured directly (if it could there would be no need to bother with surrogates). Hence it is difficult to justify fully or to refute the choice of SMRs. Three points can usefully be made. First, SMRs do have an important impact upon targets (DHSS, 1976c). This is because they apply directly to important components of targets. Second, although there is a clear need to make some allowance for morbidity, the assumption underlying the way SMRs are used is difficult to justify, this assumption being that there is a one-to-one relationship between mortality and the need for resources. Third, other mortality ratios could be used, which may be more relevant than the SMR, and the choice of ratio does have a significant impact on targets (Palmer et al, 1979).

Compensation for cross-boundary flows: The first stage of this calculation for nonpsychiatric inpatients is to apply cost estimates of treatment by speciality to the net flows of patients into or out of a region for each speciality. The sum of these products is then divided by the national cost per head of these services to convert them into a population equivalent. There are two problems with this method.

First, costs are not reported by speciality in the NHS, and so speciality costs have to be estimated. The DHSS produces estimates from regression analysis: total costs of each hospital are regressed on statistics of patient treatment in groups of specialities (see Coverdale et al, 1980). This method produces approximate estimates only. Sensitivity analysis has shown that this approach is adequate for compensation for flows between regions, but, below that level, targets are sensitive to changes in cost estimates.

The second problem arises in the translation of costs into population data using the national admission rates. Since the rates of admission vary about this mean rate, there is no guarantee that the net effect of the population adjustments made will add up to the population actually served (Senn and Shaw, 1978). Again, this does not matter for regions, but could lead to the perpetuation of inequalities if applied subregionally. Consider, for example, two neighbouring districts, A and B, with A having better-than-average services and a higher-than-average admission rate and B having worse-than-average services and a lower-than-average admission rate. Every patient that A receives from B, rather than from its own district, results in a net gain in A's population, and the converse applies to B. This has the opposite impact on targets to what would be required to indicate equality.

Adjustments for 'old long-stay' patients who are mentally ill or mentally handicapped: These adjustments are made by estimating the numbers of these patients for whom each region ought to be providing care. These estimates are derived by multiplying the national proportions of such patients in the total population in England by the population of each region. Adjustments are then made on the assumption that regions with less than these estimates are having people who originally came from this region looked after by those regions which are caring for more patients than their estimates.

This weakness is a general criticism made of the RAWP methods, which base their allocations on priorities of expenditure during the past at a time when these priorities are supposed to be changing. The significance of these shifts in priorities on targets is generally negligible—although national statements of priorities may appear to have greater force if these are seen to be coherent with and used in methods of deciding future allocations. The general criticism, however, is particularly important for services for the mentally ill and the mentally handicapped. This is because the intention is to run down the numbers of patients in these hospitals and to develop community-based services. Regions vigorously pursuing such a policy would be penalised because they would have less than the national proportion of patients in these large long-stay institutions.

4 Methods used to calculate resource targets subregionally

In this section, we discuss modifications made by regional working parties in the calculation of revenue and capital targets. We draw on reports of methods used to calculate revenue targets of the following RHAs: East Anglia (EARHA, 1978; 1981, North Western (NWRHA, 1979), Oxford (ORHA, 1978; 1980), South Western (SWRHA, 1979; 1982), Trent (TRHA, 1981), and West Midlands (WMRHA, 1982); and the joint working group, with representatives from the DHSS and the four Thames Regional Health Authorities—known, and referred to here, as 'the Thames RAWP' (DHSS, 1979b; 1981). Few RHAs have established working parties for capital targets, and here we refer only to the working parties of East Anglia, the North West, and the South West. Of course, many of these working parties were making their recommendations in the context of the 1974 organisational structure (in which RHAs were making allocations to AHAs) and of limited growth in allocations to RHAs. We have also spoken to officers in the following RHAs: East Anglia, North East Thames, North West Thames, South East Thames, South West Thames, South Western, Trent, and West Midlands. In the final part of this section, we briefly mention how relevant these recommendations were believed to be for the new structure against the prospects of cuts in allocations to some RHAs.

4.1 Calculating revenue targets

We have learnt about methods recommended for ten of the fourteen RHAs and are therefore able to give a survey of general responses to the problems identified in the previous section: the choice of year for the population base; the use made of SMRs; the method of compensating for cross-boundary flows; and the provision of services for the mentally ill and the mentally handicapped.

Choice of year for the population base: The East Anglia, Trent, and Oxford RHAs use projected populations for the year of allocation. The Trent RHA has a major programme of new hospital building and attempts to forecast the effects of this on the populations served by the hospitals of each district. The East Anglia RHA commented on the problems resulting from the projections by the Office of Population Censuses and Surveys (OPCS) and local authorities being different (when they can be compared) and from the need to use forecasts by local authorities for the new DHAs (OPCS forecasts are not available at the district level).

Use made of SMRs: In the national method the nonpsychiatric inpatient component of a region's target is calculated using SMRs by condition in each age/sex group. Below regional level the numbers of deaths by condition in each age/sex group can be small and can vary considerably from year to year. The Thames RAWP recommended avoiding problems that arise from fluctuations in these numbers in their disaggregated form by using the total SMR across conditions. The Oxford RHA working party recommended aggregating SMRs over those conditions where there are significant fluctuations. The most common approach is to take averages over a number of years.

The East Anglia and West Midlands RHAs use SMRs only where these are shown to be strongly correlated with the use of hospital services.

The Thames RAWP weighted SMRs in an attempt to take account of social deprivation. Each AHA was given a score (of high, medium, or low) against three criteria: percentage of new commonwealth immigrants, percentage of households lacking one basic amenity, and percentage of pensioners living alone. If the high or low 'scores' were in the majority, then the area was classed as high or low overall. Otherwise a medium 'score' was given to the area. The total SMR for each area was then multiplied by 1.05 for a high 'score', by 1.03 for a medium 'score', and by 1.00 for a low 'score'.

Compensating for cross-boundary flows: Compensating for these flows raises two kinds of problems. One involves a policy decision as to whether such flows should continue or cease, and therefore whether compensation is appropriate. The second is, given that compensation is to be made, that of obtaining reliable data on these flows and on the costs of treatment.

Regional specialities are essentially scarce and expensive. An underlying assumption of the RAWP methods is that each authority (and district) ought to be self-sufficient; that is, capable of supplying a comprehensive service to its residential population. There was a mistaken belief, following the publication of the RAWP Report, that district self-sufficiency was departmental policy. It makes no sense for each district to aspire to have, for example, its own facilities for open-heart surgery, radiotherapy, and the treatment of haemophilia. But the way the RAWP methods allow for flows of patients within a region to the one centre where treatment is given offers no guarantee that they will be adequately protected.

The Thames RAWP recommended that:

"RHAs should identify and formally recognise for the purposes of securing their costs when assessing target allocations: regional services which the RHA decides should serve more than one Area and a catchment population of approximately one million; which are appropriately sited in relation to other services and which provide units which are viable on clinical, service and economic grounds; and which enable optimum use to be made of scarce resources of manpower and equipment" (DHSS, 1979b, page 27).

The Thames RAWP further recommended that regional specialities be directly funded as a first charge on the region's total revenue, and that targets be applied for the distribution of what remains after first charges have been made (other examples of these are clinical training of medical and dental students and regional administration). This approach is commonly known as 'top slicing' and is often adopted by RHAs. An alternative to 'top slicing' is to use a method which causes each authority to pay for regional specialities according to the use made of these by its residents. This is done by the South Western, Trent, and East Anglia RHAs. The South Western RHA has proposed that the managing authority is fully funded for the fixed cost, with the variable costs being financed by authorities in proportion to the use made of the specialities by their patients. The methods used by the South Western and Trent RHAs cause funding to be arranged separately from the calculation of targets. The East Anglia RHA, however, incorporates its arrangements for regional specialities within the target. The managing authority has the cost of the service added to its target; authorities are then charged according to the use made of the service, with these charges being deducted from their targets.

Catchment populations are used, instead of resident populations with compensation for cross-boundary flows, by the North Western and Trent RHAs for nonpsychiatric acute services. This method directly accounts for 'natural' cross-boundary flows: these flows arise when the catchment population of a hospital overlaps a number of boundaries.

Data on cross-boundary flows by patients used in the national RAWP methods come from hospital activity analysis (HAA), which is known to be inaccurate and to exclude outpatient and maternity services. The North Western RHA highlighted the problem of inadequacies of data in inpatient cross-boundary flows: these data should be recorded by HAA, which for some hospitals only covers some 70% of patients treated. Some regions considered outpatient services, but did not take action. The North Western RHA intends to have a survey of these services every three years, but recognises problems in the lack of data on costs by speciality and on flows between neighbouring RHAs. The North Western and Oxford RHAs allow for cross-boundary flows of maternity (inpatient) services (which the national method does not).

Data on costs of cross-boundary flows used by the RAWP are estimated using regression analysis by case and by speciality. The West Midlands RHA compensates for cross-boundary flows of geriatric patients on the basis of cost per day rather than cost per case. This is because there is considerable variation around the mean length of stay for geriatric cases, and to use costs per case based on the mean length of stay could significantly misrepresent the costs of services actually provided. The East Anglia RHA, for similar reasons, uses costs per day for cross-boundary flows of the mentally ill and the mentally handicapped, and, because the numbers are small, its working party recommended using three-year averages.

Provision of services for the mentally ill and the mentally handicapped: The North Western, Oxford, and West Midlands RHAs favour funding these services by top slicing. There are, however, variations in how this principle is applied: different cost levels are assumed (national averages, regional averages, or actual costs), and it is common to fund only the long-stay element of services for the mentally ill by top slicing (and to fund acute services for the mentally ill in the same way as for nonpsychiatric acute services).

4.2 Capital targets

The RAWP approach to capital has not had the same support or following as the revenue methods: the DHSS delayed the use of capital methods in making its allocations to RHAs; many regions have not bothered to set up working parties for determining capital targets; and no joint DHSS– Thames regions group has considered capital. Working parties have reported on the development of capital targets in the North Western, South Western, and East Anglia RHAs.

The North Western RHA broadly follows the RAWP methods of valuing stock—their report states that this was shown to be adequate in a pilot survey in the Region (NWRHA, 1979). But targets are not then derived from the resident population of each authority (as in the national method), but from the planned catchment populations of each authority, with account taken of regional specialities and long-stay services for the mentally ill and the mentally handicapped.

The South Western and East Anglia RHAs base their approaches on assessments of the capital stock that each authority ought to have. The South Western RHA uses national norms for three different kinds of services (mental illness, mental handicap, and other). The population base is taken to be the population served for each service. The East Anglia

RHA took a more sophisticated approach to assessing entitlement to stock for certain services (acute, maternity, and mental illness) by using projected usage rates by age/sex groups [for acute services, it drew on the methodology of the London Health Planning Consortium (DHSS, 1979a).] To reflect its 'compliance with policy', the East Anglia RHA also attempted to value existing stock by using an index of this which was given equal weighting to the index used in assessing stock in terms of its age. The index used ranged from 0.1 to 1.0. It was determined by the regional quantity surveyor on the basis of location, suitability, and concordance with the regional strategic plan.

4.3 Resource allocation to district authorities
The Thames RAWP did issue a note on the appropriateness of their methods for the restructured NHS (DHSS, 1981). This note stated that little amendment was believed to be necessary. The extra difficulties anticipated were: making adequate allowance for those DHAs with a high proportion of elderly (this is a serious problem for DHAs in the Thames regions on the South Coast); and the need to estimate, using local authority statistics, measures of social deprivation for the new DHAs. This response is similar to that of officers in RHAs who we spoke to early in 1981: no radical changes were being envisaged at that time. However, there is now concern, particularly in some of the Thames RHAs, about using RAWP-type methods to bear the burden of a policy of redistribution when the total regional budget is being cut. In section 6 of this paper, we discuss this problem further and outline an alternative approach being developed in the South West Thames RHA.

5 Models of deciding allocations of capital and revenue
The national RAWP did recommend how its methods of calculating targets could be used in making allocations to regions. For revenue allocations it recommended 'ceilings' and 'floors' on the pace of change (DHSS, 1976c). This was to avoid large sudden changes: regions receiving such increases would be unable to make good use of extra money; and regions receiving such cuts would have inadequate time to make them. Regional working parties (including the joint DHSS–Thames working group) have not generally considered how allocations should be made: their task has generally been only to consider how targets should be calculated.

RHAs have to formulate policies, first on the coverage of targets, and second on their role in influencing actual allocations. The first involves policies on whether to include capital and whether to make special provision for certain services (for example, regional specialities and services for the mentally ill and the mentally handicapped). The second involves policies on interactions between allocations of capital and of revenue, services and staffing. These are illustrated by the following questions. Should the allocations of capital and revenue be coordinated by an RHA in an attempt to minimise the risk of districts getting extra revenue without the capital stock to make good use of that revenue, and of districts having capital money to build new hospitals, but not enough revenue to run them? Should RHAs attempt to relate allocation of financial resources to the planning of services? RHAs make decisions on consultant appointments which are crucial to the development of many services; should these be tied in with decisions on resources and service development?

Raising these questions points to various possible styles of management that an RHA may choose, from a spectrum of strong central direction to considerable local autonomy. In our discussions with officers in RHAs, we have identified four models of regional styles of management.

5.1 Four models of resources policy
Devolved financial: this is the approach of the national RAWP. Targets are derived for capital and revenue, and the pace of movement towards these targets is decided independently by separate formulae [there is no funding of the Revenue Consequences of Capital Schemes (RCCSs)]. In this model, the RHA's main role is determining districts' financial allocations, and districts take the initiative and the burden of the responsibility for the development of services.

Revenue-led: revenue allocations are mainly decided by the principle of reducing the range of variation around revenue targets. The region does not fund the RCCS. A district therefore has to decide on hospital building in the light of how it will finance the running of new hospitals. This means that the revenue allocations influence the allocations of capital, and revenue dominates resource policy.

Capital-led: capital allocations are mainly decided by the principle of reducing the range of variation around capital targets. This approach provides guidance for the building of new hospitals, and the region funds the RCCS. The funding of the RCCS is the major impact upon the revenue allocations of districts, and hence capital allocations dominate resource policy.

Planning-based: the building of new hospitals is decided through the review of services, which is carried out as part of the planning process rather than through comparison with capital targets. This review is used to schedule the priorities of different districts, and capital is allocated to fund that schedule. The region funds the RCCS, which has the main impact upon districts' revenue allocations. Hence planning is the originator of changes in resources policy.

5.2 Comparing the four models with their predecessor
The different models can be compared with the model of policymaking which was dominant for many years prior to the 1974 reorganisation. Regions then made decisions on major capital development (and allocated capital accordingly), funded the RCCS (from funds earmarked for this

purpose centrally), and otherwise allocated revenue money incrementally. Regions generally have some form of revenue targets to guide allocations of revenue, and therefore aim to abandon incremental budgeting. In two of the models, regions do not finance the RCCS—some regions which do fund the RCCS only do so for those districts that are below their revenue targets. The use of targets as a basis for allocating major capital is another fundamental change, because this requires districts to take the initiative in deciding how those capital monies should be used. Though the model which is planning-based looks similar to the pre-1974 model, it differs from that in its attempt to draw the programme for capital development from the new system of service planning.

5.3 The advantages and disadvantages of a devolved style of management
The advantages of using capital targets and not funding the RCCS are the changes that result in districts' attitudes to capital. When a region offers a district a capital scheme, backed by the monies to finance its construction and running costs, the district is unlikely to question whether the region's proposal is the best way of using those monies. When the district is instead given allocations based on targets, it will be directly aware of the local opportunity costs of its choice of using capital and the revenue consequences.

The weaknesses of using a devolved style spring from three sources: the 'lumpiness' of capital and its revenue consequences, the reliability of targets, and the extent to which decisions can be devolved down to districts.

5.4 The problems of capital
A district will require, during the construction of a hospital, substantial capital monies. When the hospital is completed it will no longer require capital, but there will be a quantum jump in its revenue requirements to finance the running of the hospital (unless this is to be financed by closing other hospitals). These demands for capital and revenue cannot easily be accommodated in those regions which follow a policy of smooth movement towards targets: flexibility is likely to be needed, with districts taking turns to receive 'lumps' of capital monies and some provision being made for below-target districts (such as in the funding of the RCCS). Another option to give more flexibility is for regions to make a general allocation both of capital and of revenue and to let districts decide how to spend that allocation themselves. [This policy is favoured by the Welsh Office, which, from April 1984, is delegating responsibility for capital planning to area health authorities and will be basing allocations on their capital plans (Welsh Office, 1980).]

A particular problem in making allocations to districts is how to take account of capital stock. If the objective is to move towards equity, then it is important to derive some assessment of the value of stock, but that value crucially depends upon its physical state, its appropriateness, and its location—all of these characteristics are difficult to measure. These measurement difficulties cast doubt on the reliability of using targets to guide capital allocations, but they are intrinsic difficulties, which cause problems whatever method is used—the use of targets draws attention to them in a way that other methods do not.

5.5 The reliability of targets for inner London teaching districts

Regions do not rely on the national method to derive revenue targets: commonly they introduce modifications to take account of regional specialities and of services for the mentally ill and the mentally handicapped. The problem of using revenue targets is most severe in cases where most burden is placed upon them—in the inner London districts responsible for teaching hospitals. The targets of these districts do not depend mainly upon the residential population, but on arrangements made for regional specialities, protection for the extra costs of the clinical training of medical and dental students, and compensation for the massive cross-boundary flows which occur. In such cases the use of targets cannot provide a clear and secure basis for policy, because so many important modifications have to be made.

5.6 The need for a strategic basis for resource allocation

The position of the inner London districts with teaching responsibilities presents, in a particularly stark form, the general problems of resource management in the provision of health services. It is not reasonable to expect every district to be able to provide the same range of services: certain (regional) services will only be provided in a few centres in the region, and many other services will have to be shared. But the methods through which targets are calculated do not address systematically such questions as which cross-boundary flows should continue (because services are being appropriately provided in one district for people who live elsewhere) and which ought to stop (because people are having to travel unreasonable distances for basic services that ought to be provided locally).

As long as targets are derived from casual treatment of cross-boundary flows, they cannot provide a sound basis for major changes in subregional allocations, because the targets being aimed for are not derived from a strategy. And without a regional strategy, it is difficult to coordinate changes made by districts. If these changes are not coordinated, then some services may be excessively expanded because too many districts independently opt for the same sort of changes. It is obviously a responsibility of regions to enable districts to coordinate the changes they make; the methods based on the RAWP approach will not enable this to be done.

6 New directions in the formulation of resource policies

6.1 Finance determines services?

In this concluding section, we are concerned with a different approach to the methods recommended by the RAWP for RHAs. Before outlining that approach, it is important to raise a spectre that haunts current developments—the spectre of financial dominance. This Government's avowed policy for public services is that finance will determine what is to be provided. Within this context it is possible to see an RHA's role as concerned with moving money around, with these movements being based on financial criteria—past allocations, targets, the RCCS.

Perhaps the most important criticism of the RAWP methods subregionally, in the current climate, is that they reinforce the trend of financial dominance. The service components of targets at district level are not intended to be meaningful, because the method is too crude to work on that detail at that scale: only the total (given the target) has significance. This means that finance cannot be related to particular services using the RAWP methods subregionally. Sadly, it is plausible to imagine decisions about resources being influenced primarily by poorly understood modifications to methods to calculate targets, rather than by direct relationships to the need for services.

What is at stake is not a belief that the NHS is entitled to open-ended demands for resources: the claims of the NHS have to be set against other claims (for example, pensions, supplementary benefit, housing, social services, and education—only to mention those having some links with spending on health care). Neither is it believed that it is a straightforward matter to establish what does constitute relative needs for health services of different DHAs. The crux of the matter is that the implications of resource decisions ought to be better understood and methods ought to be developed to enable such understanding to improve.

It is equally dogmatic to assert that finance will determine services (whatever services have to be forgone at that level of finance) as to assert that finance will not constrain service development (whatever that development may cost). The former assertion may serve as a temporary corrective to the latter, but a balanced approach must consider services and finance. For this to be done, information needs to be provided on the effects of finance on services and that information can only be provided by linking finance to services at the district level.

The NHS information systems do not enable links to be easily made between finance and services. The NHS planning system was an imaginative attempt to make links on a broad scale as a basis for national policymaking and for joint planning of services for the elderly, mentally handicapped, and mentally ill. But, as has been described in this paper, the planning system gives no framework for the planning of acute services. This suggests the need for a more detailed approach based upon specialities.

The approach that we are developing is examining three kinds of specialities: regional (for example, radiotherapy), subregional (for example, ophthalmology), and district (for example, general surgery). By taking one example of each we hope to produce a method (or methods) that could be applied to any speciality.

6.2 An approach based on catchment population of specialities
The approach consists of three elements applied to each speciality. These
elements are described below.
(a) *Assessing relative deprivation and overprovision*: an average rate of
hospital utilisation by age and sex is applied to the population of each
authority. This gives, for each authority, a case-load 'norm', which can be
compared with the actual number of cases treated (at any hospital—
whether in the district or not). The difference between the two gives an
indication of *relative* deprivation and of overprovision.
(b) *Modelling the impact upon access to services of changes in location*:
a gravity model is currently being used to provide a way of modelling
flows to hospitals. It is hoped to use this model to show how changes in
location can even out some of the relative deprivation and overprovision in
a region.
(c) *Providing a framework for evaluation of changes in service location*:
element (b) gives information on moving towards equal access to services,
but other criteria are important in deciding the location of services. There
are important advantages in providing services on a certain minimal scale:
a high volume can bring economies of scale and better quality of care.
But concentration of services also causes inconvenience and raises travelling
costs.

This work is at an early stage. Its objective is not to produce a
mechanistic approach to determine the allocation of resources, but to
enable those responsible better to understand the link between decisions
on resources and services. The way we see the approach being used is as
follows. Element (a) raises the question, in DHAs where services appear to
be relatively overprovided, is there scope for cuts to be made or are those
services already at what appear to be minimally acceptable standards?
Element (b) is seen as providing information on possible alternative
locations for services (each possible location being known to be feasible, in
that it is possible to staff a hospital at each site). Element (c) is intended
to provide a framework for indicating assessments of the different costs
and benefits (not all of these will be expressed in financial terms, and they
will not be weighted and aggregated to give a total score).

The approach may not eventually point to a wholesale relocation of
acute services, but the need to develop a greater flexibility in their
organisation. Examples of this are the development of day' and outpatient
services in districts which are relatively deprived.

The approach, as seen at this time, raises more questions than it answers.
But, we believe, the questions are the right ones to be asking and provide
the appropriate foci for research. The tentative nature of what we suggest
is a product of ignorance about such a basic question as, what effect does
distance have upon access to health services (when these services are
disaggregated down to specialities). If regional scientists can provide ways
of answering this question, RHAs would have a much firmer basis for

making decisions on finance and services. This work necessarily requires technical development (much of which may be esoteric), but (unlike the resource target industry) it would be directed at answering a question, the significance of which is readily understood.

An approach based on specialities raises two kinds of problems. First, establishing what is meant by the same name in different hospitals; for example, 'general surgery' is likely to include a more complex case-mix in a large teaching hospital than in a small district general hospital. This problem requires a method of establishing what constitutes the basic building blocks of the approach. The second problem is the moving from assessments of arrangements of services by speciality to an integrated policy on staffing, capital investment, and the allocation of revenue. Rather than attempt to explicate fully how this might be done, we will conclude by indicating the guiding principles in common with and in contrast to the RAWP methods.

6.3 Towards a reappraisal of the RAWP approach

What the approaches have in common is the objective of attempting to secure equal access to health services for those at equal risk. Where the approaches differ is that the RAWP methods are based on the residential population of each authority. This makes sense for community-based services, but not, at the district level, for hospital care. The catchment populations of hospitals do not conform neatly to authority boundaries and it does not make sense to attempt to force them to do so. Although the RAWP methods do allow for cross-boundary flows, these flows are seen, in principle, to be an aberration. And in cities, these cross-boundary flows can be considerable, with half of each DHA's resident population being treated by hospitals in other DHAs. Our approach (for hospital services) is to attempt to identify catchment areas for each hospital by speciality and to fund districts on the basis of patients treated from these catchments areas.

It may not be practical to base funding on catchment areas for each speciality. It may be necessary to group specialities into classes having the same catchment population. Although there are over thirty specialities, the bulk of revenue goes on about half a dozen. This means that policy for revenue may not require detailed investigation of each speciality.

The RAWP methods relate only to work load in the way they account for cross-boundary flows. In the current climate, in which 'growth' appears to depend upon 'efficiency savings', it seems to make sense subregionally to introduce, in some form, a method that funds hospitals according to the number of patients treated. There are potential difficulties here. A hospital could practice an early-discharge policy, which enables it to sustain a high throughput. This could place a burden on community services for the authorities in which the patients live or in which those services are inadequate, and this could put patients at risk.

The effects of changes of this kind would not be picked up by hospital statistics: the annual hospital returns (SH3s), for example, do not distinguish between whether a patient is discharged alive or dead.

The approach we are developing is intended to be useful for investigating services. Indeed, the first findings will be of this kind. The approach could be generalised in two ways. First, by applying to each speciality the analysis of discrepancies between 'norms' and actual case loads by speciality for each authority. The nature of the discrepancies would indicate priorities for further investigation. Second, when the RHA is considering options for changes in services, it might find that the approach provides useful information.

Although the RAWP was concerned with the distribution of services, its report began with the following points:

"There is ample evidence to demonstrate that demand for health care throughout the world is rising inexorably. England has no immunity from this phenomenon. And because it can also be shown that supply of health care actually fuels further demand, it is inevitable that the supply of health care services can never keep pace with the rising demands placed upon them. Demand will always be one jump ahead. This is a problem for Government and society in general and not, fortunately, one to which the Working Party was called upon to address its mind. We mention it at the beginning of this Report, however, to emphasize two points. Firstly that the resources available to the NHS are bound to fall short of requirements as measured by demand criteria and secondly that supply of facilities has an important influence on demand in the locality in which they are provided" (DHSS, 1976c, page 7).

It is obviously true that there is always scope for spending more on health and that distance affects access to services. But these are empty observations for RHAs in the current climate. By taking these assumptions as the starting point for their report, the RAWP did not consider how 'government and society in general' might best decide at what point demands for more or better services ought not to be financed, or how authorities might decide the point at which distance becomes an impediment to access to services. Indeed, the RAWP methods exclude both questions, since these methods are not intended to link finance to the details of the provision of services and they are based upon population defined by authority (and district) boundaries.

What seems to be most needed now is a reappraisal of the starting points of the RAWP analysis. Is the relative overprovision of services for DHAs in the Thames RHAs excessive, or is it a reasonable level of service to which we ought to aspire? Would access to services be significantly improved by relocation of services within a region? Answers to these questions require an approach that links finance both to services and to research by regional scientists. Accepting the starting points of the RAWP and its approach subregionally, at a time of no real growth, raises the prospect of cutting services (that we ought to retain) in one place and moving them to another place in the hope that access might be made more equal.

The NHS faces an era akin to that envisaged by the Beveridge Report (1942) of stable levels of expenditure—although the scale of that level is much greater. This expectation is a product, not of a naive belief that health services make people healthier, but of austerity. This context seems to require policy analysis different from that to be expected from the DHSS—commonly the originator of innovatory approaches in the NHS. Analysis needs to be done to meet the detailed requirements of RHAs and to enable society to have relevant information about effects on services of the finance available to the NHS. Regional scientists can usefully contribute to managing the difficult future faced by the NHS, provided that they appreciate that policies for acute services involve much more than just decisions about where to locate a standard acute hospital.

Acknowledgement. This paper reports research being financed by the South West Thames RHA and the King Edward's Hospital Fund for London. It draws on material supplied by and interviews with finance staff of the RHAs mentioned. We are grateful to all of these for their assistance. Practice in this field is always developing. The paper is based mainly on the position in early 1982. Changes in national and regional methods since then do not, however, alter the arguments made about the inadequacies of the national methods for use by RHAs or the need for an alternative approach to them.

References

Bevan R G, 1982, "A critique of the medical service increment for teaching (SIFT)" RP-6, Centre for Research in Industry, Business and Administration, University of Warwick, Coventry, England

Bevan R G, Copeman H, Perrin J, Rosser R, 1980 *Health Care—Priorities and Management* (Croom Helm, Beckenham, Kent)

Beveridge Report, 1942 *Social Insurance and Allied Services* Cmnd 6404, Chairman: Sir William Beveridge (HMSO, London)

Coverdale I, Gibbs R, Nurse K, 1980, "A hospital cost model for policy analysis" *Journal of the Operational Research Society* **32** 851–864

DHSS, 1972 *Management Arrangements for the Reorganised National Health Service* Department of Health and Social Security (HMSO, London)

DHSS, 1976a *The NHS Planning System* Department of Health and Social Security (HMSO, London)

DHSS, 1976b *Priorities for Health and Personal Social Services in England. A Consultative Document* Department of Health and Social Security (HMSO, London)

DHSS, 1976c *Sharing Resources for Health in England* The Report of the Resource Allocation Working Party, Department of Health and Social Security (HMSO, London)

DHSS, 1977 *The Way Forward* (HMSO, London)

DHSS, 1978a *Health and Personal Social Services in England. DHSS Planning Guidelines for 1978/79* health circular HC(78)12, March (Department of Health and Social Security, London)

DHSS, 1978b *Health Service Development. Organisation of Radiotherapy Services for the Treatment of Cancer* health circular HC(78)32, October (Department of Health and Social Security, London)

DHSS, 1979a *Acute Hospital Services in London* profile by the London Health Planning Consortium, Department of Health and Social Security (HMSO, London)

DHSS, 1979b *Assessing Target Allocations within the Thames Regions* report of a joint working group (Department of Health and Social Security, London)

DHSS, 1979c *Health and Personal Social Services in England. DHSS Planning Guidelines for 1979/80* health circular HC(79)9, April (Department of Health and Social Security, London)

DHSS, 1980a *Health Service Development Structure and Management* health circular HC(80)8, July (Department of Health and Social Security, London)

DHSS, 1980b *Hospital Services—The Future Pattern of Hospital Provision in England* May (Department of Health and Social Security, London)

DHSS, 1981 *The Application of TSR Principles in Assessing District Health Authority Target Allocation within the Thames Regions* report of a joint working group, June (Department of Health and Social Security, London)

DHSS, 1982a *Health Services Development—The NHS Planning System* health circular HC(82)6 (Department of Health and Social Security, London)

DHSS, 1982b *Health Services Development—Resource Assumptions and Planning Guidelines: 1982-83 to 1984-85* health circular HC(82)14 (Department of Health and Social Security, London)

EARHA, 1978 *Report of Working Party on Target Revenue Allocations* (East Anglian Regional Health Authority, Cambridge, England)

EARHA, 1981 *A Framework for Capital Investment—Report of the Regional Resource Allocation Working Party* (East Anglian Regional Health Authority, Cambridge, England)

Hencke D, 1983, "More hospitals for handicapped come under fire" *The Guardian* 2 March, p 2

HM Treasury, 1983 *The Government's Expenditure Plans 1983-84 to 1985-86* volumes 1 and 2, Cmnd 8789 (HMSO, London)

Hodgart R L, 1978, "Optimising access to public services: a review of problems, models and methods of locating central facilities" *Progress in Human Geography* 2 17-48

Kay J A (Ed.), 1982, "Symposium on local government finance" *Fiscal Studies* 3 1-22

Maxwell R J, 1981 *Health and Wealth* (Lexington Books, Lexington, MA)

Mayhew L, Leonardi A, 1982, "Equity, efficiency, and accessibility in urban and regional health-care systems" *Environment and Planning A* 14 1479-1507

MoH, 1956 *Report of the Committee of Enquiry into the Cost of the National Health Service* The Guillebaud Report, Cmnd 9663, Ministry of Health (HMSO, London)

MoH, 1961 *The District General Hospital* building note 3, Ministry of Health (HMSO, London)

MoH, 1962 *A Hospital Plan for England and Wales* Cmnd 1604, Ministry of Health (HMSO, London)

MoH, 1969 *The Functions of the District General Hospital* The Bonham-Carter Report, Ministry of Health (HMSO, London)

NWRHA, 1979 *Resource Allocation—Final Report of the Regional Working Party* (North Western Regional Health Authority, Manchester, England)

OECD, 1977 *Public Expenditure on Health—Studies in Resource Allocation* (Organisation for Economic Cooperation and Development, Paris)

ORHA, 1978 *Second Report of the Regional Revenue Advisory Group* (Oxford Regional Health Authority, Oxford, England)

ORHA, 1980 *Third Report of the Regional Revenue Advisory Group* (Oxford Regional Health Authority, Oxford, England)

Palmer S, West P, Patrick D, Glynn M, 1979, "Mortality indices in resource allocation" *Community Medicine* **1** 275-281

Perrin J R, Magee M, 1983, "The cost, joint products and funding of English teaching hospitals" RP-8, Centre for Research in Industry, Business and Administration, University of Warwick, Coventry, England

Senn S J, Shaw H, 1978, "Some problems in applying the national formula to area and district revenue allocations" *Journal of Epidemiology and Community Health* **32** 22-27

SWRHA, 1979 *Regional Resource Allocation Working Party—The Distribution and Management of Capital—Final Report of the Capital Sub-Group* (South Western Regional Health Authority, Bristol, England)

SWRHA, 1982 *Resource Allocation Working Party (Officers)—Final Report* (South Western Regional Health Authority, Bristol, England)

Townsend P, Davidson N, 1982 *Inequalities in Health: The Black Report* (Penguin Books, Harmondsworth, Middx)

TRHA, 1981 *Revenue Targets and Notional Funds for the New Health Authorities* (Trent Regional Health Authority, Sheffield, England)

Watkin B, 1975 *Documents on Health and Social Services 1834 to the Present Day* (Methuen, London)

Welsh Office, 1980 *The Health Capital Programme in Wales. Report of a Working Party* (Welsh Office, Cardiff)

Winyard G P A, 1981, "RAWP—new injustice for old" *British Medical Journal* **283** 930-932

WMRHA, 1982 *Capital and Revenue Targets Working Party—Sixth Report to the RHA* (West Midlands Regional Health Authority, Birmingham, England)

Health Services Planning: Observations on the Relationship between Theory and Practice

T RATHWELL
University of Leeds

1 Introduction

The spatial implications of planning decisions have been of particular
interest to regional scientists for several years, an interest which has
tended to concentrate on the locational manifestations of such plans.
There appears to be little concern for or attempts to understand the
processes underpinning planning decisions. Although this statement may
be of less significance with respect to urban and regional planning, it is
particularly true for health services. Recently, however, some geographers
and regional scientists have begun to turn their attention towards such
services. Most of these efforts at contributing to an understanding of the
spatial implications of health services have been concerned with specific
issues, such as accessibility (Knox, 1978; Phillips, 1981; Whitelegg, 1982),
distribution of facilities and services (Giggs, 1979; Knox, 1979; Smith,
1979, particularly chapter 5), and allocation of resources (see Bevan and
Spencer, chapter 5 in this volume).

Such studies, although insightful, since they contributed to an understanding of the many variables affecting the distribution and utilization of
health care, did not "inform on how or why such changes occur" (Eyles
and Woods, 1983, page 244). Eyles and Woods (1983) argue that it is the
answers to these questions which are of fundamental importance to an
understanding of the spatial manifestation of health care, because they
ultimately determine the manner in which health services are provided.

This paper, through a study, which the author is currently undertaking,
of the effects of policymaking within the framework of the National
Health Service (NHS) planning system, attempts to explore the central
questions of how and why change occurs. The issues discussed herein are
indicative of the impressions formulated at the midpoint in the study, and
in some ways are speculative—in the sense that they have been corroborated
only informally. The study seeks to delineate the approach to health
services planning in a particular health authority by focusing on the work
of two planning teams, each of which was concerned with a specific
clientele. The objectives of the research and therefore of this paper are
twofold: to determine how the philosophy and rationale which underpins
the NHS planning system is manifested in the plans produced, and to
investigate the extent to which external factors to the organization
influence the planning process (such factors, for example, might be
government policy changes, ministerial intervention, unilateral changes in
professional practices) and the resulting policy decisions.

The paper briefly outlines the evolution of health services planning in the NHS with particular attention being paid to the development and rationale for joint-care planning. Consideration is then given to the relationship between planning and policymaking in the health sector and the constraints that such a relationship imposes upon those involved in the planning process. The paper then goes on to describe in some detail the manner in which health services planning is undertaken in the study area. Finally, a number of hypotheses are put forward as possible explanations for the observed differences expected in the approach to planning and policymaking.

2 NHS planning: origins and evolution

Health services planning has been a relatively recent phenomenon in the NHS. Introduced at the 1974 reorganization of the NHS, it was seen as a natural adjunct to the corporate management structure, which was itself based on the principle of decisionmaking by consensus. The introduction of a formal planning system (DHSS, 1976b) was an attempt to coordinate, within the framework of a single structure, the fragmented approach to planning which existed beforehand.

Prior to 1974, the predominant move of planning in the NHS was not service planning, but hospital or capital planning, a consequence of the publication in the early 1960s of *A Hospital Plan for England and Wales* (MoH, 1962). This document articulated the concept of the district general hospital, comprising a relatively standard set of medical and surgical specialities and serving a predetermined population base. It is not surprising, therefore, that planning in the NHS throughout the 1960s and early 1970s was 'capital-led'—concerned about and generally confined to buildings— rather than emphasising, other than indirectly, services to patients.

A major characteristic of NHS planning up to the mid-1970s, as identified by those who were involved, was the influence of powerful vested interests who obviously had much to gain and/or lose by its outcome. This influence, or 'planning by decibels', as it sometimes has been christened, was an acknowledgement that those powerful vested interests, notably the hospital consultants, had a major influence on and indeed were seen to dominate the policymaking process (Ham, 1981). This method of planning (responding to vocal power bases) is not unlike the 'science of muddling through' (often referred to as 'disjointed incrementalism') described by Lindblom (1959). Disjointed incrementalism is, in essence, a reactionary form of planning, in that it responds to specific events or crises as they arise and does not attempt consciously to anticipate them.

To central policymakers this 'incremental' approach to planning was considered most unsatisfactory and, consequently, a more rational and comprehensive mode of planning was required. It was considered appropriate, in connection with the reorganization of the NHS along corporate management lines, to introduce a rational comprehensive mode of planning as a key element in this management structure. The introduction of a structured planning system in the NHS followed shortly after the 1974 reorganization and adopted as its basis the 'rational comprehensive' mode. It was 'rational' in that it assumed that all planning issues could be objectively assessed and a decision taken solely on the merits of each proposal. It was 'comprehensive' in that it implied that all aspects of any particular issue or topic could be assessed and the implication of any course of action weighed accordingly, thus ensuring that the 'best' choice emerged.

Three distinct but not mutually exclusive factors can be identified to explain the movement towards, and eventual adoption of, a rational comprehensive planning model for the NHS. First, there was a growing awareness of and interest in the ideas associated with corporate management. For instance, considerable interest existed within the Department of Health and Social Security (DHSS) in employing, directly or in an amended form, techniques of PPBS (Planning, Programming, Budgeting System) which had come to dominate public sector thinking in the United States of America during the early 1960s. Second, and to some extent concomitant with the move toward a PPBS-type planning, there was increased pressure exerted on all central departments by both the Treasury and the Public Expenditure Survey Committee (PESC) to contain costs and to present their financial forecasts in a more comprehensive and rigorous manner. The third factor or pressure for a 'different' planning approach arose because of developments occurring in the NHS. The continued development and expansion of high technology medicine and the costs associated with it led the NHS to give some consideration to the manner in which care was being provided and to the ways of providing care on a more cost-effective basis. This, of course, was prompted by the change in the economic climate and the election of a government committed to reducing public expenditure to a level which it was believed the country could afford.

The rationale for establishing a formal planning system for the NHS was the concern to move away from the fragmented and 'decibel-guided' planning of the 1960s and early 1970s; the desire to integrate and improve the services for patients; and the wish to make the planning of these services more responsive to the 'needs' of the patient. This was articulated thus: "health services can only be evaluated in relation to the identifiable needs of the community for different kinds of health care [which] must be expressed in terms of proposed developments of the component parts" (DHSS, 1972, pages 50–51). In other words, planning was considered important as a means through which change could occur, while ensuring that the proposed changes were compatible with the perceived needs of the community.

The procedure for translating this philosophy of planning into reality was documented in the manual *The NHS Planning System* (DHSS, 1976b).

The cornerstone of the NHS planning system was its emphasis upon the 'health care group', which recognized that there were certain groups in society (for example, the elderly, children, handicapped) whose needs and demands for health care often encompassed much of the totality of care available: "In practice the health care needs of the community are highly diverse and a single individual or family may simultaneously require health care for several different conditions ... [therefore] it is useful for planning purposes to distinguish a limited number of broad 'health care groups' with special needs, and to differentiate some categories of care ... so as to quantify the services required" (DHSS, 1972, page 51). This then was the structure and, to some extent, the purpose of the formal NHS planning system launched nationally in 1976. The original emphasis in the NHS planning system manual on planning by care groups was given a fillip by the publication of *Priorities for Health and Personal Social Services in England* (DHSS, 1976c), which mapped out the national priorities according to this care group approach. The structure of the document with its emphasis upon care groups, rather than on facilities and services, had a considerable influence on health services planning in the NHS.

3 Joint-care planning
Not only were health authorities encouraged to plan on a health care group basis, but subsequent guidance from the DHSS also recommended a form of joint planning between health and local authorities, again on a care group basis, as even more appropriate, given the overlap or complementarities of responsibilities between authorities which existed and would continue to do so (DHSS, 1976a; 1977). It was envisaged that the health and local authorities would establish joint-care planning teams (JCPTs) composed of appropriate officers from both authorities. It was also envisaged that there would be a JCPT for each care group, corresponding to those identified in the consultative document on priorities (DHSS, 1976c).

The planning role of the JCPTs was strategic rather than operational. In the words of a DHSS circular, "they will need to consider the health and social needs of particular groups in their community, and produce proposals for the future development of the LA [local area] and AHA [area health authority] services relevant to those needs" (DHSS, 1976a, page 3). In so doing they were to take due account of 'national and regional policies', but also were expected to be flexible in modifying such policies to fit local circumstances. In other words, the JCPTs were concerned, not only with the formulation and development of policy, but with the manner in which policy could best be implemented. Thus the health and local authorities were encouraged by the DHSS to establish JCPTs (DHSS, 1976a), and, to facilitate the development of joint planning, the then Secretary of State made available to health authorities special financial resources (generally referred to as joint financing monies). Indeed, a further circular (DHSS, 1977) advocated health care planning teams be replaced by joint planning teams (JPTs), consisting of both health and local authority personnel.

Joint finance monies were allocated by the DHSS to each regional health authority (RHA) separately from the monies distributed according to the formula devised by the Resource Allocation Working Party (DHSS, 1976d) (see Bevan and Spencer, chapter 5 in this volume, for discussion of the formula). However, there were certain criteria adopted by the DHSS when distributing joint finance to regions: namely that half was allocated in proportion to population weighted by numbers of elderly persons and half in proportion to usage by various age groups of hospital facilities for mental illness and mental handicap. Joint finance was to be allocated to local authorities on the condition that the benefits of expenditure on a project would be of benefit to both parties and "[could] be expected to make a better contribution in terms of total care than if directly applied to health services" (DHSS, 1976a, page 3). However, this was a permissive power, as the decision on joint finance expenditure was ultimately a matter for the health authorities.

A detailed critique of joint-care planning is beyond the scope of this paper, as this has been done elsewhere (Shaw, 1978; Rathwell and Reynolds, 1979a; 1979b; Marslen-Wilson, 1982); however, it is worth noting that the arrangements as envisaged in the circular (DHSS, 1977) were not universally accepted and, consequently, the results of joint-care planning both in planning and policy terms have had mixed success (Booth, 1981a; 1981b; Glennerster, 1982). Briefly, however, major factors contributing to the lack of success of joint-care planning have been identified as differing political bases—members of health authorities are appointed by the Secretary of State, whereas local authorities have elected councillors; different sources of finance—health authorities are financed largely from exchequer funds, whereas local authorities by a combination of a local property tax (rates) and central government grants (rate support grant); and differing working relationships vis-à-vis officers and authority members/councillors—health authority officers seem to have considerable flexibility in determining which issues to support, whereas local authority officers are generally obliged to refer matters to the committee system before they can offer an opinion.

4 Health planning and policymaking
The introduction and implementation of the NHS planning system has not been regarded unanimously as a success (Royal Commission, 1979; DHSS, 1980). Certainly plans have been prepared by health authorities to comply with the formal requirements of the system, which may be stated as the desire to integrate and improve the services for patients and to make these services more responsive to the 'needs' of patients.

There appear to be three major factors inhibiting the planning process from obtaining its full potential as originally envisaged. These debilitating factors, so critics argue, are:

(a) The prescriptive nature of the planning system itself, which, with its emphasis on an annual time scale, precludes any detailed analysis and assessment of problems, to such an extent that most plans tend to adopt DHSS guidelines as 'de facto' appropriate levels of service (Barnard et al, 1980a; 1980b).

(b) Policy decisionmaking, rooted very much in incrementalist philosophy, has not given those involved in the planning of health services clear and succinct objectives within which to plan; planners do not know where they are going, nor how they are going to get there (Irving et al, 1981; McNaught, 1981).

(c) Satisfaction for most planners rests with the (difficult enough) task of producing the completed plan. No attempt is made to evaluate the policies arising out of the planning system in order to ascertain their impact upon the public, nor indeed to see if the original aims of the policies have been achieved (Barnard et al, 1980a; 1980b).

Policy formulation in the NHS has been designed to operate as a continuum:

national (DHSS) ↔ regional (RHA) ↔ local (DHA)[1] ,

with all elements having an equal opportunity to influence matters of policy. However, critics argue that, although the dominant direction of flow emanates from the DHSS downwards, health authorities, by and large, have paid little heed to the guidance (Brown, 1977; Rathwell, 1981). The study reported in this paper—of the relationship between health services planning and policymaking—focuses on the degree of interplay between ends of the continuum by examining three interrelated issues: directions given to planners; planners' attention to these directions; and the form in which they are implemented.

5 Health services planning in action

The application of health planning to the formulation of policy is considered through an empirical investigation of the processes involved in the development of services for two particular client groups, the elderly and the mentally handicapped, in a single health authority, the Newcastle Area Health Authority (NAHA). The NAHA has not changed in substance as a result of the restructuring of the NHS in 1982. All that changed was its designation; prior to the changeover it was an AHA (area health authority), afterwards it became a DHA. It was selected for precisely this reason, namely that any effects of the restructuring process would have minimal impact upon the research.

[1] District health authority.

The elderly have had considerable attention over the years—a reflection of the numbers and political influence of the elderly—and therefore one might expect that planning-related policy decisions would be quickly reached and the relevant policies implemented. The second group, however, apart from a number of central policy statements (NDGMH, 1976; 1977; 1980), has received very little local attention, and, because it lacks the political influence seemingly enjoyed by the elderly, one would not expect much emphasis on developing a coordinated policy for this group of people. Thus an examination of these two client groups might provide a useful insight into how the planning process handles the development and implementation of specific policies.

The investigation of the way in which the planning process impacts upon these client groups has two elements: retrospective and prospective. The retrospective part of the research is concerned with the identification of a number of potential policy issues and tracing their origins back through the records. The prospective part focuses upon the issues in their current state and is essentially concerned with the processes which they will go through before they are either adopted or rejected as policy (see Barnard et al, 1980c, for a discussion of this procedure). Particularly, interest focuses on the identification of facilitating and/or inhibiting factors, which are then tested for their relevance through interviews with a sample of the personnel involved in the policymaking process.

It is the retrospective portion of the research which is of relevance here. Access to all records, including minutes of committee meetings and planning team meetings, general correspondence, and published reports pertaining to both client groups, including those of the NAHA's planners, were kindly made available, and it is from these records that the following analysis has been drawn. However, material from the interviews has been included where appropriate, even though the interview schedule has not been completed at the time of writing.

The NAHA decided, in accordance with a DHSS circular on joint planning arrangements (DHSS, 1977), to move away from a health authority planning process to one joint with the Local Authority; in particular, for those services in which there is a considerable overlap of responsibility. Each joint planning team was charged with the responsibility of formulating health policies which its health authority could accept and implement. The NAHA was of the view that a single JCPT, instead of several, was the most appropriate forum for the formulation of health policy as it relates to both health and local authorities. In establishing the JCPT the NAHA was implicitly acknowledging that the 'needs' and demands for health care are often influenced by factors outside the health sector and, consequently, an approach based only on health services was unlikely to resolve the problems facing it. The NAHA also accepted the rationale (DHSS, 1977) for the establishment of JPTs as subgroups of the JCPT for the majority of care groups, and this policy was implemented by late 1977.

Figure 1 shows the finalised joint-care planning arrangements between the NAHA and the local authority.

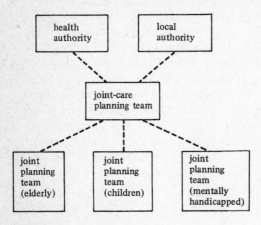

---- indicates advisory relationship

Figure 1. The joint-care planning structure.

5.1 Joint planning team for the elderly

The joint planning team for the elderly (JPTE), which replaced the health care planning team at the end of 1977, became concerned predominantly with the lack of inpatient accommodation, almost to the exclusion of all else. The NAHA, in 1978, had 352 designated nonpsychiatric beds for the elderly, split between general acute hospitals (137 beds) and long-stay/ community hospitals (215 beds) (NAHA, 1978). According to the DHSS planning norm of ten beds per 1000 persons aged sixty-five and over, the NAHA was short of some 148 beds (based on a planning population of 50 000 elderly persons). Psychiatric beds for the elderly totalled twenty-three. When set against the DHSS planning norm of between 2.5 and 3.0 beds per 1000 elderly, revealing a shortfall of 102–127 beds, it is not surprising, therefore, that concern for inpatient services should preoccupy the JPTE, particularly as the hospital consultants responsible for these services were members of the planning team. The planning team met very infrequently and appeared to be dogged by controversy from its inception. It fell foul of the national strike by social workers at the end of 1978 and early 1979, which resulted in the cancellation of all meetings until the dispute was resolved. Most of the JPTE's efforts during 1979 focused on the implications of a DHSS circular entitled *A Programme for Improving Geriatric Care in Hospital* (DHSS, 1979), which was basically about changing the attitudes of staff working with the elderly (in particular, hospital staff) to one considered to be more sympathetic towards the elderly. In other words, the stress was put on 'care'.

This circular (DHSS, 1979) caused some conflict within the JPTE, primarily because some senior officers believed that it should be given preferential treatment and that a training programme for nursing staff should be prepared forthwith. Other officers of the NAHA, in particular those concerned with planning and policy, suggested a more low-key approach to the circular and that it should be seen in context with all other issues before the JPTE. This difference of opinion was not resolved; however, it did cease to be an issue in the sense that it did not appear as an agenda item after mid-1980. This may, in part, be attributed to the fact that a new chairman was appointed to the JPTE, who may well have had a different opinion on how the JPTE should be organized and what issues should come before it. Indeed, the attention of the JPTE seemed to have transferred to a discussion on the relative merits or otherwise of 'halfway' houses for elderly patients who no longer require normal hospital-type care. By the end of 1981, the major concern of the JPTE had not changed from this preoccupation with 'halfway' houses and it had gone so far as to set up a joint working group, incorporating health, housing, and social services personnel, to look into specialist housing for the elderly. A report was presented and discussed at the July 1981 meeting of the JPTE, but no firm policies emerged.

Although the JPTE was considered to be the forum for policymaking and planning, there existed within the NAHA parallel discussions concerned with services for the elderly. It would appear that the 'real' planning was done by the NAHA planning staff, whereas the JPTE was essentially a forum for discussion and debate and therefore largely ceremonial, as none of the key issues exercising the planners were discussed, apparently, by the JPTE.

The major activity of the planners was the articulation of a strategic policy for the elderly in the NAHA. There were two related issues of immediate concern: a lack of acute and long-stay hospital-type accommodation and a lack of psychiatric services for the elderly. Two proposals were put forward for partially resolving this situation: the opening of long-stay/rehabilitation beds at hospital A (currently 'mothballed'), and the temporary closure and subsequent redevelopment of hospital B to provide a range of facilities including Local Authority services. The planners believed that the proposal for the redevelopment of hospital B provided a unique opportunity to express a positive approach to joint planning by considering more innovative ways of providing services for the elderly. In other words, it was a chance to do something different; to break away from the traditional capital-led mode of planning.

As might be expected, these proposals came under close scrutiny from a variety of sources, but not from the JPTE. A number of consultants questioned the wisdom of these proposals. One consultant, in particular, had grave reservations about the plans for hospital A and was expressly concerned about the lack of beds for elderly severely mentally infirm (ESMI) patients. As this concern did not figure prominently in the proposals originally put forward by the NAHA planners, an impasse was reached; neither side seemed prepared to alter their stance, at least not at that stage.

The RHA planners were more concerned with the proposal to redevelop hospital B; in particular, whether the necessary finance would be available and the likelihood of staffing problems. In short, the RHA planners were questioning the viability of the hospital B scheme, in accord with their overall responsibilities. However, their zealousness in this instance may well have been influenced by the fact that the RHA planners have their headquarters at hospital B, and the proposed redevelopment of the hospital appeared to jeopardize the continuation of this arrangement. Also, the proposals put forward by the NAHA planners clearly challenged the RHA planners' more traditional view of planning, which was predominantly capital-led.

This picture became even more complicated when the Local Medical Committee (LMC) expressed concern about the feasibility of the hospital B scheme and declared that action was needed now, not in the future. In response, the chief officer of the NAHA cited recruitment difficulties, in particular over nurses, as the main reason for the delay in implementing any short-term measures.

Pressure on the NAHA to take some action was stepped up when two hospital consultants enlisted the aid of the Community Health Council (CHC) to press for more acute beds in the general hospital—part of which had remained unopened because of the staff problems—as an extension to the service currently being provided at hospital B instead of at the proposed redevelopment. A third hospital consultant, not content with the efforts of the RHA, the CHC, and the LMC, wrote to his Member of Parliament (MP), and a neighbouring MP (who passed a copy of the correspondence to the Minister of Health), deploring the current shortage of beds, suggesting that the redevelopment of hospital B was unnecessary, because of unopened beds elsewhere, and alleging that the whole service was in danger of an imminent collapse. The response of the Chairman of the NAHA to these critics was to reaffirm that the policies outlined by the RHA planners were still considered to be the most appropriate strategy. Indeed, the NAHA, in an attempt to move things along, wrote to the RHA asking it to sanction an increase of twenty-five acute beds for the elderly in the general hospital, along with approval for the hospital-A and hospital-B schemes. After a considerable lapse of time, the RHA agreed to the request, with the exception of the proposal for hospital B which it considered inappropriate or unnecessary.

The position over the hospital-B scheme remained deadlocked, with continuing pressure on the NAHA to do something immediately. The NAHA planners remained adamant that the key to any improved services for it rested with the scheme for hospital B. Indeed, they were so committed to the scheme that they attempted to husband financial resources for the scheme by reallocating a small portion of the NAHA's recurring revenue to this project, with the monies being used in the short term to finance projects with nonrecurring resource implications. These tended to be one-off capital schemes or purchase of equipment. At this stage, it became apparent that a reappraisal of the proposals was warranted, and, after discussion with the clinical and other staff involved, a view emerged that a more imaginative approach to the care of the elderly than hitherto postulated was required. To this end, a feasibility study of the hospital-B scheme was undertaken, with the express objective of clarifying the policy first before commencing work on the scheme. Concurrent with this initiative, a design team was also briefed to examine possible options/ models for the scheme.

The outcome of the feasibility study was a report concluding that the initial scheme proposed for the hospital B was unrealistic and inconsistent with current thinking on care of the elderly. Concern was expressed that the concept of care originally envisaged might be counterproductive if it meant cloistering elderly people away from society. The project was reassessed within the philosophy that elderly people should maintain as independent a life as possible and the facilities of the NAHA and the Local Authority should be marshalled accordingly. How this should be done is still very much at the formative stage. It is interesting to note that this reappraisal of part of the strategy for services for the elderly occurred quite independently of the JPTE, whose energies still appeared to be concentrated on matters more operational than strategic in nature.

5.2 Joint planning team for the mentally handicapped

The joint planning team for the mentally handicapped (JPTMH) was the first joint planning team to be established (mid-1977) in the locality under the auspices of the 1977 *Joint Care Planning* circular (DHSS, 1977), and it differed significantly from the JPTE in that it also included representatives from an adjacent health authority, which provided, on a 'subcontracted' basis, all inpatient care for mentally handicapped persons from the study area. From the outset, the JPTMH concerned itself solely with policy issues and the planning of services according to declared policies. As there were no hospital-based facilities in the NAHA for the mentally handicapped, the planning team was not hindered by the existence, organization, and usage of current facilities. In other words, its room for manoeuvre was largely unrestricted.

The first task undertaken by the JPTMH was to determine the precise numbers of mentally handicapped people, children and adults alike, residing within the NAHA. The Social Services Department of the corresponding Local Authority suggested that some consideration should be given to a policy on future building requirements and the type of client such buildings would be expected to cater for. The result was a consultative paper prepared for the JPTMH outlining the proposed development of services for the mentally handicapped. This strategy for the mentally handicapped was given reasonable circulation, and comments were invited by the JPTMH. The strategy, duly amended in light of comments received, was incorporated into the NAHA's strategic plan.

The perusal of the relevant records suggested that little of importance was discussed by the JPTMH after the initial flurry of activity, other than considering the various reports and papers issued by the DHSS on behalf of the Development Team for the Mentally Handicapped—a national advisory body, established by the DHSS, whose task it was to raise the consciousness of the NHS to the plight of mentally handicapped patients. In short, the JPTMH was relatively dormant for a period of about two years, until early 1980 when it began to consider a specific proposal for two small residential homes, each to contain five places for severely mentally handicapped children. However, the need for these units was questioned by the JCPT on the grounds of the financial commitment necessary and that there were other, and more worthy, competing demands.

It was during the debate on residential homes that a number of events occurred which resulted in the virtual takeover of the JPTMH by the JCPT. The JCPT had come to the view that the JPTMH was moribund and that, therefore, a new initiative was required. This new initiative was ultimately to emerge in the form of a partnership between the NAHA and the Local Authority, with a specific remit to implement an agreed policy for the mentally handicapped.

The Social Services Department's response to an earlier NAHA strategy for the mentally handicapped was to place considerable emphasis upon community support for parents and families with mentally handicapped members. At the time a paper discussed by the JPTMH suggested that a particular unit, then being considered for closure, could be reopened as a family support unit for parents of mentally handicapped children. The JCPMH's attention to these issues was diverted by an open letter from the local CHC to Dr Vaughan, the then Minister of Health. In the letter, the CHC deplored the lack of provision for the mentally handicapped within the NAHA and further criticised the NAHA for not having a 'real' plan for future services. The letter concluded with an invitation to the Minister to enquire into the apparent lack of progress and the poor state of affairs. The response of the NAHA to the CHC's letter was to chide them for their lack of faith by saying that the NAHA believed that it was important to develop services in close cooperation with the Local Authority and that it was equally important that this be done properly and without undue haste. Indeed, the CHC were reminded that they had been party to the discussions on a possible strategy for the mentally handicapped and also that the NAHA had partly underwritten the cost of a study on services for the mentally handicapped that the CHC was conducting. The implied but unstated message to the CHC was that their activities could jeopardize the limited progress to date; progress that depended a great deal on the continuing goodwill of all parties involved.

In tandem with this activity, a number of proposals were put to the JPTMH for consideration; proposals which, in one form or another, stressed the desirability of a community-based service. An element common to all of these various papers, proposals, and reports was the need for some form of support for families, such as a resource centre or similar unit providing counselling services, information, and advice; a base for community staff; and some provision for short-term relief/day-care facilities. The culmination of this activity was the publication of a report focusing upon the needs of mentally handicapped people and their families (NAHA, 1981).

The report called for the establishment of a partnership/joint venture between representatives from the NAHA, the Local Authority, and from the community (including parents of the mentally handicapped). The report was endorsed by all concerned, and subsequently this body superseded the JPTMH, thus explicitly recognising that there were certain advantages to a jointly planned and operated service. The partnership was to be a consortium of three officers and three members from the NAHA and the Local Authority, with two places for community/voluntary groups. Not surprisingly, the local community voluntary groups were not particularly happy about having only two places on the partnership, since it could be argued that the odds tended to favour the statutory bodies; hence, they pressed for equal status. Indeed, an agreement was subsequently reached which gave the consortium of community groups equal representation on the partnership with the NAHA and Local Authority (Petfield, 1983).

Notwithstanding these teething problems, a start was made towards the establishment of the Resource Centre for the Mentally Handicapped by securing the agreement of the local CHC to the secondment of their secretary, as the interim manager for the Resource Centre. The position at the present time is that a suitable base for the Resource Centre has been found, and the partnership (through the NAHA) is in the process of advertising for a permanent replacement for its interim manager. Unfortunately, the post had not been filled at the time of writing, as it had become caught up in the "arrangements for filling the revised administrative management structure for the new District Health Authority" (Petfield, 1983, page 113).

6 Discussion
It will be evident from the foregoing analysis that, although each JPT had a common origin and overall philosophy, they chose to interpret and carry out their remit in very different ways. This involvement of separate planning and policy rationales occurred despite the fact that each planning team shared a common core membership, comprised of NAHA officers (from the policy and planning division), health professionals (particularly

medical personnel), and representatives from the Local Authority's Social Services Department. Why these two particular planning groups should follow very different paths is difficult to determine empirically, but a number of hypotheses can be advanced, with some supporting evidence.

6.1 Leadership

Battye et al (1980), in their study of *The NHS Planning System at District Level*, did not consider, inter alia, the role of the chairperson when assessing the overall effectiveness of planning teams. They did suggest, however, that the key roles in the planning process belonged to the administrator, the community physician, and the hospital consultant. It is not unusual to find one of these key actors as chairperson of a planning team.

It is clear from the assessment of how each joint planning team functioned that, not only was the role of the chairperson crucial, but so too was the supporting role played by the NAHA planning staff. The JPTE has had, since its inception, two chairpersons, both of whom have been doctors—one was community-based, the other hospital-based. The chairperson of any group can be considered, de jure, to be the leader of the group and accordingly has the opportunity to play an important role vis-à-vis the group (Fiedler, 1967). In the case of the JPTE the chairperson had considerable influence in determining which items should or should not be included on the agenda.

As stated earlier, one of the major inhibiting factors for the JPTE was the constraints imposed by the existing service provision. This particular point was discussed with those selected for interview and each interviewee agreed that existing facilities acted as a constraint on development, although they gave differing reasons in support of their view. This is an important issue, for hitherto there seems to have been, in the NHS, an unwritten law which says that existing services are sacrosanct and are therefore considered to be beyond challenge, even on grounds of effectiveness and efficiency. A central feature of the NHS is the clinical autonomy enjoyed by the medical profession, which ensures that the best clinical conditions are made available to practise medicine. A related constraint is the general power and influence enjoyed by other health professionals over matters of policy. As Illich (1978, page 342) says, "they determine *what* shall be done and for *whom*" (emphasis is original). Together these factors can be seen as imposing a formidable barrier to change—a barrier which inhibits innovation and/or experimentation and encourages planning of existing services. It is not surprising, therefore, that the JPTE, virtually to the exclusion of all else, confined its activities to a discussion of nationally or centrally derived policy issues. It allowed the JPTE to have a sense of involvement in the policymaking process, whilst at the same time avoiding the contention and fragmentation often associated with the consideration of remedies to local problems.

The behaviour of the two chairpersons of the JPTE in conducting meetings was reminiscent, in some ways, of the 'defensive leadership' described by Gibb (1971), a leadership characterized by low trust, data distortion, persuasion, and high control. Gibb's analogy does not fit exactly the role played by the chairpersons of the JPTE, but the common features of high control (manipulation of agenda items) and low trust (restricting discussion to the local significance of national policies) would suggest that those occupying the chair were more concerned with appearances than with tackling matters of substance.

It is not surprising, therefore, to find that the JPTE was bypassed by the NAHA planners, who were of the opinion that national policies for the elderly perpetuated the traditional model of planning by concentrating on improvements to existing services, which was the modus operandi favoured by the JPTE, whereas the NAHA planners favoured a new approach to local problems. In other words, the NAHA planners were concerned with local issues entirely and were less inhibited in their search for solutions. Indeed, it appeared that the planners relished their somewhat unorthodox position by challenging the conventional wisdom about what should be the overall pattern of care for the elderly. The fact that the planners did not feel constrained in the same way that the JPTE did could be attributed to the fact that they clearly saw their task as producing a policy which maximized the potential benefits for the elderly and consequently they appeared to have no qualms about pursuing a policy, however contentious, that would achieve this end. Also they did not have a constituency whose view they would have to own and represent in the JPTE's discussions, unlike the clinicians, nurses, social workers, and other providers of care (Wilding, 1982).

The JPTMH, although similar in concept and composition to the JPTE, appeared to enjoy a very different form of leadership. Why they should function differently is not clearly known, but professional background and prior experience would appear to be an important factor. In the case of the JPTMH the chairpersons were administrators, the first one from the NAHA and the second from the Local Authority's Social Services Department. The reason why these chairpersons were more successful in developing locally based policies could be attributed to the fact that they were both used to working with committees and therefore were more astute at manipulating events and guiding issues through the joint planning team. An additional and possibly related factor was the personalities of each chairperson—they were both very charismatic individuals, who, when committed to a project, were determined to see it through, and this may well have influenced other members of the JPTMH to respond accordingly.

One conclusion which could be drawn from this preliminary analysis of the relationship between planning and policymaking in one particular health authority is that the role played by the chairperson of the planning team is of crucial importance. However, as Barnard et al (1979, volume 2, page 83) concluded, "it is not enough to allocate certain roles ... and expect the system and individual to respond accordingly [since] the resources available to individuals are certainly a significant factor in the way they perform their roles as are structural and political forces". Nonetheless, the chairperson is important because of his influence over agenda items; his understanding of the political feasibility of issues being discussed; and the commitment that he brings to his position.

6.2 Politics of provision

Lee and Mills (1982) identified one of the problems of joint planning to be that it was specifically concerned with strategic or long-range planning, and consequently the issues under discussion seemed to lack a sense of urgency. Furthermore, because most local authority social services departments did not operate a forward planning system, their interests resided primarily with operational issues—that is, with issues deserving of immediate attention. To a certain extent this scenario was consistent with the position adopted by the JPTE, but these features were not present in the JPTMH.

One explanation for this difference was that the NAHA provided a service for its elderly population but not for its mentally handicapped. Arguably, existing or established services restrict any planning team's degree of manoeuvrability. For example, both the NAHA and the Local Authority provide services for the elderly, but these services are primarily based upon different philosophies of care. The NAHA services are essentially rooted in the 'medical' model of treatment and care, whereas the services provided by the Local Authority may be generalized as a 'social' mode of support and containment—an alternative for those elderly who find living alone difficult. There is a danger in polarizing the strategies in this way, but, ultimately, they do determine and condition the approach each authority will adopt to the problems at hand. It is argued that these different viewpoints were partly instrumental in the JPTE choosing to discuss policy issues emanating from the DHSS rather than to grapple with the thorny issues of determining local policies for the elderly. As Barnard et al (1979) observed, there is a tendency to concentrate on issues which "*do not immediately threaten* to disrupt people's established patterns of behaviour" (volume 4, page 30, emphasis in original). A consequence of this reluctance on the part of the JPTE to grapple cogently with local issues was that their potential for influence was usurped by the NAHA planners.

In contrast, there was no service provision for the mentally handicapped within the NAHA. Thus the planning team was not unduly constrained in its debate on the problems of the mentally handicapped and possible solutions by any predetermined service infrastructure. In other words, the absence of services and facilities meant that any inbuilt inertia or resistance to change was unlikely to be an inhibiting factor as far as the planning of future services was concerned.

6.3 Professions, planners, and planning

The role played by the various actors in the planning process also influences the degree of success achieved in formulating plans and, subsequently, in implementing the plans and policies produced. Although there are many groups involved in planning, two appear to predominate—the medical profession and administrators/planners. A prime source of their influence is their ability to determine, or at least to manipulate, the 'need' for a particular service (Illich, 1978; Wilding, 1982).

The medical profession, on the one hand, often sees issues in clear unambiguous terms; namely that, as a demand exists for a service, a requisite number of beds and resources must be provided. Historically, the medical profession has played a particularly dominant role in NHS decisionmaking and has been quite capable of ensuring that the decisions obtained were compatible with their interests (Taylor, 1977; Haywood and Alaszewski, 1980; Illsley, 1980). Lee and Mills (1982, page 141) have observed that "despite the existence of the NHS planning system and provision for the systematic consideration of projects, planners had difficulty combating the ability of influential clinicians to bypass the planning system and lobby decision-makers directly".

There is evidence to indicate that this was indeed the case for the JPTE. Several of the clinicians concerned with elderly patients became impatient with the lack of progress and voiced their concerns to higher authorities in an effort to move things along. In contrast, medical influence over the developments obtained by the JPTMH was largely negligible and can be considered to be a direct consequence of the lack of services for the mentally handicapped. Put another way, there was not a cadre of clinicians capable of influencing, in a substantial way, the deliberations of the planning team.

Many planners/administrators, on the other hand, tended to regard planning as a technical activity—whether or not a service was above or below a predetermined standard or norm. To some extent the prescriptive nature of the NHS planning system precipitated this normative approach to planning, with its emphasis on planning according to the 'needs' of the population. Unfortunately, 'need' is a concept which is very difficult to define either qualitatively or quantitatively, thus necessitating some form of shortcut, such as standards or norms against which existing services may be compared. McNaught (1981) argues that the use of norms in planning is a consequence of a 'generalist cult' in the administrative hierarchy of the NHS, which implies that administrators should be capable of a variety of tasks and activities but not necessarily expert at any. McNaught goes on to suggest that planning should be removed from the bailiwick of the generalist and given to specialist planners (also see Rathwell, 1982).

The difficulty with developing seemingly more sophisticated and specialized approaches to planning is that "policies are settled by bargaining between groups, with their own interests and frames of reference, rather than by analysis" (Brown, 1975, page 233). This is clear from the assessment of the JPTE, even though it appeared on the available evidence to be largely ineffectual in developing policies and plans. However, the planners at the NAHA were equally constrained by the ability of certain groups within the NAHA to thwart the development of policies with which they did not agree. Eckstein (1956) had referred to this as 'bounded planning', because the planning process, and indeed those operating within it, operate within very tight boundaries, reflective of their own perceived values or concerns.

Values play a very important part in planning in that they largely determine which issues are placed on the planning agendas, when, and in what form. Unfortunately there is little empirical evidence available on the impact of interests and values in NHS planning and policymaking, yet it is acknowledged as a key feature of the process (Alford, 1975; Parston, 1980). The issues discussed by both the JPTE and the JPTMH reflect, to a certain extent, the values held by the main protagonists, and it is reasonable to assume that the creation of a parallel planning group for the elderly was in part a response to differing values and perceptions. Commentators have argued that, unless the debate on policy is broadened to include notions of interest and values, it is unlikely that policies truly reflective of patients' 'needs' will emerge (Haywood and Alaszewski, 1980; Mooney et al, 1980). The evidence from the workings of the JPTE and to a lesser extent the JPTMH does suggest that disguised or unarticulated values and interests did inhibit or preempt the search for common policies.

It is useful to compare the approach to planning displayed by each joint planning team, as it sharply demonstrates the lack of continuity in planning in the NHS. It will be recalled that the JPTE produced very little in the way of proposals or plans for services for the elderly, despite a clear mandate to do so. It was left to the NAHA's planners to produce such a plan, which they did primarily via a comparison of the existing range of inpatient facilities with that indicated by DHSS planning norms. The resulting plans were a compromise between the identified number of beds required to meet the shortfall and what could reasonably be funded, given the NAHA's projected revenue allocations for the three-year planning period. The application of a rather crude analytical tool to a complex issue.

Progress for the JPTMH, or the partnership which replaced it (as described above), was seemingly much easier, as there was no base with which to draw comparisons. As often happens in discussions, issues will arise, more by accident than by design, which by general consensus are considered to be 'worth pursuing'. This was indeed the case for the mentally handicapped. It is unclear where or with whom the partnership concept emerged, but once articulated it was rapidly endorsed as offering considerable scope for progress and there was a general will to carry it through. Thus it could be argued that planning in the NHS ranges from a near slavish adherence to central planning norms (Korman and Kogan, 1978), as a surrogate for a more analytical approach, to opportunism—the ability not only to recognise opportunities but also to exploit their potential.

6.4 Consultation and collaboration

One of the key features of the NHS reorganization in 1974 was the desire
to facilitate joint discussions between the health authorities and the
corresponding local authorities. Indeed, such cooperation was enshrined
in the legislation which constituted the then area health authorities
through the establishment of a Joint Consultative Committee (JCC)
composed of health authority members and local government councillors.
The JCC, however, did not have executive powers, it was only an advisory
body, despite its legal constitution. Its creation was designed to ensure a
closer working (that is, collaborative) relationship between health and local
authorities.

'Consultation' as seen by most health authority planners consisted of
distributing copies of the draft plan to all bodies who may have an
interest in those plans, with an invitation to comment upon the contents
therein. In other words, consultation was restricted to information sharing
and did not extend to participation in decisionmaking. The comments
received through this procedure tend to fall into two categories: frivolous—
raising questions of detail rather than of substance; or nonresponse—little
in the plans of interest or no time to prepare a proper response because of
the short consultation period. As a result, the value of consultation has
become rather discredited in the NHS, because it does not provide the
response the planners want—an endorsement of their perception of how
the health service should progress. To a certain extent consultation is the
bête noire of NHS planners, because it is something they are obliged to do
but to which they carry little commitment.

This bureaucratic approach to consultation could partially explain why
very few health services plans are implemented. The answer may rest with
the limited involvement in the production of the plans of those responsible
for providing the service. An additional factor, of lesser significance, is
that it is rare for either the CHC or the public to be represented on the
planning team, thus making it difficult for the criteria of plans appropriate
to the 'needs' of the population to be satisfied. Both the JPTE and the
JPTMH followed the traditional NHS approach to consultation—comments
were invited after plans had been formulated (that is, after the event
rather than during). Furthermore, the membership of the planning teams
was composed of health and local authority professionals; no lay persons
or CHC representatives were involved. However, it is debatable whether
the inclusion of a CHC representative on the planning team would have
improved the end result of the planning process. One could speculate and
say that to do so might well improve the acceptability and hence the
commitment to the proposals put forward.

There is some limited evidence available to support the contention that the
inclusion of CHC members and/or lay people in planning does improve
the quality of the product (Jones, 1977; Ham, 1980). The 'partnership'
(see subsection 5.2) with its tripartite structure provides a good example

of the way in which the mix of professionals and lay people can produce results. It would appear that the stereotypes held by all parties are constantly being challenged, causing a reassessment of individual views and values, with the result being a more workable solution emerging. This process has not been easy; indeed it has been rather painful for many of the 'partnership' members. Yet many would agree with the assessment that the results to date from the partnership have justified the means (Petfield, 1983).

7 Conclusions

The ultimate objective of introducing a formalized planning process into the NHS was to ensure that the outcome of planning, in terms of services provided, would be commensurate with the 'needs' of the population. The health care planning team was considered to be the appropriate mechanism for achieving this objective. These planning teams were conceived as multidisciplinary groups, with members selected according to their professional skills and knowledge of health services. Furthermore, the role of the planning teams was seen as advisory rather than executive—as a forum for the discussion and formulation of plans and policies which were then forwarded to management for consideration and decision.

It is clear that the majority of planning teams failed to live up to expectations. Although a number of factors have been advanced as contributing to loss of credibility in NHS planning, four issues appear to be dominant. First, policy decisionmaking, rooted very much in incrementalist philosophy, has not given those who plan the services clear and succinct organizational objectives within which to plan: planners do not know where they are going, nor how they are going to get there. Second, since the philosophy of planning and its virtues have been given a low profile, planning has become a means unto itself, rather than the pursuit of well-chosen policy objectives. Third, the prescriptive nature of the planning system, with its emphasis on an annual timescale, precludes any detailed or long-term analysis of problems to such an extent that most plans tend to adopt DHSS guidelines as de facto appropriate levels of service. Finally, satisfaction for most planners rests with the completed plan. No attempt is made to evaluate the decision arising out of the planning system to ascertain whether or not the original aims had been achieved.

This was the environment in which planning and policymaking has taken place in the NHS. From the evidence of the local case study, it has been suggested that, for the JPTE at least, these conditions prevailed. This was not true of the partnership nor of the now dormant JPTMH. The distinguishing features which enabled the partnership scheme to progress was a committed leadership, lack of constraining services or facilities, relatively little conflict between planners and the caring professions on the type of service required, and a shared sense of urgency that something must be done.

There are many factors impinging on the planning process, some understood, some not, but what is clear is that the establishment of a planning system and the creation of planning teams to operate the system does not guarantee success. Structural changes are, at best, enabling mechanisms. It is only through a subtle blend of leadership, commitment, sacrifice, and common understanding on the part of the planners and policymakers that planning in the NHS will effect change through a considered process of assessing alternatives and determining priorities capable of being implemented.

References

Alford R R, 1975 *Health Care Politics* (University of Chicago Press, Chicago, IL)

Barnard K, Lee K, Mills A, Reynolds J, 1979 *Towards a New Rationality—A Study of Planning in the NHS* four volumes (Nuffield Centre for Health Services Studies, University of Leeds, Leeds)

Barnard K, Lee K, Mills A, Reynolds J, 1980a, "NHS planning: an assessment" *Hospital and Health Services Review* **76** (8) 262–265

Barnard K, Lee K, Mills A, Reynolds J, 1980b, "NHS planning: an assessment concluded" *Hospital and Health Services Review* **76** (9) 301–304

Barnard K, Lee K, Reynolds J, 1980c *Tracing Decisions in the NHS* project paper RC16, King's Fund Centre, 126 Albert Street, London NW1 7NF

Battye G C, Burdett F, Candin D B, Smith M J, 1980 *The NHS Planning System at District Level* revised edition (Centre for Health Services Management, Leicester Polytechnic, Leicester)

Booth T, 1981a, "Collaboration between the heatlh and social services: part I" *Policy and Politics* **9** 23–49

Booth T, 1981b, "Collaboration between the health and social services: part II" *Policy and Politics* **9** 205–226

Brown R G S, 1975 *The Management of Welfare* (Martin Robertson, Oxford)

Brown R S G, 1977, "Accountability and control in the NHS" *Health and Social Services Journal* **87** (4564) B9–B16

DHSS, 1972 *Management Arrangements for the Reorganized National Health Service* Department of Health and Social Security (HMSO, London)

DHSS, 1976a *Joint Care Planning: Health and Local Authorities* HC(76)18/LAC(76)6 (Department of Health and Social Security, London)

DHSS, 1976b *The NHS Planning System* (Department of Health and Social Security, London)

DHSS, 1976c *Priorities for Health and Personal Social Services in England. A Consultative Document* (Department of Health and Social Security, London)

DHSS, 1976d *Sharing Resources for Health: The Report of the Resource Allocation Working Party* Department of Health and Social Security (HMSO, London)

DHSS, 1977 *Joint Care Planning: Health and Local Authorities* HC(77)17/LAC(77)10 (Department of Health and Social Security, London)

DHSS, 1979 *A Programme for Improving Geriatric Care in Hospital* HN(79)35 (Department of Health and Social Security, London)

DHSS, 1980 *Patients First* (Department of Health and Social Security, London)

Eckstein H, 1956 "Planning: a case study" *Political Studies* **4** 46–60

Eyles J, Woods K J, 1983 *The Social Geography of Medicine and Health* (Croom Helm, Beckenham, Kent)

Fiedler F E, 1967 *A Theory of Leadership Effectiveness* (McGraw-Hill, New York)

Gibb J R, 1971, "Dynamics of leadership and communication" in *Leadership and Social Change* Ed. W R Lassey (University Associates Press, Iowa City, IA)

Giggs J A, 1979, "Human problems in urban areas" in *Social Problems and the City* Eds D T Herbert, D M Smith (Oxford University Press, London)

Glennerster H, 1982, "Barter and bargains" *Health and Social Services Journal* **92** (4802) 771–773

Ham C, 1980, "Community health council participation in the NHS planning system" *Social Policy and Administration* **14** 221–231

Ham C, 1981 *Policy-making in the NHS: A Case Study of the Leeds Regional Hospital Board* (Macmillan, London)

Haywood S, Alaszewski A, 1980 *Crisis in the Health Service* (Croom Helm, Beckenham, Kent)

Illich I, 1978, "The image makers" in *The Professions and Public Policy* Eds P Slayton, M Trebilcock (University of Toronto Press, Toronto)

Illsley R, 1980 *Professional or Public Health?* The Nuffield Provincial Hospitals Trust, 3 Albert Road, London NW1 7SP

Irving D, Butts M S, Whitt C N, 1981, "Planning inaction?" *Hospital and Health Service Review* **77** (4) 101–103

Jones D T, 1977, "Consulting the public: some recent findings" *British Medical Journal* **2** 1101–1102

Knox P L, 1978, "The intra-urban ecology of primary medical care: patterns of accessibility and their policy implications" *Environment and Planning A* **10** 415–435

Knox P L, 1979, "Medical deprivation, area deprivation and public policy" *Social Science and Medicine* **13D** 111–121

Korman N, Kogan M, 1978, "Planning system in a region, case study 1" in research paper I entitled "The working of the National Health service" prepared for the Royal Commission on the National Health Service (HMSO, London)

Lee K, Mills A, 1982 *Policy-making and Planning in the Health Sector* (Croom Helm, Beckenham, Kent)

Lindblom C, 1959, "The science of 'muddling through'" *Public Administration Review* **19** 79–88

McNaught A, 1981, "The neglect of planning in health districts" *Hospital and Health Services Review* **77** (8) 241–243

Marslen-Wilson F, 1982, "Lessons in cooperation" *Health and Social Services Journal* **92** (4800) 706–708

MoH, 1962 *A Hospital Plan for England and Wales* Cmnd 1604, Ministry of Health (HMSO, London)

Mooney G, Russell E, Weir R, 1980 *Choices for Health Care* (Macmillan, London)

NAHA, 1978 *Area Operational Plan, 1978/79 to 1980/81* volume two; Newcastle Area Health Authority. Available from the Newcastle Health Authority, Scottish Life House, 2–10 Archbold Terrace, Newcastle upon Tyne, NE2 1EF

NAHA, 1981 *Mentally Handicapped People and their Families—A Blueprint for a Local Service* Newcastle Area Health Authority; available from the Newcastle Health Authority, Scottish Life House, 2–10 Archbold Terrace, Newcastle upon Tyne, NE2 1EF

NDGMH, 1976 *Mental Handicap: Planning Together* pamphlet 1, National Development Group for the Mentally Handicapped, London; available from the Department of Health and Social Security, Alexander Fleming House, Elephant and Castle, London SE1 6BY

NDGMH, 1977 *Mentally Handicapped Children: A Plan for Action* pamphlet 2, National Development Group for the Mentally Handicapped, London; available from the Department of Health and Social Security

NDGMH, 1980 *Improving the Quality of Services for Mentally Handicapped People* National Development Group for the Mentally Handicapped, London; available from the Department of Health and Social Security

NRHA, 1979 *Regional Strategic Plan 1979-1988* Northern Regional Health Authority, Benfield Road, Walker Gate, Newcastle upon Tyne, NE6 4PY

Parston G, 1980 *Planners, Politics and Health Services* (Croom Helm, Beckenham, Kent)

Petfield B Le G, 1983, "Services for the mentally handicapped in Newcastle—an adventure in partnership" *Hospital and Health Services Review* **79** (3) 111-114

Phillips D R, 1981 *Contemporary Issues in the Geography of Health Care* (Geo-Abstracts, Norwich)

Rathwell T, 1981, "Politics of persuasion" *Times Health Supplement* 18 December issue,

Rathwell T, 1982, "Planning in the NHS—1982 onwards" *Hospital and Health Services Review* **78** (5) 139-141

Rathwell T, Reynolds J, 1979a, "Conflicts in cooperation" *Health and Social Services Journal* **84** (4658) 1114-1115

Rathwell T, Reynolds J, 1979b, "Keeping up the pioneer spirit" *Health and Social Services Journal* **89** (4659) 1172-1173

Royal Commission, 1979 *Royal Commission on the National Health Service—Report* Cmnd 7615, Chairman: Sir Alexander Walter Merrison (FRS, DL) (HMSO, London)

Shaw S H A, 1978, "The pleasures and perils of joint care planning" *Royal Society of Health Journal* **98** 165-172

Smith D M, 1979 *Where the Grass is Greener: Living in an Unequal World* (Penguin Books, Harmondsworth, Middx)

Taylor R, 1977, "The local health system: an ethnograph of interest groups and decision-making" *Social Science and Medicine* **2** 583-592

Whitelegg J, 1982 *Inequalities in Health Care: Problems of Access and Provision* (Straw Barnes, Retford, Notts)

Wilding P, 1982, *Professional Power and Social Welfare* (Routledge and Kegan Paul, Henley-on-Thames, Oxon)

Hospital Planning and New Town Development: Examples from North East England [†]

J MOHAN
Birkbeck College, University of London

1 Introduction

Although the NHS and New Towns Acts were passed in the same year, 1946, relatively few studies exist of the interrelationship between health service planning and new town development (for an exception, see Parston, 1980). In this paper, I seek to further an understanding of this issue by discussing the problems posed for hospital planners in North East England by the development of the new towns of Peterlee and Washington (hereafter referred to as PNT and WNT, respectively). At one level this problem is simply one of responding to rapid localised population change, but, at another level, a number of questions are raised concerning the roles and relationships of several state agencies. For this to be interpreted satisfactorily, a fuller consideration of the role of the state is essential, but this is left to the concluding section (for contrasting reviews of theoretical positions on the state, see Frankel, 1979; Giddens, 1982; Gold et al, 1975; Habermas, 1976; Jessop, 1977; 1982). Furthermore, a theory of the state must be embedded within an appropriate 'theory of society' (Dear, 1978), though the construction of such a theory is problematic (see Anderson, 1978; Carney, 1973; Gregory, 1978; Lewis and Melville, 1978; Mohan, 1983b). Rather than enter into such debates at this stage, the evidence is divided into three sections. First, an outline is presented of the decisions to develop PNT and WNT, and the response of the Newcastle Regional Hospital Board (NRHB) to the development of these new towns is discussed. Hospital strategy for the areas in which these towns are located has been disputed at various times, and the most recent manifestations of such disputes are examined (section 2). Second, consideration is given to attempts to solve these problems by technical procedures (section 3); ultimately these attempts were inadequate and so an account is given of the resolution of these disputes, summarising the criteria taken into account by various agencies (section 4). In a concluding section I draw

† This paper is based on numerous unpublished items of correspondence, minutes of meetings, and background papers held in health authority files. For section 2, I drew on material held in the Newcastle Regional Hospital Board's (NRHB's) files 47A (correspondence with Peterlee New Town Development Corporation) and 47B (correspondence with Washington New Town Development Corporation), as well as on occasional items in the minutes of the NRHB Planning Committee and Capital Development Subcommittee. Discussion of events since 1974 was based on papers held in the Northern Regional Health Authority Planning Division's files on *Sunderland Area Health Authority—Major Development* and similar unpublished papers relating to the Durham Area Health Authority made available to me by officials of that authority.

together the implications of this evidence, with reference to the role of
the state and to the adequacy of geographical approaches to public facility
location problems.

2 Spatial policy, new town development, and hospital planning

Historical accounts of state spatial policies in North East England have
been presented elsewhere (Carney and Hudson, 1974; 1978; Hudson, 1976;
Robinson, 1978), and in this section, therefore, I briefly consider the factors
which underlay the designation of PNT and WNT before discussing more
fully the response by the NRHB to the development of these new towns.

A persistent theme in intraregional spatial policy in North East England
has been the assertion that industrial development must of necessity
proceed unevenly within the region and that, as a consequence, public
sector investment should be channelled only to selected locations (Carney
and Hudson, 1974; 1978), it being tacitly assumed that the requisite
labour force would move to the areas specified, given suitable employment
opportunities and a modern environment (Pepler and MacFarlane, 1949,
pages 63 and 267-268). New town development offered one means
whereby such general objectives could be attained. Formally accepted as a
policy instrument in 1946, new towns were to be developed to facilitate
decentralisation of population and also to concentrate population in areas
of dispersed settlement. The recommended population of such towns—
30000-50000—represented a compromise between being large enough to
support social facilities and to provide a sufficiently large labour force for
industrial development, and being small enough to provide a sense of
community. The attraction of stable male employment was a key goal;
indeed, this was essential if new towns were not to become dormitory
settlements. However, social goals were often vague and idealistic, and no
legislative action was taken to ensure the cooperation of other relevant
planning agencies. Thus joint planning between New Town Development
Corporations (NTDCs) and the National Health Service (NHS), for instance,
has been somewhat ad hoc in character, and it is perhaps not surprising,
therefore, that there is a considerable gap between the stated intentions
and the actual results of new town development (Robinson, 1978, page 29).

As regards the designation of PNT and WNT, the former had been
favoured as a site in the interwar years; it would avoid local urban sprawl
and ribbon development, and would improve local living conditions, this
being seen as a prerequisite for the retention of labour force adequate to
the needs of the coalmining industry in the area. After extensive
negotiations (reported in Leishman, 1971; Robinson, 1978; and Steele,
1962), Peterlee was designated as a new town in March 1948, with a target
population of 30000.

Though Washington had been proposed as a new town site in the
influential Pepler-MacFarlane report (Pepler and MacFarlane, 1949), not
until the early 1960s were definite steps taken to locate a new town there.

In accordance with the proposals of the Hailsham report (Board of Trade, 1963), favouring a rapid rise in public sector investment in the North East as a means of modernising the region's infrastructure to facilitate industrial development, Washington was designated as a new town early in 1964. Its target population—80000—reflected the importance attached to it by the Hailsham report; Washington was intended to: "stimulate faster progress in raising the scale and quality of the region's urban development generally" (Board of Trade, 1963, page 27).

Thus the designations of PNT and WNT reflect the differing political circumstances of 1948 and 1964. The former was intended principally as a focus for settlement in the eastern County Durham area, whereas the latter was to play a considerably more active part in stimulating the region's industrial development. The response to these developments by the NRHB is now considered. Figure 1 shows the location of Peterlee and Washington in relation to the hospital facilities available in 1960.

Hospital planning in postwar Britain took as its point of departure the evidence and recommendations of the wartime hospital surveys (MoH, 1946). These proposed serving the Peterlee/Easington area with the hospitals at Sunderland and Hartlepool (MoH, 1946, pages 59 and 90). This ante-dated the decision to locate a new town at Peterlee, after which it became clear that Peterlee was regarded as the NRHB's third-highest priority for new hospital development (NRHB, 1950, page 10).

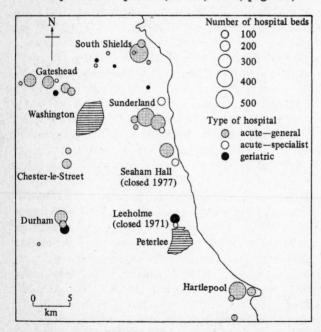

Figure 1. Location of Washington and Peterlee in relation to hospitals in eastern County Durham (source: MoH, 1962).

However, the conflicting intentions of the NRHB, the NTDC, and the National Coal Board (NCB) were to hinder this proposal's implementation. In conveying land to the NTDC, the NCB had insisted that their approval be sought for future surface developments. Clearly, construction of a large building such as a hospital would demand particular caution with regard to choice of site. By late 1953 the NCB's programme for coal extraction was behind schedule and this would delay the availability of the land previously offered to the NRHB. However, the same land could be used almost immediately for light structures, such as housing. Because of resource constraints on new hospital investment, the NRHB was unlikely to be able to provide a hospital for some time. The NTDC were therefore anxious not to leave an 'undeveloped hole' in Peterlee. The NTDC also felt that unless they were able to minimise disturbances to and restrictions on the extraction of coal, they could hardly expect much help from the NCB in developing Peterlee. Thus the NTDC's wish to develop social provision in Peterlee was subordinate to the NCB's requirement to maximise coal production. The NRHB, therefore, was offered an alternative site.

Though Peterlee had been a high priority for hospital development in the early postwar years, it evidently slipped down the list of the NRHB's priorities from the mid-1950s onwards. This was partly because of its slow growth, but it is also clear that there were pressures on the NRHB to switch its investment priorities towards Teesside. Changing attitudes to hospital size may have swayed the NRHB against Peterlee, and, as the NRHB pointed out, there existed four hospitals in close proximity to the town. Finally, the rundown of the coal industry from 1958 (see Krieger, 1979) and the uncertain prospects for the attraction of other sources of local employment combined to make it uncertain whether the anticipated population growth in the Easington area would take place. Hence the NRHB felt that the evidence did not warrant developing a new hospital in the Peterlee area, a view endorsed in *A Hospital Plan for England and Wales* (MoH, 1962). The question of hospital provision for the Peterlee area did not reappear on the political agenda until the late 1970s (see below). Before discussing this, the NRHB's response to the development of WNT is examined.

The *Hospital Plan* (MoH, 1962) had proposed that the Sunderland area should be served by district general hospitals (DGHs) in Sunderland and Ryhope (figure 1). The NRHB was initially unwilling to locate a hospital at WNT, on the basis that there was no 'natural drainage' of population to the new town. However, this opinion was subsequently revised, and this seems to have been motivated by the possibility that WNT's population might seek hospital facilities in Gateshead; the DGH there was only three miles from WNT (figure 1). This would be a 'serious embarrassment' to the NRHB, as it would greatly overload the capacity of Gateshead's hospitals; hence the NRHB's provisional agreement to the development of a hospital in WNT.

However, and as at PNT, the precise *timing* of such a development remained open to question. It could not be accommodated in the NRHB's ten-year capital programme, and, for the NTDC, this posed the problem of 'sterilising' thirty to forty acres of land. For this reason the NTDC offered the NRHB a site on the periphery of the town, since they could not be seen to leave a more central location undeveloped. Though they accepted this site, the NRHB nevertheless felt that WNT might never reach its projected size. Its target population (80000) was regarded as an *upper* limit to growth, and, according to the master plan for WNT, it was "largely a matter of speculation" how much of the migration to WNT would be made up of overspill (Llewelyn-Davies, Weeks and Partners, 1966, page 40). Since the master plan did not envisage much overspill in the early years of WNT's development, voluntary migration would be crucial in the town's expansion. Such migration was, by definition, beyond the NTDC's control, and the NRHB, therefore, felt justified in delaying hospital development in WNT. Attempts were made to provide a 'hybrid' type of health care, for example by providing specialist services at a health centre; this was based on a number of similar experiments at other new towns (see Parston, 1980). However, development of a DGH was effectively out of the question, particularly in view of the proposals of the Bonham-Carter report (CHSC, 1969), which advocated a considerable spatial concentration of hospital services into units of over 1000 beds, serving populations in excess of 200000. On such criteria neither WNT or PNT could be considered seriously as hospital sites.

However, a rather different emphasis in policy emerged from the mid-1970s onwards. Whereas hospital policy had previously stressed the virtues of centralisation, the accessibility and public expenditure implications of DGH development prompted moves towards a smaller scale of hospital provision, reflected, for example, in plans for community hospitals (DHSS, 1974). Such developments once again raised the possibility of providing hospitals in Peterlee and Washington.

In the case of Peterlee, a protracted dispute developed between the Durham Area Health Authority (DAHA) and the Northern Regional Health Authority (NRHA), concerning hospital location in the Durham Health District (DHD). The 1974 NHS reorganisation had set up regional and area health authorities (RHAs and AHAs) whose functions were potentially in conflict. Broadly speaking, the AHA's obligation to provide comprehensive health care for its resident population could be held to be at variance with the RHA's responsibility for efficient strategic management. It became apparent, in mid-1979, that the DAHA and NRHA differed somewhat in their proposals for the DHD. The formal allocation of the Easington Local Government District (LGD) to the DAHA from 1974 (figure 2) had increased the population of the DHD to around 240000. The hospital capacity for such a population could not be accommodated at Dryburn Hospital, Durham (the DHD's main facility) because of constraints on land availability. In seeking an alternative, the DAHA proposed developing a complementary general hospital in the Easington area (DAHA, 1979, page 41); this reflected its concern at the lack of local hospital facilities for approximately 105000 people resident in the Easington LGD. For reasons discussed later (section 4) this was not acceptable to the NRHA; broadly speaking, it contradicted the NRHA's regional strategy and was considered uneconomic (NRHA, 1979, pages 36–37). The DAHA therefore commissioned an assessment of hospital location from myself, and this is reported in the next section.

As for Washington, two developments had necessitated a reexamination of hospital strategy for the Sunderland AHA (SAHA). One of these—the emergence of proposals for a rather smaller scale of hospital provision—has been discussed already. Of more importance, however, were the direct political pressures stemming from the 'Hospital for Washington Campaign'. This had started as a 'spontaneous movement' in early 1979. Six months later, some 22000 people had signed a petition calling for the construction of a 500-bed general hospital in the town. This was in direct opposition to the SAHA's declared strategy of concentrating hospital development on the Sunderland DGH, with a second general hospital at Ryhope (figure 3). The campaigners stressed the rapid growth of Washington (its population, by 1979, was approximately 50000) and its high birth rate, which, at 22/1000, was almost twice that for the SAHA as a whole. The SAHA's intention to locate its second maternity unit at Ryhope would therefore be 'disastrous'. The campaigners also emphasised that a hospital would facilitate industrial development. Washington was allegedly 'the only growth point for industry in the Northern Region', and it was claimed that industrialists were 'disconcerted' to find that there was no hospital

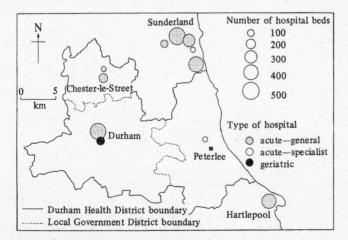

Figure 2. The Durham Health District (source: DAHA, 1979).

available[1]. In the light of these pressures, the NRHA reassessed their
strategy for the Sunderland area.

Clearly, then, the development of PNT and WNT has at various times
posed problems for NHS planners in North East England. Moreover, these
problems have never been resolved to the satisfaction of all parties
concerned. Though the NRHB was undoubtedly keen to provide hospitals
in both these towns, uncertain NHS capital allocations and changing policy
on hospital size prevented this intention from being realised. This also,
incidentally, caused problems for the NTDCs concerned, who had to
consider whether to leave undeveloped areas of land in their towns in
expectation of future hospital development. Indeed, this reflects a more
general problem of developing social facilities appropriate to the needs of
new towns. Although NTDCs cannot be seen to leave large areas of land

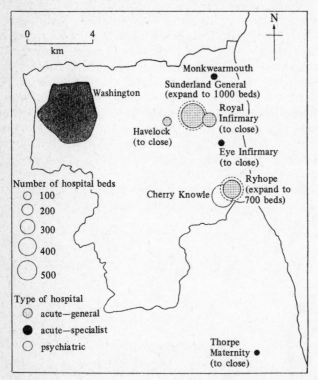

Figure 3. Location of hospitals in the Sunderland Area Health Authority (SAHA) and
the SAHA's proposals for future development (source: SAHA, 1979).

[1] In these foregoing few paragraphs, I have summarised the arguments of the Hospital
for Washington Campaign, as set out in a letter (1980) to the Ministry of Health. A
copy of this letter is held in the NRHA Planning Division's file on *Sunderland Area
Health Authority—Major Development*.

undeveloped, they are nevertheless dependent on the decisions of various other statutory agencies concerning the nature and timing of service provision. Nor can NTDCs guarantee that they will attain their population targets, since they depend to a considerable extent on voluntary migration. The more general implications of this evidence will be taken up later; at this point consideration is given to attempts to resolve these planning disputes on a technical level.

3 Technical solutions to hospital planning problems
Clearly, the problems of providing appropriate hospital facilities for PNT and WNT had been a matter for dispute over several years. Attempts were subsequently made to resolve them on purely technical grounds and these are now examined.

In the case of Peterlee, the DAHA commissioned, from the author, an assessment of alternative hospital strategies for the DHD. This has been reported in more detail elsewhere (Mohan, 1983a) and here only its main features are summarised. In planning future hospital services for the DHD, the DAHA made allowances for certain cross-boundary patient flows; the proximity of parts of the DHD to hospitals in Sunderland and Hartlepool meant that these were almost inevitable, and the area to be served by the DHD facilities is shown in figure 4. The total population of this area was estimated at 212000 in 1979 and, by comparing existing hospital provision with what would be predicted by an application of NHS 'norms' for hospital services, it was revealed that an additional 175 hospital beds

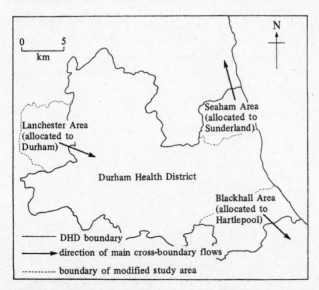

Figure 4. The Durham Health District (DHD), showing modifications to reflect patterns of patient flow (source: Mohan, 1983a).

would be necessary if the DHD was to become self-sufficient in hospital provision. Given the constraints on developing Dryburn Hospital, Durham, this necessarily implied examining other potential sites, and so alternative strategies for hospital provision were assessed.

This involved using the Tornqvist computer algorithm (Tornqvist et al, 1971), the value of which had been demonstrated in several analyses (for example, Robertson, 1976; 1978). The technique involves minimising the aggregate travel function generated by providing m facilities to serve n demand points. Mathematically this can be stated as:

$$\text{minimise } C = \sum_{j=1}^{m} \sum_{i=1}^{n} p_i d_{ij} \, ,$$

where

C is the total cost function;

p_i is the demand at point i; and

d_{ij} is the distance between demand point i and supply point j.

Since more extensive accounts of such methods are available, they are not discussed at greater length (see Beaumont, 1980; Hodgart, 1978). The measures of demand and distance used were, respectively, total population in each one-kilometre grid square and straight-line distance. Analysis proceeded through an assessment of the aggregate travel function for the existing hospital sites (table 1) to a consideration of where best to locate an additional facility. It was shown that locating an additional hospital in PNT would reduce the aggregate travel function for the DHD from 1 570 021 km to 794 306 km—a reduction of 49%. In these terms it

Table 1. Aggregate and average travel statistics for various combinations of hospital locations.

Location	Population served	Aggregate distance (km)	Average distance (km)
Dryburn	162606	1431227	8.80
Chester-le-Street	49442	138794	2.80
Total [a]	212048	1570021	7.40
Dryburn	98194	457905	4.76
Chester-le-Street	49439	138745	2.80
Third facility	66415	197656	2.97
Total [b]	212048	794306	3.74
Dryburn	144485	845021	8.85
Second facility	67363	209295	3.09
Total [c]	212048	1053316	4.97

[a] For the existing hospital sites at Dryburn and Chester-le-Street.

[b] For the two existing hospitals plus a third facility optimally located [in the new town of Peterlee (PNT)].

[c] For two facilities, one at Dryburn and the other optimally located (in PNT).

could be argued convincingly that access to hospital services in the DHD would be greatly improved if a hospital were to be located in Peterlee. An alternative strategy was also considered, involving closure of the facilities in Chester-le-Street and searching for the optimum location of a new facility, assuming that Dryburn remained the major facility in the DHD. This would reduce the aggregate distance function by 32.7%, from 1570021 km to 1054316 km. In terms of *average* travelling distance to each facility, the present arrangements give figures of 2.80 km to Chester-le-Street and 8.80 km to Dryburn. An additional facility at Peterlee would incur average travelling distance ranging from 4.76 km (Dryburn) to 2.97 km (Peterlee), and therefore this clearly reduces inequalities in access to services within the DHD.

Certainly, this analysis is limited by comparison with some of the more sophisticated location–allocation methods now available (for instance, see Beaumont, 1980). Use of total population as a measure of demand is clearly an overgeneralisation, since it ignores variations in and constraints upon the expression of demand imposed by class, space, culture, and gender. Likewise, in no sense does straight-line distance provide a sophisticated measure of accessibility. However, the crucial point here concerns not so much the technical merits of the procedure used but rather the reasons for its commissioning and the use to which it was put. In this context this study is compared with similar work carried out by the NRHA.

This work had considered not just the DHD but also the presence of hospital facilities in adjacent areas which might be able to guarantee the necessary level of service provision for the Easington area (figure 2). A new hospital at Peterlee could be expected to reduce patient flows into the DAHA, thus reducing the population seeking services at Ryhope General Hospital. However, the consequences for the Hartlepool Health District were more serious. The anticipated reduction in patient flow to Hartlepool could seriously threaten the viability of some clinical units. Although general hospital facilities would be brought within easy reach of the population of the Easington area as a consequence of the DAHA's proposals, the NRHA felt that this ought not to be overstressed, since the access problems imposed by existing arrangements were 'not excessive'[2]. The NRHA also presented an assessment of public transport in the DHD (table 2), which, it was claimed, supported the NRHA's views. The NRHA remained convinced, therefore, that the Easington area could best be served by Hartlepool and Sunderland rather than by Durham.

In considering the consequences of these studies, the claims made for the studies by the NRHA and the DAHA are considered. The DAHA felt that the work reported above had vindicated their arguments and confirmed the

[2] See the NRHA's *Report on the Pattern of Hospital Provision in Durham AHA* (1979), a copy of which is held in the NRHA Planning Division's files.

strategy previously referred to—acute hospitals in Peterlee and Durham, plus a community hospital in Chester-le-Street—as the 'optimum arrangement' of services. By contrast, the NRHA claimed that they had looked closely at 'the geography of and lines of communication within' the Easington area and had concluded that this area could best be served from Hartlepool and Sunderland. The crucial point here is not the objectivity and/or precision of these studies, nor the competence of those who conducted them, but rather *the use to which they were put.* This in turn links them to assessments of spatial aspects of the problems of hospital planning in the SAHA.

The point at issue here was whether to locate the second DGH in the SAHA at WNT or at Ryhope. The NRHA evaluated two sites according to various criteria. On *accessibility*, Ryhope was felt to be superior, as it was only four miles from Sunderland General Hospital, whereas WNT was five-and-a-half miles away. This simplistic assessment subsequently exposed the NRHA to the charge of catering only for the needs of medical staff and administrators. On other criteria, Ryhope was considered superior because of the large site there (250 acres, as opposed to sixty acres at WNT); also, the Ryhope site was already in NHS ownership. In neither case was staff recruitment seen as a problem, though Ryhope had the advantage of a long tradition of employment in local hospitals. Hence the local labour force was likely to include appropriately qualified staff[3].

Table 2. Public transport in the Easington area: frequency of service and travel time from selected centres to existing hospitals [source: NRHA's *Report on the Pattern of Hospital Provision in the Durham Area Health Authority* (1979, unpublished), a copy of which is held in the NRHA Planning Division's files].

From	To							
	Hartlepool		Ryhope		Sunderland		Durham	
	F	T	F	T	F	T	F	T
Seaham Harbour	1	15	4	12	4	20	1	55
New Seaham	2	50	8	6	8	15	1	40
Murton	–	–	3	18	3	25	1	30
Easington	4	40	2	15	4	30	1	70
Easington Colliery	2	30	–	–	2	38	1	60
Horden	3	25	–	–	–	–	3	60
Peterlee	5	35	2	30	3	35	5	50
Shotton	2	45	2	30	2	40	4	35
Wingate	2	25	1	35	1	45	1	55
Blackhall	7	18	–	–	–	–	2	55

Key: F ≡ frequency (number of buses per hour); T ≡ travel time (minutes).

[3] In this paragraph, I have summarised the arguments of the NRHA's consultation paper on *Long Term Hospital Strategy for the Sunderland Area* (1980). A copy of this is held in the NRHA Planning Division's file on *Sunderland Area Health Authority— Major Development.*

However, these proposals were objected to on technical grounds. Officials at Tyne and Wear County Council (TWCC) had carried out an independent investigation of spatial aspects of this dispute (reported in Riley, 1982). Since the NRHA had not made explicit their patient referral policies, several options were explored. These were, first, allocation of patients to *all* general hospital beds in the SAHA (including either Ryhope or WNT), and, second, allocation of patients to beds in Sunderland General Hospital and WNT or Ryhope. In neither situation was there a sizeable difference between WNT or Ryhope (table 3). But, with the exploration of various options, such as capacity-constrained solutions with varying referral policies (either to the nearest hospital or to the nearest available bed), a location at WNT began to show clear advantages, of the order of 10% in aggregate distance terms (table 3). This was felt to be 'significant'

Table 3. Summary of location–allocation analysis carried out by the Tyne and Wear County Council (TWCC) on alternative hospital strategies [source: unpublished report to the TWCC on *Hospital Strategy for the Sunderland Area* (16 February, 1981), a copy of which was made available to the author by M Riley of the TWCC].

Strategy	Town [a]		R−WNT	R−WNT/R (%)
	WNT	R		
NRHA policy				
(i) allocation to all general-hospital beds in the district including WNT or R	7532520 (25.9)	7525335 (25.9)	−7185 (0)	−0.0 −0.0
(ii) allocation to general-hospital beds in Sunderland General and in either WNT or R	7698583 (26.5)	7688788 (26.5)	−9795 (0)	−0.0 −0.0
TWCC policy				
(i) uncapacitated allocation to the nearest of all hospitals, plus either WNT or R	4345473 (14.9) (0.57)*	5029764 (17.3) (0.66)*	684291 (2.4)	15.7 15.7
(ii) uncapacitated allocation to the nearest hospital—either Sunderland General or either of WNT and R	5509096 (18.9) (0.72)*	6123727 (21.0) (0.81)*	614631 (2.1)	11.1 11.1
(iii) capacitated allocation to the nearest of all general-hospital beds, plus either WNT or R	4713318 (16.2) (0.62)*	5587338 (19.2) (0.73)*	874020 (3)	18.5 18.5
(iv) capacitated allocation to the nearest general-hospital beds in Sunderland General and in either WNT or R	5764607 (19.8) (0.76)*	6469813 (22.3) (0.85)*	705206 (2.5)	12.2 12.2

[a] Figures are total travel times (in minutes); figures in brackets are average travel times; figures in brackets with an asterisk indicate proportion of NRHA policy time.
Key: NRHA ≡ Northern Regional Health Authority; R ≡ Ryhope; WNT ≡ Washington New Town.

in a land-use transport planning context, and, indeed, an official of TWCC suggested that siting the hospital at WNT would save the TWCC some £5 000 000 over ten years. These savings would accrue from not having to repair and/or replace roads in the Ryhope area, and indeed in the Sunderland area more generally, as a result of WNT's superiority in terms of accessibility and traffic generation (Riley, 1981). There was little to choose between the sites in terms of space for car parking or access by public transport, but it was felt that the benefits of a hospital at WNT would be more widely dispersed throughout the western part of the SAHA[4]. Hence TWCC favoured WNT on the grounds of what they saw as its superiority in locational terms. However, this was rejected by the NRHA on the grounds that the TWCC's conclusions could be accounted for by the margin of error attached to such calculations, though the NRHA did not indicate the criteria which they would have used in such an analysis. Clearly, then, the NRHA's preferred policy option was open to criticism on technical grounds. More seriously, the strategy proposed by the NRHA failed to satisfy the Hospital for Washington Campaign and the WNT Development Corporation (WNTDC); indeed, the campaigners and the WNTDC alike were vociferous in their criticism (the subsequent debates are considered in section 4).

In summary, neither of these disputes were resolved by the application of purely technical methods. For instance, although the studies of hospital location in the DHD both claimed to be objective analyses of the same issue in the same area, they came to different conclusions and were used in support of competing views. This can partly be explained in terms of the use of different analytical methods, but of more importance is the fact that the divergent intentions and perceptions of the NRHA and the DAHA were influential in defining the way the problem was to be analysed. It is therefore essential that the emergence of such conflicts is adequately understood; this, in turn, would permit analysis of why and under what conditions certain techniques are employed in planning. These remarks are amplified later (section 5); first, however, the resolution of these two disputes is considered.

4 The resolution of the disputes
In proposing that a new hospital be built in the Easington/Peterlee area, the DAHA had stressed that, although they had never envisaged a totally *independent* hospital in that area, they wished nevertheless to develop a substantial hospital presence. In this regard they appealed to the DHSS's (1980) changing attitude to the scale of DGH development, arguing that rigid definition of hospitals as either 'DGHs' or 'community hospitals' was unwise in the light of varying local circumstances. Greater flexibility

[4] This information is contained in an unpublished report to the Tyne and Wear County Council (TWCC) on *Hospital Strategy for the Sunderland Area* (16 February, 1981), a copy of which was made available to the author by M Riley of the TWCC.

was required, and the DAHA wished to develop an ad hoc or 'hybrid' type of hospital, which would include acute and psychiatric facilities[5]. The DAHA's appeal to the DHSS's revised hospital policy is of interest. Although this policy's stress on a more spatially dispersed pattern of services would appear to support the DAHA's case, one option excluded from this document was the provision of new hospitals in communities currently lacking them, such as new towns. Such an option might be regarded as an inescapable consequence of this change in policy; its exclusion reinforced the fears of NHS administrators that the rhetoric of this policy document concealed a wish to restrain new capital development (see also Mohan, 1983b, chapter 7). It was therefore unlikely that the DAHA would receive support for its proposals.

Thus the DAHA's proposals were based upon a recognition of local need and upon a desire to serve its resident population more adequately. By contrast, the NRHA did not regard the provision of a fully comprehensive hospital service as one of the principal tasks of an AHA. Cross-boundary flows of patients were acceptable in the interests of regional strategy and efficient management (NRHA, 1979, page 36). Indeed, the NRHA felt that the DAHA had given only limited consideration to the strategic implications of their proposals, in that they had considered the subject 'only in the context of the Durham area itself'. By contrast, the NRHA felt that a DGH in Peterlee could not be viable, since its catchment population was unlikely to exceed 60000. In addition, such a development would involve providing hospital services for the DHD from three hospitals (Durham, Peterlee, and Hartlepool) instead of from two (Hartlepool, Durham). This could not be considered a cost-effective solution and, indeed, it could have threatened the viability of the DGH at Hartlepool. The NRHA therefore favoured locating a community hospital at Peterlee, linked to and supported by the DGH at Hartlepool; in this way the viability of the Hartlepool facility would not be threatened[6].

Though there was apparently a deep-rooted conflict—broadly speaking, between interests of regional strategy and local need for and access to services—a consensus was reached with surprising speed. The NRHA considered that there was a "substantial measure of basic agreement ... and acceptance of the regional strategy". This seems to have emerged in the wake of assurances from the NRHA that their approach to hospital provision for the Easington area would be flexible and that outpatient facilities would be available at Peterlee. The NRHA also agreed to provide maternity facilities in the Easington area; there was likely to be a 'considerable public outcry' if they did not do so, since Thorpe Maternity Hospital was likely to close[5]. At one level this dispute exemplifies the

[5] See "Notes of a meeting between representatives of the NRHA and DAHA, 11 March, 1980", a copy of which is held in the NRHA Planning Division's files.

[6] See the NRHA's *Report on the Pattern of Hospital Provision for Easington District* (1979), a copy of which is held in the NRHA Planning Division's files.

'equity versus efficiency' trade-off: compare the DAHA's emphasis upon local need for and access to services with the NRHA's stress on broader issues of regional strategy. At another level, however, it could be argued that the two authorities were seeking to reconcile incompatible objectives. The DAHA's responsibility to provide a comprehensive health service for its resident population was clearly at variance with the NRHA's duty to ensure the efficient management of health facilities in the whole of the NRHA. Clearly, the NRHA felt unable to permit a full DGH development in the Easington area and offered the compromise of a community hospital in PNT.

In the case of WNT, considerable opposition developed to the NRHA's intention of locating the second DGH in the SAHA at Ryhope. Before considering this opposition, it is worth noting that, whereas the NRHA's strategy had favoured Ryhope on essentially *technical* criteria—land and labour availability, for instance—there is some evidence that direct political pressures led the NRHA (and also the SAHA) to favour Ryhope. A draft version of the NRHA's *Hospital Strategy for the Sunderland Area*[7] argued that acceptance of Ryhope as a site for the second DGH in the SAHA had been influenced by recollection of 'local political pressure' after the closure of Seaham Hall Hospital (see figure 1) in 1977. This had provoked a considerable local reaction (for example, see the *Newcastle Journal*, 1977a; 1977b; 1978a; 1978b), and, since the Ryhope Hospital was a major employer in an area of high unemployment, the NRHA anticipated 'strenuous local political activity' should that hospital be run down or closed. The NRHA was clearly unwilling to risk a repetition of events at Seaham Hall, and it would seem that this was an important, though not necessarily a decisive, factor in favour of Ryhope. However, the final (public) version of the NRHA's strategy made no mention of this point, emphasising, rather, that Ryhope's advantages were land ownership, its potential for development, and the ready availability of trained personnel.

Despite this, considerable opposition was mounted against the NRHA's proposals. The WNTDC claimed that the NRHA was defending a predetermined conclusion and had given scant consideration to the views of the local community, in particular to the 'vigorous, comprehensive, and nonpolitical' case pursued by the Hospital for Washington Campaign. The proposed strategy ignored the needs of the young and growing population of WNT and was oriented more towards the convenience of administrators and staff than to the interests of patients and visitors. The WNTDC also felt that the lack of a hospital in WNT could hinder the attraction of industry—an argument rejected as 'not relevant' by the NRHA. The TWCC also objected to the proposals on technical grounds (see section 3). Against this, the Gateshead and South Tyneside AHAs supported the NRHA on the grounds of the potential threat to staff recruitment if a

[7] Unpublished report (1980), a copy of which is held in the NRHA Planning Division's file on *Sunderland Area Health Authority—Major Development*

hospital were to be built in WNT, and the Durham Community Health Council stressed that additional travel would be imposed on those residents of the Easington LGD who havitually sought hospital care in the SAHA[8].

The NRHA's strategy had clearly generated considerable dissatisfaction— reflected, for example, in an appeal to the Minister of Health by the Hospital for Washington Campaign—but, despite this, the NRHA's strategy was carried through. The NRHA stressed the problems posed by the delays inherent in this dispute; the progress of various other schemes in the SAHA was contingent on agreement being reached on a strategy for the SAHA as a whole, and the delays were lowering staff morale at Ryhope and hindering the disposal of surplus NHS land adjacent to Ryhope. The NRHA did offer, at one stage, a strategy whereby all development in the SAHA would be concentrated at Sunderland General Hospital (figure 3); this came after an indication that the DHSS would consider a somewhat larger scale of development than formerly envisaged (in DHSS, 1980) if cogent arguments could be advanced in favour of such a scheme. In proposing a 1200-bed hospital in central Sunderland, the NRHA claimed that this would offer the most accessible pattern of hospital services from the point of view of the SAHA as a whole. There was some force in this insofar as it reduced *disparities* in access as between WNT and Ryhope, though the provision of two facilities would have almost certainly reduced aggregate distance travelled. The attraction of such a proposal may well have been that it compromised between the WNT and Ryhope sites, rendering the two locations virtually equidistant from a DGH. For various reasons, however, it proved impossible to find either a way of concentrating all DGH development on one site or a suitable alternative site in central Sunderland. The NRHA therefore reaffirmed its original strategy; although it was conceded that WNT may have been the more accessible site, such considerations 'could not be the key determinant' between alternative locations[9]. The NRHA therefore resolved that hospital development in the SAHA would be based on DGHs at Sunderland and Ryhope, with complementary community hospitals in Sunderland, Houghton-le-Spring, and Sunderland (figure 3).

Clearly, then, considerable problems were experienced in agreeing on hospital strategies for eastern County Durham and the SAHA. Yet in both cases policies were produced which both minimised disturbances to existing arrangements (for example, by avoiding interruptions to the NRHA's capital development programme) and, at the same time, apparently

[8] In this paragraph, I have summarised the views presented in the NRHA's document on *Hospital Services in the Sunderland Area: Results of Consultation* (1981), a copy of which is held in the NRHA Planning Division's file on *Sunderland Area Health Authority—Major Development*.

[9] See the NRHA's report on *Sunderland Hospitals Strategy* (16 November, 1981), a copy of which is held in the NRHA Planning Division's file on *Sunderland Area Health Authority—Major Development*.

made material concessions to those pressing claims for new hospital development (decisions to provide community hospitals in WNT and PNT could certainly be interpreted in this light). In no sense, however, could these disputes be said to have been resolved on a purely technical level; even after the analyses reported above (section 3) were carried out, considerable discussion took place. This raises important issues concerning the role of the state, which are taken up in the concluding section.

5 Concluding remarks

The foregoing evidence traced the emergence and resolution of two spatial health service planning problems. It did so by considering the decisions to develop PNT and WNT and the response of the relevant health authorities (section 2); by assessing attempts to resolve these issues on essentially technical grounds (section 3); and by summarising the criteria taken into account in the resolution of subsequent debates on hospital location (section 4). These concluding comments concern the role of the state and the use of knowledge in planning.

Regarding the role of the state, three points are clear from the foregoing discussion: these concern the constraints under which the state operates, the divergent intentions of various state agencies, and the process of state policy formulation.

First, irrespective of the intentions of particular state agencies, their scope for manoeuvre is constrained in several ways. Whereas the NRHB was undoubtedly keen to provide hospital services in PNT and WNT, its ability to do so was limited by financial restraints and a shift in investment priorities (PNT) and by changing attitudes to hospital size (PNT and WNT). In turn, these constraints should not be interpreted at the level of changes in the subjective intentions of key politicians and planners. Rather they reflect the changing character of the British state since 1948 [see Mohan (1983b; 1984) for the broader implications of these changes for hospital planning].

The divergent intentions of state planning agencies forms a further important theme. NTDCs, for example, were given no statutory obligation to provide health services, nor were appropriate mechanisms set up to ensure coordinated planning. In these circumstances, NTDCs were almost wholly dependent on decisions taken by authorities over whom little influence could be exerted. Moreover, the NRHB, not surprisingly, proceeded cautiously in response to the development of WNT and PNT, as is illustrated by the NRHB's concern that these towns might not attain their stated population targets. Further pressures are imposed on NTDCs by these problems: on the one hand it is clear that the NTDCs at Washington and Peterlee were keen to provide a site for a hospital, but, on the other hand, both expressed considerable misgivings about leaving land undeveloped for considerable periods of time. Hence service provision has lagged behind population growth (see Robinson, 1978; and, more generally,

Wirz, 1975). Furthermore, both Washington and Peterlee were intended to modernise social conditions in their respective localities, but this goal has not been achieved in terms of hospital provision, and in a sense this exemplifies the limited role of new towns as a policy instrument. Whereas expenditure on the provision of industrial infrastructure (advance factories and so on) was regarded as a legitimate role for NTDCs, advance provision of social facilities was not so regarded (Robinson, 1978, page 303). In Offe's (1974; 1976) terminology, this could be seen as evidence of the 'selectivity' of the state, whereby expenditure on (at least some of) the preconditions for capital accumulation is deemed legitimate, whereas expenditure designed to improve social facilities is not.

As to the process of state policy formulation, this emerges less as the systematic and coordinated pursuit of stated objectives than as a series of ad hoc responses to changing sociopolitical and economic circumstances. Hence the appropriate strategy for hospital provision for these new towns (and the areas surrounding them) has never been agreed to the satisfaction of all parties concerned. This is clear from disputes between the state and those it serves (WNT), between different branches of the state (WNT and PNT), and even within the NHS itself (PNT). If there is a common theme to these disputes, it is that the policies produced emerge as "cautious crisis management and long-term crisis avoidance strategies" (Offe, 1976, page 415), as the various branches of the state sought to resolve the competing demands placed upon them. Nor can these disputes be interpreted solely in terms of the subjective intentions of the agencies concerned, since this would take no account of the constraints on the state's scope for manoeuvre (Frankel, 1979; Habermas, 1976). Such constraints pose serious problems for policy formulation; public decisions regarding the provision of welfare services cannot be resolved solely by reference to technical or bureaucratic procedures (Offe, 1975a; 1975b; see also Jessop, 1982, pages 106–112). This brings my discussion to the second point in this conclusion, which concerns the use of knowledge in planning.

It should be clear from the above that, whatever the merits of the respective cases put forward by different parties, the extent to which these could in any sense resolve the disputes was limited. Irrespective of the technical merits of the analyses put forward, their practical effect was relatively marginal, because of the practical problems of agreeing on a strategy for hospital location in these areas. This in turn raises questions about the possibility of resolving what are essentially political problems in purely technical terms. Since the aims to be achieved by hospital strategies were open to dispute, so too were the criteria against which alternative proposals were to be assessed. In these circumstances the extent to which facility location decisions can be 'optimised' in the manner suggested by several analysts (for example, Beaumont, 1980; Leonardi, 1981) seems questionable. More generally, it is important to examine whether techniques such as location-allocation models provide anything other than technical solutions to planning problems; indeed, as Lewis and Melville (1978) imply, such methods may offer no more than a technology for the partial control of social processes. At the very least those involved in practical issues (such as NHS planning) have a duty to point out the limitations of their methods. However, it is also essential to examine why disputes (such as those recorded here) should arise. For this to be interpreted satisfactorily some consideration of the role of the state is essential. Without an awareness of this broader context, analyses of spatial aspects of health service planning must remain limited to providing purely technical solutions to political problems.

Postscript

After the decision to develop the second DGH in the SAHA at Ryhope, the Hospital for Washington Campaign continued to pursue its case and on 24 February 1982 met the Minister of Health. In addition, Sunderland Borough Council (who had favoured a hospital at Washington) and the WNTDC continued to seek alternative sites for a hospital. Two potential locations were identified, at Castletown and at Middle Herrington; both of these were on the western margin of Sunderland and were therefore much closer to WNT than the Ryhope site. After a meeting on 5 April 1982 between the Minister of Health, the SAHA, and the NRHA, the NRHA's Architect was requested to assess the feasibility of DGH development at Middle Herrington. However, to the surprise of the NRHA, it was subsequently announced that a full appraisal *both* of the Middle Herrington site and of the Ryhope site had been requested (*Hansard* 1982). The NRHA carried out this appraisal and, at their meeting in September 1982, endorsed their previous support of the Ryhope site. This decision was subsequently communicated to the Minister of Health, but not until *September 1983* did he respond, favouring the Middle Herrington site. No reasons were given for this decision and the NRHA resolved to accept it, though they expressed their disappointment at what seemed a purely political concession by the Minister of Health to the various demands for a hospital in, or near to, WNT. Such a decision merely reaffirms the need for analyses of public sector location problems to move beyond narrowly technical considerations towards an explicit consideration of the political nature of public provision.

Acknowledgements. Thanks to Dr R Hudson (Geography Department, University of Durham) for comments on a previous draft of this work, and to Mr A Garland (Northern Regional Health Authority) for making available unpublished material upon which this paper draws heavily. Thanks also to Mr C Nelson (Northern Regional Health Authority) for the information given in the postscript. The views expressed are those of the author and are in no sense indicative of views held by individuals or agencies referred to herein.

References

Anderson J, 1978, "Geography, political economy and the state" *Antipode* **10** 87-93
Beaumont J R, 1980, "Spatial interaction models and the location-allocation problem" *Journal of Regional Science* **20** 37-51
Board of Trade, 1963 *The North East: A Programme for Regional Development and Growth* Cmnd 2206 (HMSO, London)
Carney J, 1973, "Urban public goods: positivist and radical positions" *Area* **4** 175-177
Carney J, Hudson R, 1974, "Ideology, public policy and underdevelopment in the North East" WP-6, North East Area Study, Department of Geography, University of Durham, Durham, England
Carney J, Hudson R, 1978, "Capital, politics and ideology: the North East of England, 1870-1946" *Antipode* **10** 64-78
CHSC, 1969 *The Functions of the District General Hospital* Central Health Services Council (HMSO, London)
DAHA, 1979 *Strategic Plan 1979-88* (Durham Area Health Authority, Durham, England)
Dear M J, 1978, "Planning for mental health care: a reconsideration of public facility location theory" *International Regional Science Review* **3** 93-112
DHSS, 1974 *Community Hospitals: Their Role and Future Development in the NHS* (Department of Health and Social Security, London)
DHSS, 1980 *The Future Pattern of Hospital Services in England and Wales* (Department of Health and Social Security, London)
Frankel B, 1979, "On the state of the state: Marxist theories of the state after Lenin" *Theory and Society* **7** 199-242
Giddens A, 1982 *A Contemporary Critique of Historical Materialism* (Macmillan, London)
Gold D, Lo C, Wright E O, 1975, "Recent developments in Marxist theories of the capitalist state" *Monthly Review* **27** 29-43 (part 1); **27** 36-51 (part 2)
Gregory D, 1978 *Ideology, Science and Human Geography* (Hutchinson, London)
Habermas J, 1976 *Legitimation Crisis* (Heinemann Educational Books, London)
Hansard 1982, Written Answers, column 327, 17 June (HMSO, London)
Hodgart R L, 1978, "Optimizing access to public facilities: a review of problems, models and methods of locating central facilities" *Progress in Human Geography* **2** 17-48
Hudson R, 1976 *New Towns in North East England* final report HR 1734 to the Social Science Research Council, Hamilton House, Temple Avenue, London EC4, England
Jessop R, 1977, "Recent theories of the capitalist state" *Cambridge Journal of Economics* **1** 353-373
Jessop R, 1982 *The Capitalist State* (Martin Robertson, Oxford)
Krieger J, 1979, "British colliery closure programmes in the North East: from paradox to contradiction" in *London Papers in Regional Science 9. Analysis and Decision in Regional Policy* Ed. I G Cullen (Pion, London) pp 219-232
Leishman A D, 1971 *New Town Politics* MA thesis, Department of Geography, University of Durham, Durham, England
Leonardi G, 1981, "A unifying framework for public facility location problems" *Environment and Planning A* **13** 1001-1028 (part 1); 1085-1108 (part 2)
Lewis J, Melville B, 1978, "The politics of epistemology in regional science" in *London Papers in Regional Science 8. Theory and Method in Urban and Regional Analysis* Ed. P W J Batey (Pion, London) pp 82-100
Llewelyn-Davies R, Weeks and Partners, 1966 *Washington New Town Master Plan and Report* Washington Development Corporation, Washington, Tyne and Wear, England
MoH, 1946 *The Hospital Services of North East England* (Ministry of Health, London)

MoH, 1962 *A Hospital Plan for England and Wales* Cmnd 1604 (Ministry of Health, London)

Mohan J F, 1983a, "Location-allocation models, social science and health service planning: a case study from North East England" *Social Science and Medicine* **17** 493-499

Mohan J F, 1983b *State Policies and Public Facility Location: The Hospital Services of North East England, 1948-82* PhD thesis, Department of Geography, University of Durham, Durham, England

Mohan J F, 1984, "State policies and the development of the hospital services of North East England, 1948-82" *Political Geography Quarterly* (forthcoming)

Newcastle Journal 1977a, "D-day for hospital closure" 7 October, p 7

Newcastle Journal 1977b, "Watchdogs fight hospital closure" 17 September, p 5

Newcastle Journal 1978a, "Campaign to save hospital" 24 January, p 5

Newcastle Journal 1978b, "War over hospital" 17 January, p 7

NRHA, 1979 *Regional Strategic Plan 1979-88* (Northern Regional Health Authority, Newcastle, England)

NRHB, 1950 *Annual Report* (Newcastle Regional Hospital Board, Newcastle, England)

Offe C, 1974, "Structural problems of the capitalist state" in *German Political Studies* Ed. K Von Beyme (Sage, London) pp 31-57

Offe C, 1975a, "Introduction to part III" in *Stress and Contradiction in Modern Capitalism* Eds L N Lindberg, C Offe, C Crouch, R Alford (D C Heath, Lexington, MA) pp 245-249

Offe C, 1975b, "The theory of the capitalist state and the problem of policy formation" in *Stress and Contradiction in Modern Capitalism* Eds L N Lindberg, C Offe, C Crouch, R Alford (D C Heath, Lexington, MA) pp 125-144

Offe C, 1976, "Political authority and class structures" in *Critical Sociology* Ed. P Connerton (Penguin Books, Harmondsworth, Middx) pp 388-421

Parston G, 1980 *Planners, Politicians, and Health Services* (Croom Helm, Beckenham, Kent)

Pepler G, MacFarlane P W, 1949 *The North East Area Development Plan: Interim Confidential Edition* (Ministry of Town and Country Planning, London)

Riley M, 1981, personal communication, 11 August

Riley M, 1982, "Accessibility to hospitals: a practical application" *Environment and Planning A* **14** 1107-1111

Robertson I, 1976, "Accessibility to services in the Argyll District of Strathclyde: a locational model" *Regional Studies* **10** 88-95

Robertson I, 1978, "Planning the location of recreation centres in an urban area: a case study of Glasgow" *Regional Studies* **12** 419-428

Robinson J F F, 1978 *Peterlee: Aspects of New Town Development* PhD thesis, Department of Geography, University of Durham, Durham, England

SAHA, 1979 *Area Strategic Plan 1979-88* (Sunderland Area Health Authority, Sunderland, England)

Steele D B, 1962 *The Origin of Peterlee New Town and some Features of its Subsequent Development* MA thesis, Department of Politics, University of Durham, Durham, England

Tornqvist G, Nordbeck S, Rystedt B, Gould P, 1971 *Multiple Location Analysis* Lund Studies in Geography series C(12) (Lund, Sweden)

Wirz H, 1975 *Social Aspects of Planning in New Towns* (Saxon House, Farnborough, Hants)

Elderly Severely Mentally Infirm (ESMI) Units in Lancashire: An Assessment of Resource Allocation over Space

J R BEAUMONT
Birkbeck College, University of London

A SIXSMITH
Kings College, University of London

1 Introduction

Since 1948, with the formation of the National Health Service (NHS), everyone in the United Kingdom, in theory, has had free access to medical care. Though all the ideals and principles of the welfare state, in general, and of the NHS specifically, are founded on equal accessibility to free public services according to 'need', the spatial organisation of hospitals and the distribution of potential users mean that access to health facilities varies greatly between individuals. Although a degree of inequality is inevitable, because of the discrete location of facilities to serve a continuous distribution of population, spatial maldistributions in provision exist and produce unnecessary inequities in access opportunities on 'life chances' and raise the question of 'territorial justice' (Davies, 1968). This situation is especially worrying, since it is suggested that it is reinforced by the so-called 'inverse care law' (Tudor Hart, 1975); that is, the level of provision of good medical care tends to be inversely related to the requirements of the population served. This important general issue of inequality has been examined recently both from a social and political perspective (Dahrendorf, 1980) and from a geographical perspective (Smith, 1979), and the specific issue of 'who gets care where', which often can be literally a matter of life or death, has been addressed in detail by the Department of Health and Social Security's (DHSS, 1980a) research working group on inequalities in health and by Townsend and Davidson (1982).

Obviously, it can be argued that analyses of health care provision are important studies that possess both direct practical relevance and general theoretical interest. Although variations arising from society's structure are clearly of fundamental importance, attention should continue to focus on locational effects [possibly in a broader context than recent studies— for example, see those being undertaken by the Health Research Group in Geography at Queen Mary College, London (Cornwell et al, 1982)].

In this paper, particular attention focuses on mental health, which has generated much recent interest [for example, see Dear and Wills (1980) and Smith (1977)], and specifically on mental health care for the elderly [note Warnes's (1981) general discussion on a geographical contribution to gerontology]. In section 2, a background discussion of elderly severely mentally infirm (ESMI) units provides the foundation for the entire paper.

The broad implications of the changing philosophy towards community-based services are examined. In section 3, a selective overview of location–allocation models indicates how useful information can be provided to decisionmakers on the implications of alternative location strategies. The models are straightforward conceptually, but they address directly the goals of community-based mental care provision. This provides a foundation for the detailed case study examining the problem of locating a set of new ESMI units in Lancashire and for the prescriptive policy suggestions that are presented (section 4). Finally, in section 5, the general approach to location planning is augmented by a consideration of the wider context of the decisionmaking process. It is stressed that location analysis cannot be divorced from its social, economic, and political context.

2 ESMI units: a background

2.1 Introduction

Health care for the elderly has traditionally been a cinderella branch of the NHS. However, the number and proportion of old people has increased steadily throughout this century, and, by 1981, 17.7% of the population (then 55 676 000) was of pensionable age (compared with 16.3% in 1971), with an increasing number over seventy-five years of age. Consequently, it is not surprising that the elderly have become an increasingly significant component of social policy generally and of health care provision specifically. After the 1974 reorganisation of the NHS, the DHSS produced two reports, *Priorities for Health and Personal Social Services in England* (DHSS, 1976) and *The Way Forward* (DHSS, 1977), in which the general requirements and targets for the health and personal social services were established. Specifically, the need for an expanded and improved service for the elderly was stressed. More detailed examinations of the particular problems of providing services for the elderly were contained in two recent government publications, *A Happier Old Age* (DHSS, 1979) and *Growing Older* (DHSS, 1981).

To date, special provision for psychogeriatrics has been extremely limited in the United Kingdom. When the elderly mentally infirm have required hospitalisation, this has tended to be provided in either the old, large, isolated mental institutions or in hospital wards which were not designed for such purposes. This almost complete lack of specific facilities for psychogeriatrics has caused a great deal of unnecessary suffering both for confined elderly persons and for their families and friends. However, associated with changes in treatment (Klerman, 1977), government guide-lines, and public attitudes (Rabkin, 1974), a growing desire for community-based care can be discerned (with the concomitant running-down of the old mental hospitals). This change in philosophy has direct implications regarding spatial organisation; a dispersed pattern of a larger number of smaller facilities would replace the centralised pattern of a small number of larger facilities.

The North West Regional Health Authority's (NWRHA's) policy (under which the Lancashire Area Health Authority was placed) is to provide the ESMI service in standard purpose-built units throughout the Region. It is deemed that it is desirable to separate these facilities from the more general health services, because severe behavioural problems are often encountered in demented old people, and, to a large extent, their needs are unique. Anyway, it should be noted that the construction of purpose-built units for different specialities is not uncommon.

Although chronological age provides a useful operational definition, mental illness in old age is heterogeneous, and, for convenience, a tripartite division can be recognised: functional psychosis, reversible organic psychosis, and irreversible organic psychosis. For the purpose of the present discussion, it is sufficient to point out that the last disorder is essentially incurable and the first two disorders can be treated with successful patient rehabilitation. Consequently, ESMI units are designed to cater for both short-term and long-term patients by offering facilities for active treatment and rehabilitation alongside the caring facets of the service. A standard unit consists of two wards with a total of fifty-six beds, and a day centre that can cater for an additional fifty patients. The day centre provides a service for all types of ESMI patients who are capable of living at home given adequate support from family, friends, and social services, and also for some patients from the wards who are not too disturbed or disruptive. (Later, this community link is considered in more detail, and it is argued that it is a decisive factor in siting ESMI units.)

The NWRHA has shown a real commitment to provide 'an adequate service for psychogeriatrics, and its proposed programme of development has been seen as one of the major achievements of health planning in the Region. Clearly, the issue of psychogeriatrics' care is both difficult and controversial, and, in deciding upon a system of ESMI units, the health planners' problem involves providing a service from scratch, a rare feature today but one that presents obvious challenges. For example, Dear (1978) suggests that planners should look at public facility location in its widest context in order to address problems such as facility externalities. However, the main focus of this chapter is user access, and the wider issues are examined in the concluding section.

2.2 ESMI unit location

Simply stated, one of the underlying reasons for a decentralisation policy is that, in general, individuals' accessibility to facilities should be enhanced [which is important in public service provision—there is empirical evidence to indicate that accessibility directly affects the level of utilisation (see later)]. In locating facilities, a basic objective is to match resource allocation with need; more specifically, the spatial distribution of need with the allocation of resources over space.

To determine the required level of service and the number of ESMI units, a simple procedure was adopted by the NWRHA. The service is viewed as local in nature, and, consequently, individual facilities would provide for well-defined catchment areas. ESMI service provision would be based on the residential population aged sixty-five years and above (rather than involve additional weights). The spatial distribution of the elderly population in Lancashire is shown in figure 1. In the consultative document, *The Way Forward* (DHSS, 1977), a provision norm of 2.5–3.0 beds and two to three day-places per thousand people aged sixty-five years and above was proposed, and, therefore, it is a straightforward arithmetic exercise to determine the desired level of service. The jurisdictional level for planning ESMI units is the district level, but there must be coordination between districts to ensure a suitable pattern of services for the region.

Table 1 indicates the existing service provision for the Lancashire Area Health Authority (LAHA), which reinforces the earlier comment that planners face the general problem of determining the location of a set of new facilities. At present, no ESMI units are found in some districts,

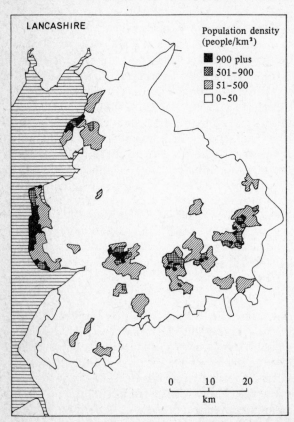

Figure 1. Population density of people aged sixty-five years and over, Lancashire.

although it is intended to have rectified any shortfalls in provision by 1988, the end of the current ten-year strategic plan.

More specific details can be taken from the 1979 Strategic Plan for the LAHA (1979), although it should be appreciated that these plans are still tentative; at present, building of the majority of the ESMI units in Lancashire has yet to commence and the majority remain at the planning stage (see table 2 and figure 2). In essence, the eventual pattern of service provision is not finalised and may be different from the existing plan. The majority of the ESMI units will be of the standard form, although, again, this could be subject to alteration. For example, the proposed unit at Victoria Hospital may be shelved in favour of an alternative strategy if no suitable site is available. ESMI services not provided in a standard unit will be offered in conventional hospital wards that have been adapted for ESMI care.

It is this situation which provides both the underlying motivation and the opportunity to undertake this study: specifically, to assess the spatial efficiency and equity of the proposed spatial organisation of ESMI units and, generally, to examine the ramifications of alternative patterns of service provision. The analytical part of this study involves the application of so-called location–allocation models [see Beaumont's (1981) review paper] to address these issues.

Although the concept of a community-based service has obvious locational implications within neighbourhoods, no explicit statement about siting ESMI units has been forthcoming beyond a statement in the 1979 Regional Strategy Plan that:

"The general policy is for ESMI beds, apart from those in the District assessment unit, to be located away from the District General Hospitals though this is not the case at present in the Region, and indeed because of local factors several new units have been sited at District General Hospitals" (NWRHA, 1979, page 103).

Table 1. ESMI requirements and provision: Lancashire Area Health Authority.

District	Resident population [a] (1000s)	Service level required [b,c]	Existing provision [c]	New facilities required [c]
Lancaster	23.7	71 (71)	0 (0)	71 (71)
Blackpool	68.8	206 (206)	147 (100)	59 (106)
Preston and Chorley	45.7	137 (137)	112 (100)	25 (37)
Blackburn	38.7	116 (116)	0 (0)	116 (116)
Burnley	33.4	100 (100)	66 (0)	34 (100)
Ormskirk	14.2	43 (43)	0 (0)	43 (43)

[a] In 1991 of persons aged sixty-five years and above.

[b] Using a norm of three beds and three day-places per 1000 residents aged sixty-five years and above.

[c] Figures represent number of beds; those in brackets number of day-places.

Although the location of ESMI units should take account of the overall spatial organisation of health care and social services facilities, it is interesting to note that the proposed units have not been sited away from the existing hospitals (see table 3). Such locations are often attractive because of available space on owned land. However, specifically in relation to the association with district general hospitals (DGHs), it should be appreciated that, recently, there has been a policy of general decentralisation of health care [see the DHSS (1974) report on community hospitals and DHSS (1980b)]. Consequently, it is possible that ESMI units planned for DGHs will be located elsewhere, which, for example, has occurred in the Rochdale District of Greater Manchester.

Although planners must consider a variety of aspatial aspects, attention must be given to the accessibility of facilities for patients, because, as stated earlier, it affects the level of utilisation. Using published activity

Table 2. Existing and planned ESMI units: Lancashire Area Health Authority.

District	Existing facilities			Planned facilities [a]		
	hospitals	beds	day-places	hospitals [b]	beds	day-places
Lancaster				Victoria	56	50
				Lancaster Moor	?	?
Blackpool	Wesham Park*	35		Fleetwood	56	50
	Devonshire Rd	56	50	Devonshire Rd	56	50
	Lytham	56	50	Lytham	56	50
				new DGH	56	50
Preston	Ribbleton	56	50	Ribbleton	56	50
and	Chorley			Chorley		
Chorley	and District	56	50	and District	56	50
				Preston		
				new DGH	56	50
Blackburn				Accrington		
				Victoria	56	50
				Queens Park	56	50
				Clitheroe CH	?	?
				Ribchester CH	?	?
Burnley	Burnley			Burnley		
	and District**	28		and District	56	50
	Rossendale	38		Pendle*	28	
Ormskirk				Ormskirk		
				and District**	28	50
				Skelmersdale CH*	28	?

Note: all provision is in the form of standard units, consisting of fifty-six beds and fifty day-places, except where indicated (that is, * represents a hospital ward and ** a standard unit only partially devoted to ESMI services).
[a] Shortfalls in the Burnley District are to be met outside the planning period.
[b] DGH ≡ District General Hospital; CH ≡ Central Hospital.

patterns, preliminary studies of the Beechurst ESMI unit at Chorley and District General Hospital, for instance, indicate that such difficulties are particularly significant for day patients. The basic problem is one of long journey times (in ambulances), and, therefore, as well as examining location of ESMI units and linkages with other services, it is important to consider the organisation and level of ambulance (and public transport) provision.

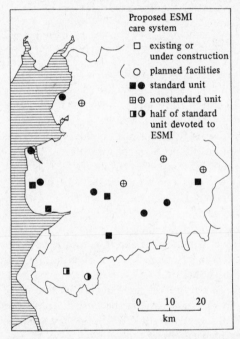

Figure 2. Existing and proposed pattern of ESMI facilities in Lancashire.

Table 3. Proposed location of ESMI units in Lancashire.

District	District General Hospital (DGH) site	At other hospital sites
Lancaster		Victoria Hospital
Blackpool	New DGH	Fleetwood Devonshire Road Lytham
Preston and Chorley	Preston new DGH Chorley and District	Ribbleton
Blackburn	Queens Park	Accrington Victoria
Burnley	Burnley and District	
Ormskirk	Ormskirk and District	

(Accessibility is not only a problem of the relative location of demand and supply, but is also concerned with the mobility of individuals, particularly the differential mobility of different groups of people such as the elderly and the poor.) Indeed, Rigby (1978) suggests that improving the level of individuals' mobility is the most practical means of improving access to hospitals, given the existing stock of facilities. Alternatively, as the final location of the ESMI units has to be decided, it is pertinent to try to maximise patients' accessibility.

3 Location–allocation models: a background
3.1 Introduction
Location–allocation models, jointly optimising the location of facilities and the spatial allocation of customers to them, now forms an extensive literature on private- and public-sector facility location (for example, see Beaumont, 1981; Hodgart, 1978; ReVelle et al, 1970; Rushton, 1979; Scott, 1971). More specifically, various formulations employing different criteria have been applied to examine the problem of locating health facilities (for example, see Calvo and Marks, 1973; Dokmeci, 1977; Gould and Leinbach, 1966; Mayhew and Leonardi, 1981; Morrill and Kelly, 1970; Rigby, 1978). Different criteria are appropriate in different situations, particularly with regard to the type of hospital and the service it provides. For instance, in the provision of emergency medical services the minimisation of maximum travel distance (or time) would be apposite. In contrast, in the present context, the criterion of minimising the aggregate distance travelled by patients to an ESMI unit (given specified capacity constraints), which usually results in patients being allocated to their nearest unit, is relevant, at least in the first instance, because it is consistent with the community concept. Moreover, current NWRHA policy sees each ESMI unit as serving a strictly defined catchment area. This induced users' behaviour usually follows the simple nearest-facility allocation rule. Extensions can be made to enhance the information that is available to planners.

In this section, a discussion of the basic multifacility location–allocation problem involving the minimisation of aggregate weighted distance is considered as a problem on a plane and on a network. In the latter, it is possible to incorporate an assessment of the optimal pattern from a set of specified sites. This idea is developed further in a capacity-constrained location–allocation model, which incorporates a spatial interaction model. Throughout the discussion, emphasis is placed on the usefulness of undertaking comparative analyses of the results of different models, and this is stressed in a discussion of the trade-off between spatial efficiency and spatial equity. With regard for the greater involvement of decisionmakers, for completeness, attention is drawn to the appropriateness of computer graphics in the presentation of information and the potential applicability of microcomputers.

3.2 Minimising aggregate weighted distance on a plane

Simply stated, the basic rationale underlying location–allocation problems is optimising (either maximising or minimising) the value of an objective function subject to a set of specified constraints. Hodgart (1978) recognises three types of location as access problems: the general problem of multifacility location, which assumes no facilities exist already; the incremental location problem, which involves locating additional supply capacity given an existing distribution; and the facility reorganisation problem, which consists of closing some existing facilities and possibly opening new ones. In relation to the present discussion of locating ESMI units in the LAHA the problem, as stated earlier, involves locating a complete system of new facilities. Therefore, a major question is deciding upon the number of facilities to be located, which is determined primarily by the availability of financial resources. Fortunately, the NWRHA intends to provide a full level of service, and, therefore, this problem is one of satisfying the need from units of specified size. Hence, it is possible to calculate the number of units directly. However, some ESMI units are already established, and, therefore, the problem is incremental in nature. In fact, interesting information can be forthcoming through a consideration of the impact of the constraint of the existing facilities by comparing the optimal spatial patterns for the general and the incremental problems.

The elementary and fundamental form of the location–allocation problem involves locating optimally a set of p facilities (ESMI units) to minimise the aggregate transport costs contracted in serving a set of n specified-demand locations. The problem is uncapacitated; that is, there is no upper capacity limit on the number of patients catered for by a specific ESMI unit, and, consequently, at optimality, it is assumed that each patient is allocated to his or her nearest unit. This continuous-space location–allocation problem can be written as

$$\text{minimise } C_T = \sum_{i=1}^{n} \sum_{j=1}^{p} O_i \lambda_{ij} c_{ij} , \qquad (1)$$
$$\{s, \lambda\}$$

subject to

$$\sum_{j=1}^{p} \lambda_{ij} = 1 , \qquad i = 1, ..., n , \qquad (2)$$

where

C_T represents aggregate transport costs;

s is a vector of supply points, (x_j, y_j);

O_i is an index of need at location, (x_i, y_i);

c_{ij} is a generalised measure of transport costs between demand point i and supply point j, which is usually taken to be the Euclidean distance metric $c_{ij} = [(x_i - x_j)^2 + (y_i - y_j)^2]^{\frac{1}{2}}$;

λ_{ij} is a binary variable, possessing a unitary value if patients residing at i
       are allocated to the ESMI unit at j, and zero otherwise.
The constraints ensure the 'all-or-nothing' allocation procedure.

Given the obvious importance of operationability, it is important to
appreciate that other data requirements are not excessive. Population
forecasts based on current figures for different areas provide the basis for
the definition of need. Specifically, as described in the preceding section,
and along the lines of the recommendations contained in the Resource
Allocation Working Party's report (DHSS, 1976b), the number of people
aged sixty-five years and above gives this measure based on specified
standards of provision. As figure 1 indicates, there is a spatial variation in
the distribution of need, and, therefore, it is insufficient to plan a relatively
uniform distribution of units; such complex combinatorial location
problems require the information offered by computer-based models. In
terms of modelling public facility location problems, it has been argued
that such representations are restrictive, because it is assumed that there is
a perfectly (price) inelastic demand situation [for instance, see Beaumont
(1981) and Leonardi (1981)]. In fact, empirical evidence indicates that,
for specific types of public services, aggregate utilisation levels depend
upon consumers' proximity to facilities and therefore upon the spatial
organisation of the services (Smolensky et al, 1970). In the context of
mental health services, however, as stated earlier, the level of utilisation is
independent of the spatial pattern; it is only the allocation of patients to
particular units that is dependent on their distribution. It is, therefore,
apposite to employ this relatively simple representation.

As the problem is formulated, the distance matrix, $[c_{ij}]$, is determined
endogenously given the coordinates of the demand points. It is assumed
that the ESMI units can locate anywhere within the jurisdictional boundary
of the LAHA. It would be possible, however, to determine optimum
location patterns for specified transport networks, although this requires a
large quantity of data. For example, Bach (1981, pages 976–977), in
describing the application of location–allocation models to assist planners
in Dortmund, West Germany, highlights the tedious nature of deriving a
coded transportation network, which is either not available at all or not at
the required level of disaggregation:

"The semiautomatic coding of x and y coordinates and the computation
of the 286 × 286 matrix of Euclidean distances with the help of a
computer took two days. The manual coding of the street network
took about three months" (Bach, 1981, pages 976–977).

Clearly, one must consider whether this effort is rewarded (assuming the
manpower is available)!

The only additional information that is required is the number of ESMI
units that have to be sited. In the most recent NWRHA strategy plan
(NWRHA, 1979), it was stated that, by 1991, a system of about fourteen
ESMI units should have been established. Though it would appear a

straightforward problem to locate fourteen units, it is important to consider this specific problem in conjunction with others that involve locating optimally different numbers of units. It not only facilitates greater comprehension of the particular problem of interest, but it also provides relevant information regarding opportunities for phasing developments of ESMI units and for deciding their spatial organisation beyond the current planning period (which is important for such a long-term investment).

The above location–allocation model, which has the basic characteristic that patients are allocated to their nearest unit, is termed an unconstrained and uncapacitated problem. However, the lack of a capacity constraint results in an enormous variation in the optimum size of the units. This provides useful comparative information for results generated by a so-called unconstrained and capacitated problem. As stated earlier, it is necessary to assume that the capacity of all the units is identical. Formally, the problem can be written as

$$\text{minimise } C_T = \sum_{i=1}^{n} \sum_{j=1}^{p} O_i P_{ij} c_{ij} \,, \tag{3}$$
$$\{s\}$$

subject to

$$\sum_{i=1}^{n} O_i P_{ij} < K \,, \qquad j = 1, ..., p \,, \tag{4}$$

where P_{ij} is the proportion of patients at i allocated to a unit at j, and K is the specified upper capacity constraint.

Finally, as indicated in section 2, some ESMI units have been established already, and, clearly, to avoid wastefulness regarding existing stock, planning should determine the optimum pattern of units given this stock. Fortunately, this so-called constrained and capacitated location–allocation problem can be solved using Goodchild's (1973) computer program, LAP, which is based on Cooper's (1963) heuristic solution algorithm[1]. Using this formulation, it is possible to extend assessments of the overall efficiency of the existing pattern and of the proposed final pattern by offering prescriptive suggestions on how future development from the present situation should take place.

3.3 Minimising aggregate weighted distance on a network

The previous models are continuous-space location–allocation problems; that is, the optimum facility locations can be at any point in the study area (Beaumont, 1981). However, a system's morphology need not be restricted to analysis on a plane. For example, ReVelle et al (1970) and ReVelle and Swain (1970) have proposed the following p-median problem for optimally locating p facilities to minimise aggregate weighted distance

[1] When using such iterative procedures, it is necessary to undertake a number of computer runs with different starting values to try to ensure the solution is a global, rather than a local, optimum. Interestingly, from experience, the efficiency of this algorithm is much greater for the constrained, rather than the unconstrained, problem.

on a network. The search for the solution to this problem is assisted by Hakimi's (1964) theorem, which shows that the optimum solution involves locating facilities at the network's nodes (although equally good solutions involving locations on the network's links exist occasionally). Hillsman (1980) provides a number of generations of the ALLOC computer program to solve this particular problem. In the present context, the program is useful, in that possible sites are specified exogenously as nodes. Also, a location constraint can be introduced to force units to be located at specified nodes. Thus it is possible to formulate an incremental problem which takes account of the existing stock of ESMI units.

The results of the above problems are presented in the next section, and they provide further information for decisionmakers to assess the ramifications of alternative patterns of ESMI units in Lancashire.

4 An exploratory description of ESMI units in Lancashire using location–allocation models
4.1 Introduction
NWRHA planners outlined the proposed system of ESMI units for Lancashire in their 1979 *Regional Strategic Plan* (NWRHA, 1979) (see figure 2), and this is unlikely to be modified greatly. Indeed, a number of units have been completed already and the majority of the remaining units are scheduled for completion by the mid-1980s. In this section, the proposed system of ESMI units is evaluated using location–allocation models, and a description of the results provides the basis of alternative strategies. The results are presented in a series of maps, and, to a large extent, these are self-explanatory.

Simply stated, the problem is to locate a specified number of ESMI units in the District Health Authorities (DHAs) in Lancashire (the administrative boundaries are shown in figure 3). The required number of beds and day-places is determined, as stated earlier, by current government and NWRHA benchmarks. The projected 1991 population of people aged sixty-five years and above is 219 500, which requires approximately 680 beds and 680 day-places. Given the size of the standard ESMI units, a system comprising of approximately twelve to fourteen units would be expected. As indicated in figure 2, the number of facilities proposed by the NWRHA is slightly different, because a small proportion of the services may be provided in smaller nonstandard units. This aspect of capacity, particularly the effects of uniform sizes, is addressed in more detail below.

Although the basic problem can be thought of as locating a specified number of new ESMI units to complement those which are finished or nearly completed, it is important to consider this specific problem in conjunction with others that involve locating optimally different numbers of units. It not only facilitates greater comprehension of the particular problem of interest, but it also provides useful information regarding opportunities for future developments.

Throughout the analyses, aggregate weighted distance for patients travelling to facilities is minimised. In the next subsection, a range of so-called unconstrained and uncapacitated problems with different numbers of units is examined. That is, none of the units have their possible locations constrained (or fixed), and it is assumed that there is no upper capacity limit on the number of beds and day-places available in any facility. The lack of a capacity constraint results in an enormous variation in the optimum size of the units, but it does provide a basis for assessing the influence of establishing units of an equal size, particularly as all patients are no longer allocated to their nearest unit. In subsection 4.3, the results of introducing an upper capacity constraint are described. In all cases, it is assumed that the capacity of each unit is identical, and, consequently it is consistent with the NWRHA standards only when there are sufficient facilities. It is reasonable to assume that equal pressure would be placed on services if there were insufficient units, although an indication of any unequal pressure is provided by the preceding uncapacitated problems.

For comparison, a location constraint is introduced into an uncapacitated problem. To date, a total of six ESMI units have been either built or are under construction, and it is apposite, therefore, to examine the problems in which the optimum location of additional units are determined. A description of the variations in optimum size, particularly if there is an

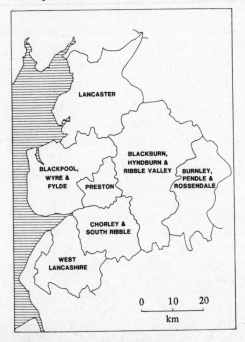

Figure 3. Lancashire Health Districts.

indication of underutilisation of any of the six existing units, again offers useful information.

In essence, however, these subsections provide the background for a description, in subsection 4.5, of the results of constrained and equal-capacity problems. An alternative type of location constraint is considered in the following subsection. As proposed in section 2, in practice it is often useful to determine the set of feasible sites from which the optimum configuration is derived. As an illustration of this approach, the set of feasible sites is defined as all the local hospital sites, and two kinds of problems are addressed: first, determine the optimum pattern of a specified number of units; and, second, determine the optimum pattern of a specified number of units given the six 'existing' units.

Finally, given that the planning of ESMI units is district-based, some attention is given to whether planning at this level is consistent with a coordinated provision for the whole of Lancashire. (Similarly, in a detailed analysis, links between location of units in Lancashire and other parts of the NWRHA should be examined.)

4.2 Unconstrained and uncapacitated problems
In this subsection, the results of a series of so-called unconstrained and uncapacitated problems are presented; that is, none of the units have their possible locations constrained (or fixed), and it is assumed that there is no upper capacity limit on the number of beds and day-places available in any unit.

The lack of a capacity constraint results in an enormous variation in the optimum size of the units (see figure 4), which, as figure 1 portrays, directly reflects the uneven population distribution of Lancashire, specifically in the major urban centres. This information, therefore, provides some indication of the effects of realistically assuming that all the ESMI units are a standard size. As the number of units in the system increases, the pressure on the units in the urban centres is successively reduced. Even with fourteen units, no unit is located in the very sparsely populated northeast area; a very small unit is located at Clitheroe when the system has thirteen units. As table 4 demonstrates, the mean distance between a patient and a unit is an indirect function of the number of units in the system. In addition, it is noted that, because there is no upper capacity constraint, all patients are allocated to their nearest unit.

Although the number of facilities is, to some extent, independent of the spatial issue, the scale of provision will have an important bearing on the levels of individuals' accessibility, especially their variations. Figure 5 gives the optimal solutions for locating twenty and twenty-six units, respectively. Clearly, as to be expected, a greater scatter of units is generated, and, again, there are large variations in the units' required capacities. Interestingly, however, the results indicate two distinct sets of sizes for the ESMI units; the larger urban units are complemented by smaller units in rural centres.

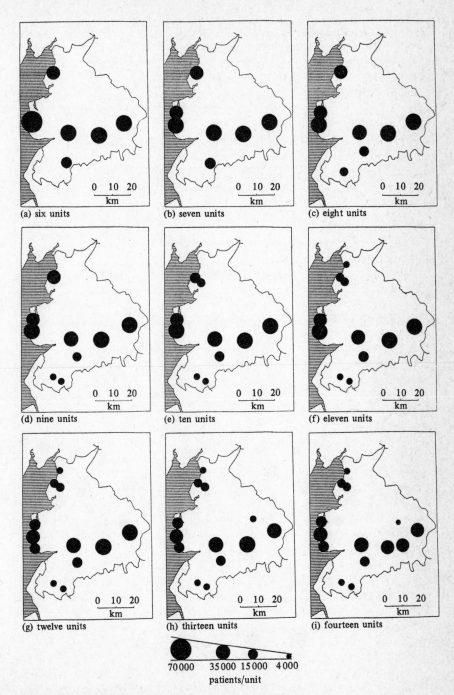

Figure 4. Unconstrained and uncapacitated solutions, Lancashire.

Table 4. Location-constrained and equal-capacity model; mean distances and standard deviations of distances for a given number of units.

Number of units [a]	Mean distance [b] (km)	Standard deviation [c]
6 (0)	12.82	7.12
7 (1)	12.08	9.14
8 (2)	7.86	4.38
9 (3)	7.4	5.4
10 (4)	7.4	5.28
11 (5)	6.5	3.4
12 (6)	6.33	4.2
13 (7)	5.5	3.4
14 (8)	5.89	3.94

[a] Figures in brackets represent number of unconstrained units.
[b] Between a patient and a unit.
[c] Equal to $[(\Sigma x^2/n) - x^2]^{1/2}$, where n represents the number of units.

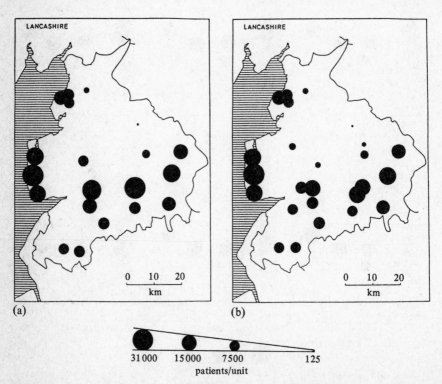

Figure 5. Optimal solutions for (a) twenty units, unconstrained and (b) twenty-six units, unconstrained.

This seems to suggest that the current policy of providing a system of standard units is somewhat insensitive to the spatial variations in population distribution, and, consequently, it may be beneficial to consider nonstandard ESMI care provision. Specifically, it may be useful to have the standard units in areas of high (elderly) population density and to provide a smaller scale service in other areas. This type of policy, in fact, has been adopted in some parts of Lancashire. For example, the proposals for Blackburn District, which is the largest in Lancashire and is characterised by the densely populated urban areas of Blackburn, Accrington, and Darwen in the south and by the sparsely populated rural areas in the north [figure 6(a)], comprise of two standard units in the urban areas with a smaller amount of nonstandard provision at Ribchester and Clitheroe [figure 6(b)].

Clearly, this issue of standard sizes for the ESMI units is not divorced from the location problem, and it is likely to be especially significant in the districts, such as Lancaster, with the large rural areas.

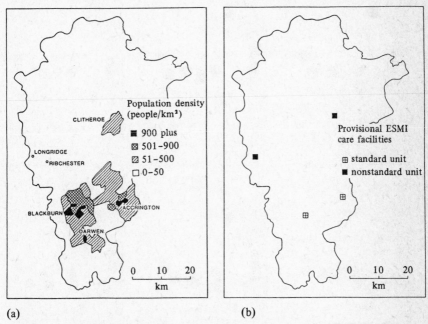

(a)   (b)

Figure 6. (a) Density for population aged sixty-five years and above, and (b) provisional ESMI facilities, Blackburn District.

4.3 Unconstrained and capacitated problems
As stated in section 2, in general all the ESMI units are to be built at a standardised size, and, therefore, in modelling the location problem, it is appropriate to locate optimally a set of equal-capacity units. In this subsection, the results of a series of so-called unconstrained and capacitated problems are presented.

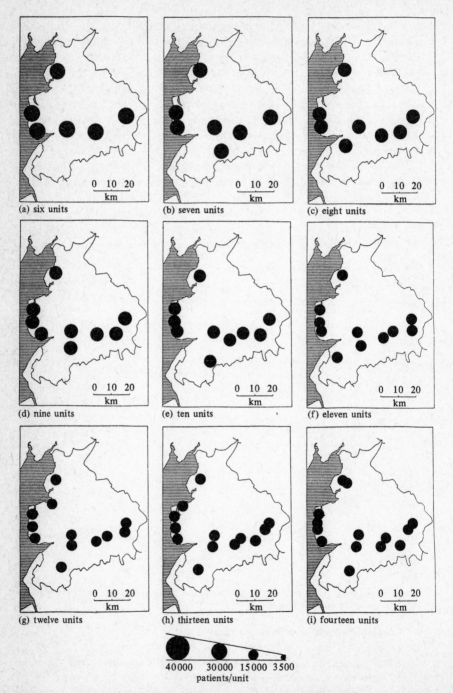

Figure 7. Unconstrained and (equally) capacitated solutions, Lancashire.

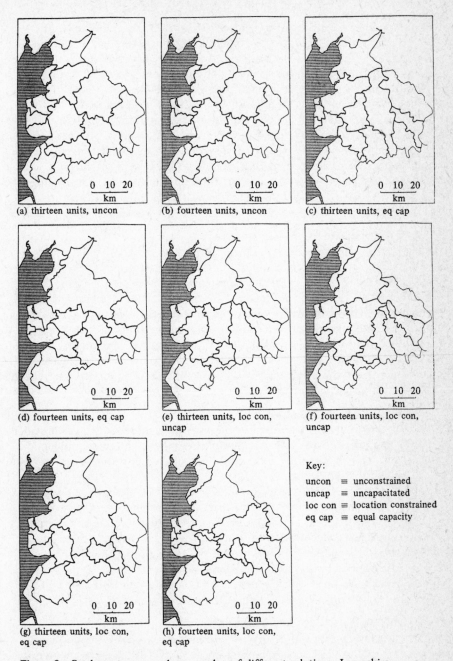

(a) thirteen units, uncon

(b) fourteen units, uncon

(c) thirteen units, eq cap

(d) fourteen units, eq cap

(e) thirteen units, loc con, uncap

(f) fourteen units, loc con, uncap

(g) thirteen units, loc con, eq cap

(h) fourteen units, loc con, eq cap

Key:

uncon	≡	unconstrained
uncap	≡	uncapacitated
loc con	≡	location constrained
eq cap	≡	equal capacity

Figure 8. Catchment areas under a number of different solutions, Lancashire.

Although the major urban centres remain important locations, the optimum solutions tend to mirror the local concentrations of elderly people (see figure 7). For example, the Fylde coast, which has the highest concentration of people in the sixty-five-years old and above age group, has four units located in it when the system has fourteen units. It is important to note that, though the units are of equal capacity, the distances travelled by patients exhibit a large variation. Figure 8 describes the catchment areas for the optimally located systems of thirteen and fourteen units under different combinations of constraints on capacity and location. We can note that considerable differences in catchment-area size and configuration arise under these different alternatives; for instance, the mean distance travelled to a unit in Lancaster is three-times the mean distance for the whole system and fifteen-times the smallest mean distance.

4.4 Constrained and uncapacitated problems
For further comparison, as there are at present six ESMI units which are either built or under construction, in this subsection the results of a series of constrained and uncapacitated problems are presented. Again, the variations in the capacities required by the optimally located units vary enormously (see figure 9). However, this type of problem does give some indication of the relative pressure on the existing units (if patients are allocated to their nearest unit). Throughout the series of results, the ESMI unit at Devonshire Road has the most pressure on it, and, of the set of existing units, the ESMI unit at the Ormskirk and District Hospital has the lowest pressure on it.

4.5 Constrained and capacitated problem
Although the results presented in the preceding subsections have provided some insights into the effects of specifying slightly different problems, realistically it is necessary to consider capacitated problems given the six existing ESMI units.

Interestingly, the pattern of results generated by the previous problems is reflected in the solutions to this particular problem (see figure 10). Simply stated, the locations are in the major urban centres and there is also a relative concentration of units on the Fylde coast. Again, the adoption of standard sizes means that the units which cater for patients living in rural areas have relatively large catchment areas (figure 4 presents the catchment areas when fourteen units are located optimally). Of course, the number of units affects the mean distance travelled.

4.6 Minimising the weighted distance on a network
In this subsection, some results are presented concerning the optimal location of facilities for minimising the weighted distance on a network. The centroids of each of the original population areas are assumed to be demand nodes. As stated in section 2, in practice the set of all the possible sites for locating facilities is often known a priori, and, therefore,

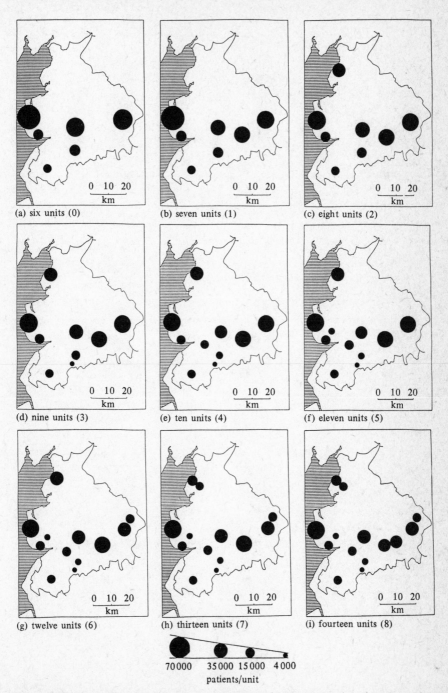

Figure 9. Location-constrained and uncapacitated solutions, Lancashire (numbers in brackets indicate number of 'unconstrained' units).

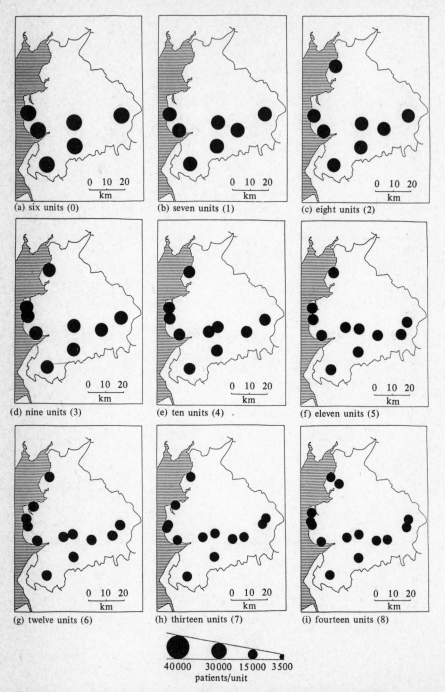

Figure 10. Location-constrained and (equally) capacitated solutions, Lancashire (numbers in brackets indicate number of 'unconstrained' units).

the problem involves determining the optimum combination from this feasible set. In this particular problem of interest, given that the location of the initial ESMI units has been associated with existing hospitals in Lancashire, the set of possible supply nodes was defined as all the hospital sites in Lancashire; this totalled fifty-five sites. Simply stated, two types of problem are examined below according to the above criterion: first, given the set of possible sites, determine the optimum pattern of a specified number of units; and, second, given the set of possible sites and the location of the existing units, determine the optimum pattern of a specified number of additional units. The results of both these problems for different numbers of units are presented, and, for completeness, some comparisons are made with the results given in the preceding subsections. No equal-capacity constraints are included, but the information on the levels of service required if patients go to their nearest unit provides insights into possible under' and overutilisation. Clearly, it would be wasteful to shut any of the existing ESMI units, and, therefore, the basic question is whether the selection of a few additional locations can significantly improve the population's accessibility to facilities.

Existing ESMI units are located at Devonshire Road, Lytham, Ribbleton, Chorley and District, Burnley General, and at Ormskirk and District Hospital. A series of problems in which a different number of units (from six to fourteen) were optimally selected from the possible sites were studied, and it is important to note that none of the solutions included one of the existing units. These results, however, provide an interesting benchmark for comparison. For instance, the total weighted distance for the present system is 37% more than for the optimal location of six facilities. In general, given the constraint of the established units, the solutions to locating a different number of additional facilities indicated a core of stable sites, such as Lostock Hall, West Preston, and Beaumont (see table 5). This feature is especially useful in planning the growth of an integrated and coordinated system of service. The information on the marginal reduction in the aggregate weighted distance, which decreases as more facilities are added, could be used to help determine what is the desirable number of ESMI units. Similarly, it is shown that the addition of Moss Side to make a system of fourteen units only serves 3.7% of the total demand and only reduces the pressure on two of the thirteen units. In terms of levels of utilisation, as to be expected, the smallest is always one of the established units (usually Devonshire Road), but the unit at Ormskirk and District Hospital always makes a significant contribution.

In summary, although this type of analysis could be undertaken in more detail, sufficient details have been presented to indicate the pertinence of this kind of study. Clearly, a fundamental requirement is an unambiguous definition of a set of feasible sites (taking into account land availability, acceptance by the neighbourhood, and so on). For completeness, it is instructive to note that the results of this analysis are consistent with those of the preceding sections, because they reflect the general configuration of urban centres (although, in this case, no ESMI unit would be sited in the middle of Blackburn).

Table 5. Optimal location of new ESMI units given the established facilities.

Number of new ESMI units	Percentage reduction [a]	Percentage increase [b]	Optimal location of ESMI units
1	21.8	18.4	Reedyford
2	31.5	13.6	Royal Lancaster, Reedyford
3	36.8	12.3	Royal Lancaster, Lostock Hall, Reedyford
4	43.2	8.6	Lostock Hall, Beaumont, West Preston, Reedyford
5	45.9	11.5	Bull Hill, Lostock Hall, Beaumont, West Preston, Eaves Lane
6	48.8	11.5	Bull Hill, Victoria, Lostock Hall, Beaumont West Preston, Eaves Lane
7	51.4	11.4	Bull Hill, Victoria, Lostock Hall, Beaumont, Withnell, West Preston, Eaves Lane
8	53.7	13.4	Bull Hill, Victoria, Lostock Hall, Beaumont, Withnell, West Preston, Eaves Lane, Moss Side

[a] In the aggregate weighted distance compared with the existing situation.
[b] In the aggregate weighted distance compared with optimal solutions when there are no location constraints.

4.7 Preston Health District: some comparative results

As stated earlier, jurisdictional power for the planning of ESMI units is at the District level, and, therefore, it is appropriate to consider whether the optimum patterns for Lancashire are consistent with optimum patterns for the District. For illustrative purposes, in this subsection the results of a study of Preston Health District (now Preston Health District and Chorley and South Ribble Health District) are presented. Figures 11(a) and 11(b) describe the population distribution and the proposed location of ESMI units in the Health District, respectively. There are to be three standard ESMI units in the District, which are to be located in urban areas, and two of these are currently in use. Figures 11(c)–11(f) are the results for the Preston Health District of the four types of location problem which were considered earlier for locating fourteen units in Lancashire: an unconstrained and uncapacitated problem; an unconstrained and capacitated problem; a constrained and uncapacitated problem; and a constrained and capacitated problem, respectively. As the results indicate, the proposed system for the Preston Health District is very compatible with all solutions based on Lancashire (although the constrained and uncapacitated problem locates a unit at Leyland).

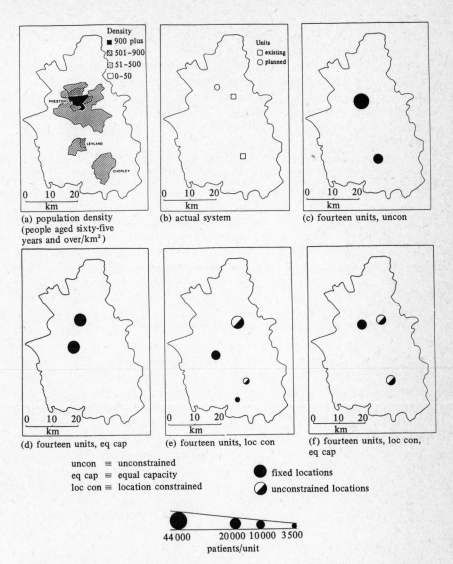

Figure 11. Preston Health District and Chorley and South Ribble Health District; some comparative results.

4.8 Concluding comments

In this section, a detailed description of various spatial characteristics of the demand and supply of ESMI units was presented as a source of valuable information about the implications of alternative location strategies. To a certain extent, it can be argued that it is often more practical to improve users' accessibility to services by enhancing their mobility rather than by relocating facilities. However, when the problem involves planning the spatial organisation of a new set of facilities, it is pertinent to address directly the issue of maximising accessibility (particularly at a time of increasing needs and decreasing resources).

From the analyses, a basic concern relates to the general principle of establishing standardised ESMI units of equal capacities. This is an unnecessary restriction which reinforces the inequities facing patients in rural areas, and it is suggested that the ESMI units should be located to reflect the configuration of urban centres and complemented by a set of smaller units serving local rural areas.

Finally, it should be appreciated that this analytic model-based approach does not provide the answers or remove the usefulness of planners. It only provides insights into one facet of a multidimensional problem, and the ultimate analysis is the decisionmakers' interpretation of the results.

It is believed that a planning process, applying location–allocation models, should develop as an ongoing and systematic extension (and perhaps reformulation) of various models within a planner–computer, interactive, decisionmaking process. This idea of a continual interactive process of problem-solving is not new, but, as planners' familiarity with computers continues to grow, such a framework offers a means of enhancing human welfare and rationalising future capital investment programmes. Furthermore, the direct involvement of the planners throughout the process seems essential, especially as it is likely to reduce resistance to the proposals. The usefulness of models is likely to be enhanced if planners feel that the results have been determined with them and not for them. Consequently, two growing areas of interest, computer graphics and micro-computing, would appear to be especially pertinent. The application of computer graphics to present the results would improve the ease of interpretation and evaluation [for example, see Goodchild's (1981) so-called ILACS system]. Moreover, given the recent advances in computer technology and the increasing availability of microcomputers at a low cost, program development of microcomputers, which usually have good colour-graphic facilities, would be a sensible direction to pursue. For example, the United Nations Centre for Human Settlements (Habitat) has successfully sponsored the development of an urban-data-management software package, which includes location–allocation models (Robinson, 1982).

5 Conclusions
5.1 Introduction
Although, the above empirical–analytic methodology is useful in assessing alternative location strategies, ultimately it is impossible for these assessments to be divorced from the socioeconomic, political, and organisational context of the decisionmaking process. For example, it is insufficient to consider only the functions of the ESMI units without reference to the wide range of health and social services required by the client group. Moreover, as formal community support is necessary (Gonen, 1977), especially in relation to the general philosophy of 'deinstitutionalisation',

consideration must be given to the attitudes and acceptance of the general public.

To incorporate a broader socioeconomic and political perspective, in a discussion of the geography of community mental health care, for instance, Dear and Wills (1980) advocate the adoption of a historical–hermeneutic approach, rather than an empirical–analytic approach per se. They suggest that the large-scale introduction of community-based mental health care can be interpreted as a combination of the following: social attitudes; social control; increasing state interventionism; and increasing professionalism. Though it is apposite to list these influences, in relation to the present discussion the suggestion of a historical–hermeneutic *or* an empirical–analytic approach seems unnecessarily restrictive. As Bernstein (1976, page xiv) demonstrates: "... empirical research, interpretation and critical evaluation dialectically involve each other".

Thus the two elements should be seen as complementary, and there remains a need to go beyond the traditional geographical studies of location simply as access. Along the lines of Dear's (1978) framework for a reexamination of public facility location theory, two additional components are discussed as a basis for future research: location as externality and the policy context for public facility planning.

5.2 Location as externality
Location as access is a component that has been widely considered. In contrast, location as externality has not been given the attention it merits. For convenience in this discussion, two types of externalities can be recognised: user externalities and nonuser externalities. User externalities can be thought of as the whole range of health and social services and voluntary contributions, such as home helps and meals-on-wheels, that are found in the community. This broader integrated provision of services is a necessary prerequisite to the successful introduction of local ESMI units, particularly for the home-based day patients. Fortunately, there seems to be increasing recognition of this situation [for example, see the DHSS's (1975) White Paper entitled *Better Services for the Mentally Ill*], although, clearly, recent public expenditure cuts do not facilitate the required scale of such developments.

In the context of this paper, it is the nonuser externalities that have direct ramifications for the location of ESMI units. Simply stated, the issue relates to the community's acceptance of the location of such a facility within their neighbourhood, and it is important because a significant characteristic of the proposed community-based care is a reduction in the distance (both geographical and social) between the mentally ill patients and the general public. Although one argument behind this deinstitutionalisation policy is that incarceration of patients in large asylums is unhelpful, and may even be regressive, what are the attitudes of the general public, particularly those people living in the neighbourhood of a proposed ESMI unit, to this redirection? This is of fundamental importance, because the success of this community-based care depends on the acceptance of the mentally ill, in both a passive and an active sense, by the neighbourhood. An important case study on this neglected component of the locational analysis was undertaken by Smith and Hanham (1981) in a survey of residents in two neighbourhoods of Norman, Oklahoma, one of which was adjacent to a large mental health facility. The interested reader is encouraged to read their paper and to consider the ramifications for greater public education campaigns about mental illness and for location decisionmaking. In relation to the siting of ESMI units in Lancashire, it should be noted that Smith and Hanham's investigation was concerned with an existing facility, and people's opinions may change (often becoming increasingly tolerant) once a facility has been introduced.

It is suggested that a useful preliminary exercise in the planning process determining the sites of the ESMI units would be a sample survey of residents' attitudes to the location of an ESMI unit in their proximity. Although variations can be expected related to the socioeconomic characteristics of the residents (Segal and Aviram, 1978), such a study would help determine a set of suitable and acceptable sites. In terms of planning policy, Dear and Wittman (1980, page 358) indicate that

"... a 'risk aversion' strategy has become common. This involves seeking out locations where no community opposition is anticipated, or where controversial facilities would go unnoticed".

One potential defect of such a system, however, would be the differential political pressures that communities could exert to avoid the location of an ESMI unit in their neighbourhood. Having argued about the development of an 'asylum without walls' in the inner cities (Dear, 1977), Dear (1981, page 494), in a discussion that implicates both the community and the state in this isolationist process, declares that:

"... the formal mechanism of state planning policy is brought to bear on the exclusion process. While some neighbourhoods are excluding the mentally disabled, other neighbourhoods (with less political clout) are being saturated by mental health facilities".

5.3 Policy context
The socioeconomic and political context is especially important in a consideration of the provision of new mental health services, particularly given the current Government's mandate to continue public expenditure cuts and the increasing incidence of private health care[2].

[2] Fortunately, there is a growing research interest in the role of the state, although this role is seen not only as an investor in public services, but also, more fundamentally, as a basic element in the organisation and operation (and even maintenance) of capitalist societies. Important references include Dear and Scott (1981); *Environment and Planning A* and the *International Journal of Urban and Regional Research*; and, two papers on contemporary perspectives on health and health care, which reemphasised the need for a broader socioeconomic, political, and historical context (Eyles, 1982; Smith, 1982).

As alterations in professional and public judgements and desires about
the form of confinement for the mentally ill have occurred, an increasing
trend towards community-based care or deinstitutionalisation has resulted.
In the preceding discussion about externalities, it was argued that the
interdependences between health and social services should be recognised
explicitly. That is, the provision of ESMI units must be viewed as part of
a larger reorganisation of health and social services in general. Though
recent organisational changes have resulted in some (hopefully, temporary)
instability, it is much more fundamental to appreciate that the planners
deciding the spatial pattern of ESMI units are constrained by available
financial resources and the organisational backcloth on which they make
their decisions.

References
Bach L, 1981, "The problem of aggregation and distance for analyses of accessibility
    and access opportunity in location–allocation models" *Environment and Planning A*
    13 955-978
Beaumont J R, 1981, "Location–allocation problems in a plane: a review of some
    models" *Socio-Economic Planning Sciences* **15** 217-229
Bernstein R J, 1976 *The Restructuring of Social and Political Theory* (Basil Blackwell,
    Oxford)
Calvo A B, Marks D H, 1973, "Location of health care facilities" *Socio-Economic
    Planning Sciences* **7** 407-422
Cooper L, 1963, "Location–allocation problems" *Operations Research* **11** 331-343
Cornwell J, Coupland V, Eyles J, Smith D M, Woods K J, 1982 *Contemporary
    Perspectives on Health and Social Care* OP-20, Department of Geography, Queen
    Mary College, University of London, London, England
Dahrendorf R, 1980 *Life Chances: Approaches to Social and Political Theory*
    (Weidenfeld and Nicolson, London)
Davies B, 1968 *Social Needs and Resources in Local Services* (Michael Joseph, London)
Dear M J, 1977, "Psychiatric patients and the inner city" *Annals of the Association of
    American Geographers* **67** 588-594
Dear M J, 1978, "Planning for mental health care: a reconsideration of public facility
    location theory" *International Regional Science Review* **3** 93-112
Dear M J, 1981, "Social and spatial reproduction of the mentally ill" in *Urbanization
    and Urban Planning in Capitalist Society* Eds M J Dear, A J Scott (Methuen,
    London) pp 481-497
Dear M J, Scott A J (Eds), 1981 *Urbanization and Urban Planning in Capitalist Society*
    (Methuen, London)
Dear M J, Wills T, 1980, "The geography of community mental health care" in
    Conceptual and Methodological Issues in Medical Geography Studies in Geography 15;
    Ed. M S Meade (University of North Carolina Press, Chapel Hill, NC) pp 263-281
Dear M J, Wittman I, 1980, "Conflict over the location of mental health facilities" in
    Geography and the Urban Environment: Progress in Research and Applications
    Eds D T Herbert, R J Johnston (John Wiley, Chichester, Sussex) pp 345-362
DHSS, 1974 *Community Hospitals: Their Role and Development in the National
    Health Service* Department of Health and Social Security (HMSO, London)
DHSS, 1975 *Better Services for the Mentally Ill* (Department of Health and Social
    Security, London)
DHSS, 1976a *Priorities for Health and Personal Social Services in England: A
    Consultative Document* (Department of Health and Social Security, London)

DHSS, 1976b *Sharing Resources for Health: The Report of the Resource Allocation Working Party* Department of Health and Social Security (HMSO, London)
DHSS, 1977 *The Way Forward* Department of Health and Social Security (HMSO, London)
DHSS, 1979 *A Happier Old Age* (Department of Health and Social Security, London)
DHSS, 1980a *Inequalities in Health* (Department of Health and Social Security, London)
DHSS, 1980b *The Future Pattern of Hospital Provision in England* (Department of Health and Social Security, London)
DHSS, 1981 *Growing Older* (Department of Health and Social Security, London)
Dokmeci V F, 1977, "A model to plan regional health facility systems" *Management Science* 24 411-419
Eyles J, 1982, "Health and medicine in urban society: the social construction and fetishism of health" in *Contemporary Perspectives on Health and Health Care* OP-20, Department of Geography, Queen Mary College, London; pp 12-33
Gonen A, 1977, "Community support systems for mentally handicapped adults" DP-96, Regional Science Research Institute, Philadelphia, PA, USA
Goodchild M F, 1973, "LAP: location-allocation package" in *Computer Programs for Location-Allocation Problems* Eds G Rushton, M F Goodchild, L M Ostresh; monograph 6, Department of Geography, University of Iowa, Iowa City, IA, USA; pp 85-114
Goodchild M F, 1981, personal communication, September
Gould P R, Leinbach T R, 1966, "An approach to the geographic assignment of hospital services" *Tijdschrift voor Economische en Sociale Geografie* 57 203-206
Hakimi L S, 1964, "Optimum locations of switching centres and the absolute centres and medians of a graph" *Operations Research* 12 450-459
Harvey D W, 1973 *Social Justice in the City* (Edward Arnold, London)
Hodgart R L, 1978, "Optimising access to public services: a review of problems, models and methods of locating central facilities" *Progress in Human Geography* 2 17-48
Klerman G L, 1977, "Better but not well: social and ethical issues in the deinstitutionalisation of the mentally ill" *Schizophrenia Bulletin* 3 617-631
LAHA, 1979 *Strategic Plan for Lancashire Area Health Authority* (Lancashire Area Health Authority, East Cliff, Preston)
Leonardi G, 1981, "A unifying framework for public facility location problems—part 1: A critical overview and some unsolved problems" *Environment and Planning A* 13 1001-1028
Morrill R L, Kelly M B, 1970, "The simulation of hospital use and the estimation of location efficiency" *Geographical Analysis* 2 283-300
NWRHA, 1979 *Regional Strategic Plan* (North West Regional Health Authority, Manchester)
Rabkin J G, 1974, "Public attitudes toward mental illness: a review of the literature" *Schizophrenia Bulletin* 10 9-33
ReVelle C, Marks D, Liebman J C, 1970, "An analysis of private and public sector location models" *Management Science* 16 692-707
ReVelle C S, Swain R W, 1970, "Central facilities location" *Geographical Analysis* 2 30-42
Rigby J P, 1978, "Access to hospitals: a literature review" report 853, Transport and Road Research Laboratory, Crowthorne, England
Robinson V B, 1982, "Microcomputer geoprocessing software for human settlements planning" paper presented at the 78th annual conference of the Association of American Geographers, San Antonio, USA; copy available in mimeograph form from HABITAT, Nairobi, Kenya

Rushton G, 1979 *Optimal Location of Facilities* (COMPRESS, Wentworth, USA)

Scott A J, 1971 *Combinatorial Programming, Spatial Analysis and Planning* (Methuen, London)

Segal S P, Aviram U, 1978 *The Mentally Ill in Community-based Sheltered Care* (John Wiley, New York)

Smith C J, 1977, "The geography of mental health" resource paper 76-4, Association of American Geographers, 1710 Sixteenth Street NW, Washington, DC 20009, USA

Smith C J, Hanham R Q, 1981, "Proximity and the formation of public attitudes towards mental illness" *Environment and Planning A* 13 147-165

Smith D M, 1979 *Where the Grass is Greener: Geographical Perspectives on Inequality* (Croom Helm, Beckenham, Kent)

Smith D M, 1982, "Geographical perspectives on health and health care" in *Contemporary Perspectives on Health and Health Care* OP-20, Department of Geography, Queen Mary College, London; pp 1-11

Smolensky E, Burton R, Tideman N, 1970, "The efficient provision of a local non-private good" *Geographical Analysis* 2 330-342

Townsend P, Davidson N, 1982 *Inequalities in Health: The Black Report* (Penguin Books, Harmondsworth, Middx)

Tudor Hart J, 1975, "The inverse care law" in *A Sociology of Medical Practice* Eds C Cox, A Mead (Collier Macmillan, West Drayton, Middx) pp 189-206

Warnes A M, 1981, "Towards a geographical contribution to gerontology" *Progress in Human Geography* 5 317-341

Resource Allocation in Multilevel Spatial Health Care Systems †

L D MAYHEW, G LEONARDI
International Institute for Applied Systems Analysis

1 Introduction

In recent years a number of models have been developed within the
Operational Research Service of the Department of Health and Social
Security (DHSS) and at the International Institute for Applied Systems
Analysis (IIASA), in Austria, for exploring different ways of allocating
health care resources in a region or country (Gibbs, 1978; Hughes and
Wierzbicki, 1980; Mayhew, 1980; 1981; Mayhew and Taket, 1980a;
1980b; Aspden et al, 1981; Mayhew and Leonardi, 1982). These
models, which are linked through a common set of underlying behavioural
assumptions (see sections 2 and 3), are at varying stages of development,
with some now being used in a routine decisionmaking environment and
others still at the refinement stage. The model discussed in this paper falls
into the second of these categories and builds on the approach first given
by Mayhew and Leonardi (1982). This considered competing methods for
allocating resources in a region, so that the outcomes are consistent with
stated equity or efficiency criteria, but which also include provision for
the geographical choice behaviour of patients as between different
hospitals. Whereas the variables in these methods were highly aggregate
and therefore suitable mainly for the strategic level of planning, the
discussion here considers the allocation process on a more disaggregate basis,
either by medical speciality [1] or by disease condition. In making this
step, however, it was realised that the original approach would have to be
extended to take into account a variety of other factors. These include
the relative priorities of different services and their commands over
available resources, and also those of a more political or economic nature,
which are powerful considerations in any health care system. The model
that emerges is, nevertheless, simple in principle: it seeks to allocate
resources to each locality or place of treatment in proportion to potential
(not actual) demand. The particular allocation rule on which it is based is
therefore essentially an extension of the efficiency principle given by
Mayhew and Leonardi (1982), except in this case there is more than one
patient category. The use of the label 'efficient' is perhaps unusual in that
the approach excludes any reference to output measures or financial
criteria, although some of the reasons for this will become apparent in
section 2. Instead, an efficient allocation of resources is defined as one

---

† This paper is based on work carried out partly at the Istituto di Ricerche Economico-
Sociali del Piemonte, Turin and partly at IIASA.

[1] See editor's note, page 6.

that is consistent with patients' preferences for treatment in particular locations. This objective is achieved by combining the morbidity or patient-generating potential of an area with the accessibility costs to different places of treatment in order to create an allocation of resources that maximises their accessibility to the population.

Various factors, of course, will prevent the system from obtaining the prescribed ideal pattern (that is according to potential demand, resource levels, and accessibility costs) and so constrain the number of allocative options. The idea is that these factors are simultaneously taken care of in the model by three sets of parameters termed priorities, thresholds, and bounds, whose interpretation and use are described below. Last, before we proceed, it should be stressed that the efficiency principle is only one of several allocation rules that might receive broad acceptance by actors in a health care system. Nevertheless, investigations have shown that there is considerable scope for embedding other systems objectives within the same model framework.

2 Background
In a health care system, resources are scarce, with the result that there is often considerable pressure on available beds, doctors, nurses, and support services. The dilemma faced by providers is that, despite substantially increased budgets in many countries for health care during the last thirty years, this pressure has not slackened. Priorities over resources arise for medical reasons, teaching obligations, research needs, or because a government or health authority wants to devote special attention to certain services. However, if the population structure in a region is changing, and when there are other factors influencing the uptake in services, then there is a high chance of the resultant allocation process becoming haphazard.

In an ideal world it would be correct to base allocations on strictly defined medical grounds. However, such is the breadth of services covered by a health care system, and because the outcomes and benefits of so many medical procedures involved are so hard to evaluate, this ideal is simply impractical as yet. The approach considered here is rather more pragmatic; it argues that allocations are part of a behavioural process in which the principal driving force among the various actors is to satisfy potential demand. It recognises, however, that there are many constraints, side objectives, and pressures in the system that prevent this objective being met. In the approach adopted in this paper, the idea is that these aspects are taken care of by two sets of factors called thresholds and bounds.

Thresholds are based on the minimum acceptable level of potential demand before a service can be provided in a particular treatment district. They can be regarded as service norms or certificates of need laid down by health ministries, authorities, agencies, or by medical opinion. Alternatively, they may arise from economic considerations internal to the system, such as economies of scale, or they may reflect certain licensing laws if there are legal restrictions on the provision of some services. For those services involving specialised and expensive therapeutics, thresholds will be high relative to potential demand; for other services they may be nonexistent, in which case provision will be completely routine.

Bounds, by contrast, are constraints on the total allocations to any places of treatment in a locality. They represent a variety of considerations such as physical restrictions on facility expansion and the availability of finance capital. They can also be influenced by political considerations, teaching and training needs, community pressure, and other factors, preventing the rundown or closure of facilities that might otherwise be expected to take place. What the model does is simply to choose a path through both sets of factors—thresholds and bounds—consistent with the efficiency principle.

The intention is that the resultant model outputs will be used both in the study of incremental change to existing services (which to increase or decrease), and for the planning of longer-term change involving substantial rearrangements of resources or the building of new facilities. Although, in the short run, it might be expected that relatively few changes occur in well-established systems, the contrary is often true because of the flexibility derived from more mobile resources such as manpower, which can be used to increase hospital throughput and hence case loads. Thus, potential applications cover a wide range of routinely encountered problems.

3 The model

The principle of satisfying potential demand is dealt with in the model by a utility function. This function assumes that a higher utility is always derived from treating more patients regardless of category, but that the gains in utility increase at a decreasing rate. The function describes a system in which actors collectively strive to satisfy potential demand, but in which the priority they give to different groups of patients varies and the resources they can allocate are constrained by their total availability. The specific mathematical form of the function has arisen from the accumulated experience over several years of applications in the health field, rather than from any particular theoretical basis (McDonald et al, 1974), although Gibbs (1978) gives an interesting economic interpretation. However, there are connections with more traditional benefit or entropy-type objective functions; moreover, the spatial allocation submodel is related to some in common use in the regional science field and for locational analysis (Wilson, 1974; Leonardi, 1980). The submodel in question is an attraction-constrained gravity model which was developed independently of the utility approach for use by the London Health Planning Consortium (LHPC, 1979; Mayhew and Taket, 1980a; 1980b; 1981) before being transferred for use by the four Thames Regional Health Authorities in Southeast England. The main feature, in a health context, of this submodel is that it presumes that all the resources in health districts

are used to capacity. Though, as will be seen, the reality is slightly more
complex, this assumption is largely in harmony with the observed behaviour
of the health care system (Feldstein, 1963; DHSS, 1976; Gibbs, 1978);
that is demand tends to rise to meet the level of supply. In the next section
the model is developed in detail, but further considerations, including the
part of the problem involving the use of bounds, will be presented elsewhere
at a later time. The main objective of this paper is a presentation of the
utility function and the derivation of the efficiency criterion; this is
followed by a description of the algorithm needed to solve for allocations
with thresholds and the presentation of some early results.

4 The problem
The full problem may be stated as follows:

$$\underset{D_{jk}}{\text{maximise}} \sum_{jk} \delta_{jk} g_k(D_{jk}) , \tag{1}$$

subject to

$$\sum_{jk} D_{jk} \delta_{jk} = Q , \tag{2}$$

$$R_j \leqslant \sum_k D_{jk} \delta_{jk} \leqslant S_j , \tag{3}$$

$$D_{jk} \geqslant A_k , \qquad \text{if } \delta_{jk} = 1 . \tag{4}$$

Equation (1) is the function to be maximised, where $g_k(D_{jk})$ is a utility
function (see section 4.1), D_{jk} are the (as yet) unknown resources (measured
in case loads) allocated to destination j in service category k, and where
δ_{jk} is a binary matrix in which elements are set to 1 if a service k is
provided in j and 0 otherwise.

Equation (2) is a budget constraint based on the total treating capacity,
Q, of the system. Condition (3) represents the upper and lower bounds
on the allocations to a destination (S_j and R_j, respectively). Condition (4)
is the threshold principle in which the threshold in service sector k is given
as A_k. Note also that the objective function is presumed to operate over
the whole system, implying the existence of a high-level decisionmaking
authority, but where local conditions are taken care of in condition (3).
When bounds are tight, either this implies a lot of friction in the system
(because of lack of finance, say) or it suggests a high degree of local
autonomy. In both cases, it would mean less room for manoeuvre at the
higher level. In section 4.3, we contrast the utility at this higher-level with
utility at the local level, which is based on which particular patients to treat.

4.1 The utility function
The utility function used in this version of the model has the same
mathematical form as the one described by Aspden (1980). It is given by:

$$g_k(D_{jk}) = \frac{\phi_{jk}}{\alpha_k} \left[1 - \left(\frac{D_{jk}}{\phi_{jk}} \right)^{-\alpha_k} \right] , \tag{5}$$

where

ϕ_{jk} is a nonnegative quantity proportional to the ideal level of demand for service category k in location j; from now on it will be called the *potential demand*;

α_k is a positive parameter reflecting the priority the system gives to service category k.

The function defined in equation (5) is clearly increasing with respect to the allocation variable D_{jk}. As for its behaviour with respect to ϕ_{jk}, it is easily shown by elementary calculus that it is increasing when ϕ_{jk} is within the interval

$$0 \leqslant \phi_{jk} \leqslant D_{jk}\left(\frac{1}{1+\alpha_k}\right)^{1/\alpha_k}, \tag{6}$$

while it is decreasing outside this interval. Although the existence of a decreasing portion of the utility function makes no sense intuitively, its disturbing effect can be easily eliminated in practice. Again elementary calculus yields the inequality

$$\exp(-1) \leqslant \left(\frac{1}{1+\alpha_k}\right)^{\alpha_k} \leqslant 1, \tag{7}$$

therefore a sufficient condition for the utility function being increasing with respect to ϕ_{jk} is

$$\phi_{jk} \leqslant \exp(-1)D_{jk} = 0.37D_{jk}. \tag{8}$$

The optimisation problems to be considered in this paper can always be formulated in such a way as to meet the above inequality in the meaningful range of feasible solutions. Indeed, constraint (4) is enough to conclude that, if D_{jk} is positive, it is larger than a given threshold A_k, which is typically a large number (several thousands). But, the quantities ϕ_{jk} are defined up to a multiplicative constant, so that they can be arbitrarily rescaled to be made less than 1, say (or any other positive number one wishes), hence the above statement follows.

In section 4.3 of the paper when the link is made with the gravity model, we shall be more specific about assumptions concerning ϕ_{jk}. Here it suffices to say that in general

$$\phi_{jk} = f(W_{ik}, \omega_{jk}, c_{ij}, \beta_k). \tag{9}$$

That is, ϕ_{jk} is a function of the patient-generating factor W_{ik} in place of residence i, category k; a factor ω_{jk}, presumed constant, related to the importance of satisfying potential demand and the prestige of the facilities in j offering k; accessibility costs c_{ij}; and a space discount parameter β_k.

The parameter α_k, meanwhile, reflects the priority given to services at different budget levels, Q. A service is said to be inelastic (high α), for example, if treatment cannot easily be deferred without causing physical distress and medical complications. In this case, case loads change proportionately very little. By contrast, services that are elastic (low α), because treatment can be deferred, respond proportionately more when budgets rise or fall.

Before proceeding, it should be noted that the approach ignores possible variations in treatment *standards*, which are also elastic to different budget levels (Gibbs, 1978). Though it is possible to allow for this in the methods, it is presumed for current purposes that the subset of services being examined have relatively constant treatment requirements. This assumption would be met if the services being considered were in certain acute categories.

4.2 Spatial and sectoral allocations without constraints

If there are no bounds, the sectoral allocation problem separates from the spatial problem. Further, if there are no bounds *and* no thresholds then sectoral allocations are consistent with potential demand ϕ and medical priorities. First, define the following

$$D_k = \sum_{j \in L_k} D_{jk} \, , \tag{10}$$

the resources allocated to sector k, and define p_{jk}, the share of resources for k allocated to zone j, such that

$$\sum_{j \in L_k} p_{jk} = 1 \, . \tag{11}$$

In equations (10) and (11) L_k is the set of destinations with k allocated (that is, $\delta_{jk} = 1$); and D and p are related by

$$D_{jk} = D_k p_{jk} \, . \tag{12}$$

4.2.1 *Spatial allocation*

Substituting equation (12) into equation (5), one gets:

$$\bar{g}_k(D_k, p_{jk}) = g_k(D_{jk}) = \frac{\phi_{jk}}{\alpha_k} \left[1 - \left(\frac{D_k p_{jk}}{\phi_{jk}} \right)^{-\alpha_k} \right] \, , \tag{13}$$

where $\bar{g}_k$ is g_k expressed as a function of D_k and p_{jk}.

When the sectoral allocation D_k is held constant, the spatial allocation is obtained by solving for each k the following optimisation problems

$$\underset{p}{\text{maximise}} \sum_{j \in L_k} \bar{g}_k(D_k, p_{jk}) \, , \tag{14}$$

subject to constraint (11).

Although it is not strictly needed now, it is also useful to keep in mind the constraint on sectoral allocation,

$$\sum_k D_k = Q \, . \tag{15}$$

The spatial allocation solution is given by the optimality conditions,

$$\frac{\partial}{\partial p_{jk}} \bar{g}_k(D_k, p_{jk}) = \lambda_k ,$$ (16)

where λ_k is the Lagrange multiplier for constraint (11). That is,

$$D_k \left(\frac{D_k p_{jk}}{\phi_{jk}} \right)^{-(1+\alpha_k)} = \lambda_k .$$ (17)

Defining

$$\psi_k = \frac{1}{D_k} \left(\frac{\lambda_k}{D_k} \right)^{-1/(1+\alpha_k)} ,$$ (18)

we have

$$p_{jk} = \psi_k \phi_{jk} .$$ (19)

From constraint (11), however,

$$1 = \psi_k \sum_{j \in L_k} \phi_{jk} .$$ (20)

Letting

$$\phi_k = \sum_{j \in L_k} \phi_{jk} ,$$ (21)

from constraints (19) and (20) we see that

$$p_{jk} = \frac{\phi_{jk}}{\phi_k} .$$ (22)

Thus, the spatial allocation of resources is independent of the sectoral allocation. It depends on the potential demand incident on j in k and on the total potential demand in all j. This result is hence a generalisation of the efficiency principle to many services (Mayhew and Leonardi, 1982).

4.2.2 Sectoral allocation

Sectoral allocations are those to each k. Substitute equation (22) in equation (1) and consider the following problem

$$\underset{D_k}{\text{maximise}} \sum_k \sum_{j \in L_k} \bar{g} \left(D_k, \frac{\phi_{jk}}{\phi_k} \right) ,$$ (23)

subject to constraint (15). The optimality conditions are

$$\left(\frac{D_k}{\phi_k} \right)^{-(1+\alpha_k)} = \lambda ,$$ (24)

where λ is the multiplier for constraint (15). Hence,

$$D_k = \phi_k \lambda^{-1/(1+\alpha_k)} .$$ (25)

For a given L_k, λ is found as the root of the equation

$$Q = \sum_k \phi_k \lambda^{-1/(1+\alpha_k)} , \tag{26}$$

which can be found by using the Newton–Raphson method.

4.2.3 Allocations with thresholds

When a particular allocation does not meet a threshold, then resources must be reallocated. This process is called allocation by forced substitution. From equation (22) and from the definition of p_{jk}, we have

$$D_{jk} = D_k \frac{\phi_{jk}}{\phi_k} . \tag{27}$$

To cross the threshold A_k, therefore,

$$D_k \frac{\phi_{jk}}{\phi_k} \geqslant A_k , \tag{28}$$

or

$$D_k \geqslant \frac{A_k \phi_k}{\phi_{jk}} , \qquad \forall j \text{ and } k , \tag{29}$$

otherwise there are forced substitutions. The optimality conditions for this problem are, from equations (15), (20), and (29)

$$\left(\frac{D_k}{\phi_k}\right)^{-(1+\alpha_k)} - \lambda + \xi_k = 0 , \tag{30}$$

where ξ_k are the multipliers for constraint (24) and where $(\lambda - \xi_k) > 1$. Multiplier ξ_k is active (that is, nonzero) when

$$D_k < \frac{A_k \phi_k}{\min_{j \in L_k} \phi_{jk}} . \tag{31}$$

Combining equations (30) and (31) yields for forced substitutions

$$\lambda > \min_{j \in L_k} \left(\frac{\phi_{jk}}{A_k}\right)^{1+\alpha_k} . \tag{32}$$

Conversely, no forced substitutions occur whenever

$$\lambda \leqslant \min_{j \in L_k} \left(\frac{\phi_{jk}}{A_k}\right)^{1+\alpha_k} . \tag{33}$$

Although the details of the algorithm to solve the combinatorial problem of meeting thresholds will not be given, its main ideas will be outlined here.

First of all, it should be noted that, because of the way the utility function is built, an optimal location policy will always try to open as many locations as possible and with the highest possible potential.

Second, if one defines the coefficients as

$$C_{jk} = \left(\frac{\phi_{jk}}{A_k}\right)^{1+\alpha_k}, \tag{34}$$

then condition (33) can be rewritten as

$$\lambda \leqslant \min_{j \in L_k} C_{jk} . \tag{35}$$

It follows that the set of optimal locations for service category k, L_k, must be of the form

$$L_k = \{j: C_{jk} \geqslant \lambda\} , \tag{36}$$

for some root λ of equation (26). Of course, many pairs $\{(L_k), \lambda\}$ exist which are consistent with the above form (and the corresponding L_k are all *subsets* of the optimal ones), but only one of such pairs has the highest cardinality for the L_k (that is, the maximum number of open locations) and this is the optimal solution.

The algorithm which has been devised is an iterative procedure which produces increasingly tighter upper and lower bounds on λ and on the L_k, thus converging to the optimal pair.

To show how the algorithm works, the first two steps will be described. Start with $L_k^0 = \{j: j = 1, ..., N\}$, that is, with *all possible locations open*. This is clearly an *upper bound* on L_k, that is,

$$L_k \subseteq L_k^0 ; \tag{37}$$

and also the root of equation (26), λ_0, is an upper bound on λ, that is,

$$\lambda \leqslant \lambda_0 . \tag{38}$$

To get a first lower bound, consider the sets

$$L_k^1 = \{j: C_{jk} \geqslant \lambda_0\} , \tag{39}$$

and find the corresponding root λ_1 of equation (26).
The following statement is straightforward,

$$L_k^1 \subseteq L_k \subseteq L_k^0 , \tag{40}$$

$$\lambda_1 \leqslant \lambda \leqslant \lambda_0 . \tag{41}$$

Thus the first two steps of the iterations have produced upper and lower bounds for the optimal solution. For the second two steps, one finds the sets

$$L_k^2 = \{j: C_{jk} \geqslant \lambda_1\} , \tag{42}$$

and the corresponding root of equation (26), λ_2 and the sets

$$L_k^3 = \{j: C_{jk} \geqslant \lambda_2\} , \tag{43}$$

and the corresponding root of equation (26), λ_3. It can be easily shown that

$$L_k^1 \subseteq L_k^3 \subseteq L_k \subseteq L_k^2 \subseteq L_k^0 , \tag{44}$$

$$\lambda_1 \leqslant \lambda_3 \leqslant \lambda \leqslant \lambda_2 \leqslant \lambda_0 . \tag{45}$$

Therefore the bounds on the estimate of the optimal solution have been tightened. Repeating the same procedure over and over, the tightest possible bounds on the solution are obtained in a finite number of steps. The algorithm will eventually lead to a single solution, which is of course the optimal one (this often happens in actual computational experience), or to a small subset of feasible solutions, on which refined search to detect the optimal one can be easily performed. It should be remarked, however, that this final step is often uninteresting for practical purposes, since the last lower bound produced by the iterations is usually indistinguishable from the 'true' optimum, both in terms of the value of the objective function and in terms of the corresponding location pattern.

4.3 The gravity mechanism

The spatial mechanism is, as was seen in section 4.1, implicit in the methods developed. So far, we have allocated resources to destinations and sectors, but not to places of residence. For this we need the gravity model, but to use standard gravity parameters in the previous methods (see condition 3, section 4.1, β_k), we have to make the links explicit. In doing so, it is important to emphasise that, in contrast to the utility of the allocation decisions originating higher up in the system, the decision on *which* particular patients to admit are purely local ones. Thus, it is necessary to maximise the utility only of the treatment destination, once the resources it has to dispense to the surrounding population have been determined. Accordingly, we define the following new maximisation problem

$$\underset{T_{ijk}}{\text{maximise}} \left[- \sum_i \frac{\phi_{ijk}}{\alpha_k} \left(\frac{T_{ijk}}{\phi_{ijk}} \right)^{-\alpha_k} \right] , \tag{46}$$

subject to

$$\sum_i T_{ijk} = D_{jk} , \tag{47}$$

where T_{ijk} is the number of patients from i treated in j, service category k, ϕ_{ijk} ($\phi_{jk} = \sum_i \phi_{ijk}$) is the potential demand incident on j from i in k, and constraint (47) is the resource constraint on the destination arising from higher-level allocation processes, the effects of the bounds and thresholds having already been taken into account.

This is hence something like before except that we are just summing over places of residence i and not over j and k. Note also that α_k does not take into consideration possible differences between each j.

In a well-organised system, with a free flow of information, medical priorities should be perceived in more or less the same way, independently of location, but some empirical work may be necessary to check this. Continuing with the maximisation problem, we have the following optimality conditions

$$\lambda = \left(\frac{T_{ijk}}{\phi_{ijk}}\right)^{-(1+\alpha_k)} , \tag{48}$$

so that

$$T_{ijk} = \phi_{ijk}\lambda^{-1/(1+\alpha_k)} . \tag{49}$$

From constraint (47), however,

$$D_{jk} = \lambda^{-1/(1+\alpha_k)} \sum_i \phi_{ijk} . \tag{50}$$

Hence,

$$T_{ijk} = \frac{D_{jk}\phi_{ijk}}{\sum_i \phi_{ijk}} . \tag{51}$$

Letting,

$$\phi_{ijk} = \omega_{jk}W_{ik}\exp(-\beta_k c_{ij}) , \tag{52}$$

where the right-hand variables were defined in section 4.1, and substituting in condition (51), we have, on cancelling the ω_{jk} a standard attraction-constrained gravity model,

$$T_{ijk} = B_{jk}D_{jk}W_{ik}\exp(-\beta_k c_{ij}) , \tag{53}$$

where

$$B_{jk} = \left[\sum_i W_{ik}\exp(-\beta_k c_{ij})\right]^{-1} . \tag{54}$$

In words, equation (53) states that the flow of patients between i and j in patient category k increases in proportion to the treating capacity of j and the morbidity or patient-generating factor in i, but decreases inversely with the accessibility costs c_{ij}. The term B_{jk} ensures the constraint in equation (47) is met; that is, the number of cases generated by all i and treated in j does not exceed the available case load of j.

5 First results from Massachusetts
Several applications of one or more of the above or related methods are in hand or under way. The necessary data for the application described here were obtained for a 28 x 23 origin–destination system, the 23 destinations corresponding to the health planning subareas in the State of Massachusetts. Apart from providing the first opportunity to study the overall approach, the US health care system presents several distinct challenges to the regional scientist. With no central decisionmaker, corresponding to a strong regional health authority, there is a high degree of local autonomy,

implying (in our context) tight lower bounds because hospitals do not very easily give up their 'limited' resources. But, the changing configuration of potential demand, community pressure groups, Health Service Agencies, and insurance companies act to try to counterbalance the possible mis-direction of resources. Contrary to opinion, the latter act as market mechanisms only up to a point, because of the many distortions inherent in any health care 'market'. Recently, certificates of need have become a feature of the US scene, and these represent a higher level of control than hitherto. Again, in the current context they might be said to represent thresholds.

The spatial parameter β_k was determined for four services shown in table 1 using the model in equation (49), based on population utilisation rates, patient flow data, and accessibility costs (see chapter 10 of this volume). The values of R^2 shown give the proportion of the variance explained from the regression of predicted patient flows on those observed. These results showed that the model hypothesis was appropriate for all the services considered. The parameters α_k and ω_{jk}, however, were not estimated at this stage, their values being guessed or inferred from previous studies. Also, since we do not consider the effects of bounds that would further restrict the various allocative options, the results at this stage must be regarded simply only as a test of the threshold mechanism, and not as a set of viable alternatives on which to base a health care policy for Massachusetts. Moreover, the relative values of the thresholds themselves were chosen on the basis of what seemed plausible, but their magnitudes were then deliberately exaggerated to emphasise the sorts of effects their use precipitates. Thus, for obstetrics, we set a fairly low threshold (relative to potential demand), but a high α, implying a routinely provided service that is inelastic to budget changes. Conversely, at the other extreme, we gave a much higher threshold (relative to potential demand) to acute psychiatric services and a low α, emphasising the fact that this might be considered a more specialised medical service, not always routinely available and elastic to budget levels.

Table 1. Parameter values used for each service.

Type of service	k	β_k	R^2	α_k	A_k
Medical/surgical	1	0.23	0.95	3	5000
Obstetrics	2	0.27	0.95	6	300
Paediatrics	3	0.21	0.92	2	1000
Psychiatric	4	0.25	0.96	2	300

Notes:
β_k is the spatial discount parameter,
α_k is the elasticity parameter reflecting the priorities of the system,
A_k is the thresholds on services,
R^2 is the proportion of variance explained by the gravity model,
k is the patient category.

In the following illustrative outputs (table 2 and figure 1) we consider a set of allocations without thresholds and a set with thresholds. To simplify further the comparison, the resource budget Q, based on the total case load for all of Massachusetts, is held constant at a level corresponding to the allocations for these four services in 1978. Also, no change is made to the geographical configuration of demand, although this would have been easy to do. The results in table 2, therefore, are designed to show what happens to the spatial configuration of resources under the efficiency criterion when thresholds are allowed to constrain the permissible allocations in each treatment district. Basically, the effects of this particular parameter and variable set can be considered fivefold:

(1) Six services are withdrawn from places of treatment in category one, two in two, nine in three, and eighteen in four. In two places of treatment, all services are withdrawn, illustrating the severe consequences of these particular thresholds.

(2) For a fixed budget, closing departments releases resources for other places of treatment. Thus, allocations increase elsewhere, but in accordance with α. In the four places remaining open to psychiatric services, the local budget increases by 11.1% as compared with 4.6% for obstetrics services.

(3) The proportionate increases in allocations to each destination satisfying the threshold in given service are the same, indicating that spare resources are shared out fairly. This would not have occurred had there been changes in the distribution of potential demand, since this would have affected ϕ_{jk} and the allocations would have readjusted accordingly.

(4) Total allocations for each service can rise or fall according to interactions between thresholds, elasticities, and potential demand. Here only the fourth service, acute psychiatrics, changes significantly, because of its failure to breach the threshold in so many locations.

(5) Although we do not show this, the closure of services can cause large changes in local hospitalisation rates in the same services in spite of the overall resource budget being maintained; the resources released in consequence are simply redistributed among other services and places of treatment in accordance with priorities and demand. This seems intuitive from equation (53), and should therefore be taken into account when considering the full implications of any proposed changes.

Figure 1 summarises the results in geographic form. It shows how the services are reallocated in Massachusetts, when the model is applied to the current total case load according to parameters and thresholds given in table 1. The implication is that the more heavily populated and highly accessible areas have allocated to them the full range of medical services, whereas the rural and peripheral areas unable to meet the threshold have their services withdrawn. Thus, it is clearly seen how, by manipulating the thresholds to suit particular health policies, the effects of the decisions entailed may be translated into what would be expected to occur at the local level.

Table 2. Allocations and reallocations of case loads in Massachusetts with and without thresholds (total capacity $Q = 868123$).

Treatment district	Medical/surgical services $\alpha = 3, k = 1, A_1 = 5000$			Obstetric services $\alpha = 6, k = 2, A_2 = 300$			Paediatric services $\alpha = 2, k = 3, A_3 = 1000$			Psychiatric services $\alpha = 2, k = 4, A_4 = 300$		
	without threshold	with threshold	change (%)	without threshold	with threshold	change (%)	without threshold	with threshold	change (%)	without threshold	with threshold	change (%)
1	7507	0	-100.0	1012	1059	4.6	777	0	-100.0	158	0	-100.0
2	5610	0	-100.0	626	0	-100.0	739	0	-100.0	110	0	-100.0
3	30926	33466	8.2	4565	4776	4.6	3549	3943	11.1	695	0	-100.0
4	13124	0	-100.0	2116	2214	4.6	1506	0	-100.0	303	0	-100.0
5	1655	0	-100.0	133	0	-100.0	224	0	-100.0	27	0	-100.0
6	8231	0	-100.0	1173	1227	4.6	1088	0	-100.0	175	0	-100.0
7	22166	23987	8.2	3769	3943	4.6	2944	3270	11.1	539	0	-100.0
8	24345	26344	8.2	3350	3505	4.6	2865	3183	11.1	545	0	-100.0
9	18050	19533	8.2	2240	2343	4.6	2169	0	-100.0	422	0	-100.0
10	25676	27785	8.2	2610	2730	4.6	3535	3927	11.1	477	0	-100.0
11	76806	83114	8.2	10872	11374	4.6	9439	10486	11.1	1694	1881	11.1
12	79856	86414	8.2	12799	13390	4.6	9719	10797	11.1	1856	2062	11.1
13	26873	29080	8.2	3658	3827	4.6	3672	4080	11.1	568	0	-100.0
14	45424	49154	8.2	6043	6322	4.6	5608	6231	11.1	952	1058	11.1
15	16527	17884	8.2	2823	2954	4.6	2056	0	-100.0	387	0	-100.0
16	24988	27040	8.2	4304	4503	4.6	3356	3729	11.1	577	0	-100.0
17	24542	26557	8.2	3048	3188	4.6	2552	0	-100.0	554	0	-100.0
18	8368	0	-100.0	862	902	4.6	717	0	-100.0	153	0	-100.0
19	24730	26761	8.2	3349	3503	4.6	2989	3321	11.1	523	0	-100.0
20	33542	36297	8.2	4829	5052	4.6	3967	4407	11.1	732	0	-100.0
21	39673	42931	8.2	4926	5153	4.6	4793	5324	11.1	807	0	-100.0
22	55799	60381	8.2	7041	7366	4.6	6822	7579	11.1	1155	1283	11.1
23	62299	67415	8.2	8202	8581	4.6	7247	8051	11.1	1314	1459	11.1
Total	676717	684141	1.1	94350	97909	3.8	82332	78328	-4.9	14724	7745	-47.4

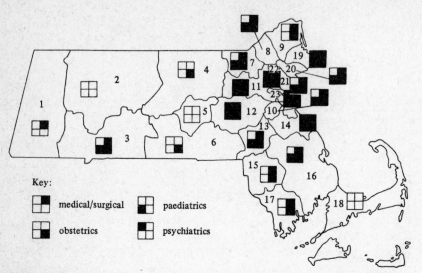

Figure 1. The geographical allocation of four health care services in Massachusetts resulting from an application of the threshold mechanism for the parameter set shown in table 1.

6 Conclusions

This paper has considered the problem of resource allocation in a multilevel spatial health care system in which there are competing priorities between services, and thresholds and bounds on permissible allocations to different places of treatment. The conceptual basis of the model rested with a utility function, which presumed that to treat more patients was better than treating less. Provision in the model was made for geographical variation in potential demand based on population structure, utilisation rates, and accessibility costs between places of residence and places of treatment. It was shown in what sense the resultant resource allocations were consistent with an efficiency criterion, and the link with the more familiar gravity model was made. Initial tests on data from Massachusetts illustrated the logical basis of the model and the way it could be used for generating the possible consequences of different health policies for different areas in a region. In future work, it will be necessary to expand the approach to deal with the question of bounds on allocations, and to incorporate other systems objectives apart from efficiency. The work presented here should be regarded as a step towards these eventual goals.

Acknowledgements. The data on patient discharges were obtained through the cooperation of the University of Massachusetts, Amherst, and the Western Massachusetts Health Planning Council. Preparation was carried out by Richard Segall, of the Department of Industrial Engineering and Operations Research at the University, and Brandon Delaney, PhD, Research Director of the Council.
    The results given in table 1 are based on work carried out by Professor E Rising at the International Institute for Applied Systems Analysis whilst he was on leave from the University of Massachusetts, Amherst, USA.

References
Aspden P, 1980, "The IIASA health care resources allocation submodel: DRAM calibration for data from the South West Health Region, UK" WP-80-115, International Institute for Applied Systems Analysis, Laxenburg, Austria
Aspden P, Rusnak M, Mayhew L, 1981, "DRAM: a model of health care resource allocation in Czechoslovakia" *Omega* **9** 509–518
DHSS, 1976 *Sharing Resources for Health: The Report of the Resource Allocation Working Party* Department of Health and Social Security (HMSO, London)
Feldstein M S, 1963, "Economic analysis, operational research, and the National Health Service" *Oxford Economic Papers* **15** 19–31
Gibbs R, 1978, "The IIASA health care resources allocation sub-model: mark 1" RR-78-8, International Institute for Applied Systems Analysis, Laxenburg, Austria
Hughes D J, Wierzbicki A, 1980 "DRAM: a model of health care resource allocation" RR-80-115, International Institute for Applied Systems Analysis, Laxenburg, Austria
Leonardi G, 1980, "A unifying framework for public facility location problems" WP-80-79, International Institute for Applied Systems Analysis, Laxenburg, Austria
LHPC, 1979 *Acute Hospital Services in London* profile by the London Health Planning Consortium (HMSO, London)
McDonald A G, Cuddeford C G, Beale E J L, 1974, "Mathematical models of the balance of care" *British Medical Bulletin* **30** 262–270
Mayhew L D, 1980, "The regional planning of health care services: RAMOS and RAMOS^{-1}" WP-80-166, International Institute for Applied Systems Analysis, Laxenburg, Austria
Mayhew L D, 1981, "DRAMOS: a multi-category spatial resource allocation model for health service management and planning" WP-81-39, International Institute for Applied Systems Analysis, Laxenburg, Austria
Mayhew L D, Leonardi G, 1982, "Equity, efficiency, and accessibility in urban and regional health-care systems" *Environment and Planning A* **14** 1479–1507
Mayhew L D, Taket A, 1980a, "Modeling patient flows: a gravity model approach" internal report for the Operational Research Service of the Department of Health and Social Security, 151 Great Titchfield Street, London W1
Mayhew L D, Taket A, 1980b, "RAMOS: a model of health care resource allocation in space" WP-80-125, International Institute for Applied Systems Analysis, Laxenburg, Austria
Mayhew L D, Taket A, 1981, "RAMOS: a model validation and sensitivity analysis" WP-81-100, International Institute for Applied Systems Analysis, Laxenburg, Austria
Wilson A G, 1974 *Urban and Regional Models in Geography and Planning* (John Wiley, Chichester, Sussex)

Patient Travel and the Use of Hospitals in Massachusetts: An Application of RAMOS[†]

E J RISING, R S SEGALL
University of Massachusetts

L D MAYHEW
International Institute of Applied Systems Analysis

1 Introduction: the decisionmaking environment

The United States of America spends over 10% of its gross national product on health and medical care. The rate of growth in costs has been approximately twice the rate of inflation, and statistics indicate that the inflationary slowdown of late is not affecting this trend. The growth is partly attributable to the ever-increasing technological needs of modern medicine, and partly also to a huge expansion in services, facilities, and equipment. At the same time, there is still a segment of population that is unable to obtain the medical care it needs, either because of the high cost or because of its unavailability in some areas.

Recognition of the twin problems of spiralling costs and a maldistribution of resources has given impetus to a number of legislative initiatives at the state and national level to improve the situation. The most recent of these was PL 93-641, the National Health Planning Resources Development Act of 1973. This specified that a Certificate of Need is required before any institution can make substantial changes to the services offered or to the deployment of capital facilities and equipment. The Act is designed to control excessive expenditure through the withholding of certificates for projected services or facilities in cases where there is danger of duplication or underutilization. Although the Act only exercises control at the margin of growth, it is argued that, if it were widely implemented and conscientiously administered, its effectiveness would increase over time as old facilities are renewed or relocated to underserved areas. At the time of enactment, this was the only kind of control on health care expenditure which was politically feasible to obtain.

The procedures for obtaining certificates of need in Massachusetts are generally similar to those in other states. The certificate is issued by the State Commissioner of Public Health on the basis of two reviews—one local and one at the State level. Initially, the decisions at both levels were based on population trends by age and sex, hospital utilization (occupancy) rates, average lengths of stay, morbidity, and other data. These data, however, were often difficult to interpret, leading in some cases to their use in supporting contrary arguments.

† This work was partially supported by the International Institute for Applied Systems Analysis, Laxenburg, Austria, and by the University of Massachusetts, Amherst, MA, USA.

The result was that the data were often ignored, and the decisions of the local health service agencies (HSAs), the State Advisory Board, and the Commissioner tended to be made instead on political grounds. As one might expect, the whole procedure became largely discredited as a rational decisionmaking procedure. Recently, the National Administration has been attempting to eliminate the programme altogether, partly because of this lack of credibility, but partly also because of its political opposition of all forms of control. So far, it has been unsuccessful, because the problems the programme was designed to combat are so severe.

It was against this background that investigations began at the University of Massachusetts to examine ways of putting the problems of health care resource allocation on a more rational footing. These investigations led to the consideration of a gravity model, of a type developed in the United Kingdom by the Department of Health and Social Security for the regional planning of acute inpatient health services. Because such a model can be used to simulate the effects on hospitalization rates in different areas from changes in supply and demand, it seemed the natural choice of analytical tool for examining the various resource implications arising from the Certificate of Need legislation in the USA. Although the model may be used in a variety of planning contexts, depending on the planning controls in the countries concerned, its most appropriate use in the USA would be to provide HSAs with a systematic method of appraising submissions from the health organisations in their localities and in deciding whether or not Certificates of Need are justified.

The name given to the gravity model is RAMOS (Resource Allocation Model Over Space), an acronym which arose following further development work at the International Institute for Applied Systems Analysis (IIASA) in Austria. Though RAMOS differs in certain important respects from other gravity models applied to health care systems, the general approach has, in fact, quite a long history in the USA. Morrill and Kelley (1970), for example, used a related model, and studies by Dhillion and Giglio (1977), also at the University of Massachusetts, and Zanakis and Neas (1981) highlighted the potential of this approach. In addition, there has been much work on the general problem of accessibility to hospitals and the utilization of health care services (for example, Schneider, 1968; Shannon, 1975; Studnucki, 1975).

The model forming the basis for this paper is an improvement in several respects on this earlier work. The specifications of the variables— particularly on the supply and demand sides—have been systematized, and all rely on routinely available population and hospital data. Also, the underlying behavioural hypothesis is more in accord with widely held views on how health care systems behave, particularly the patterns of use made by patients of facilities. Finally, more recent research has revealed the scope for broadening the model to help in the analysis of wider ranging problems [for example, see Mayhew (1980) and Mayhew and Leonardi (chapter 9, this volume)].

2 Further background: relationship between patients, doctors, and hospitals

Before considering the details of the model, it is useful to describe briefly the US practice of providing health care services, since this differs in certain important respects to that in the United Kingdom. Usually, practice varies slightly from country to country anyway, and this affects how such models may or may not be used and what data need to be collected.

The first point of importance concerns the choice of hospital. Most patients receiving inpatient care in US hospitals are referred by their local doctor, who is either on the staff of a hospital or has staff privileges. This doctor is usually responsible for the in-hospital care himself, although he may consult a specialist when necessary. Although the local doctor is thus a major factor in hospital choice, there is no compulsion or financial advantage for the patient to go to the hospital selected for him. (Possible exceptions to this would include veterans, members of armed services and their dependants, and members of the growing number of health maintenance organisations.) In any event, if a patient has strong views about a particular hospital, then he may ask his doctor for referral elsewhere. This is usually not a problem if the doctor has privileges at several hospitals, but, in any case, the patient is always free to obtain a second opinion. In an emergency this pattern differs and patients are taken to a hospital with emergency facilities that is closest at the time, but if prolonged treatment is required, the patient may later transfer to a hospital nearer home. Lastly, there are patients requiring highly specialised care who are referred to the most appropriate medical centre catering to their medical needs, often at a considerable distance from where they live. The net result of these considerations is a rich and potentially complex pattern of patient flows based on an extended freedom of hospital choice, and one of the aims of the present investigation is to see whether or not a gravity model can be used to describe this situation.

A second important factor that sets US medical practice apart from that in the United Kingdom is that patients are generally responsible for their own hospital costs. The money received by the hospital is retained as income and is used to cover running costs, although hospitals may obtain funds from endowments, grants, and other sources. Most patients are insured and do not therefore pay their bills directly, although those people whose income falls below certain levels and those over sixty-five years of age are eligible for Medicard or Medicare, a government funded system of medical insurance for which entitlements vary from state to state. In terms of current modelling approaches, such considerations may be important when specifying the demand and supply aspects of the model, since it may be necessary to stratify a population according to its ability to pay and the facilities it is eligible to use.

The final factor that should be mentioned is that the majority of hospitals are nonprofit organisations. Although they do not therefore compete in a free-market environment in the traditional sense, competition between them, in terms of research, medical reputation, and the ability to attract outstanding staff, is still very strong, and this in turn affects their relative attractiveness to different categories of patients. Again, such behaviour could affect the specification of certain variables in the basic model.

3 The basic model

The simplest version of the model, and the one we describe here, is based on the hypothesis that the flow of patients between a place of residence, i, and a place of treatment, j, is in proportion to the morbidity or patient-generating potential of i and to the resources or case-load capacity in j, but is in inverse proportion to the accessibility costs of getting from i to j. A constraint, explained more fully below, is included in the formulation of the model to ensure that the flow of patients from all patient origins, i, to a particular place of treatment, j, matches the number of patients treated in that location. Mathematically, the model is expressed as follows:

$$T_{ij} = B_j D_j W_i \exp(-\beta c_{ij}) , \tag{1}$$

where

T_{ij} is the predicted number of patients originating in i and treated in j in a speciality grouping;

D_j is the case-load capacity of health facilities in j in the same speciality grouping;

W_i is the patient-generating factor, which is the relative propensity of that area to generate patients in the same speciality grouping;

c_{ij} is the accessibility costs incurred by patients originating in i and treated in j; and

β is the model parameter, determined empirically by calibration; and

$$B_j = [W_i \exp(-\beta c_{ij})]^{-1} . \tag{2}$$

Equation (2) is the constraint or balancing factor ensuring that

$$\sum_i T_{ij} = D_j ; \tag{3}$$

that is, flows from i do not exceed the case-load capacity in j.

The detailed definitions and specifications of the model variables can become very involved, depending on region and system of interest, the specialities under consideration, and whether the model is being used for calibration or for prediction. Briefly, calibration describes the stage of parameter determination during which a value of β is selected, such that actual patient flows are correctly replicated (see also section 4). Prediction, by contrast, refers to actual simulations based on forecasts of demand and supply to see how flows change as a result of different forecasts. More details of these aspects are given in Mayhew and Taket (1980) and Mayhew and Leonardi (1982).

In terms of the input variables, the case-load capacity, D_j, is defined as the actual or predicted number of cases treated at facilities in j during a calibration or prediction year. Unlike actual case loads, for which data are available, predicted case loads require prior analysis to take account of different trends in hospital utilization and in lengths of hospital stay in each speciality, as well as information on pending or proposed hospital closures or building programmes. As for demand, this is represented by the patient-generating factor, W_i, which is an index of the propensity of an area to generate hospital cases. In the model, W_i is calculated by considering the age and sex structure of the population at risk in each area, multiplying the population in each category by the overall rates for that category, and then summing the whole. The difference between calibration and prediction values of W_i is that the latter are based on demographic forecasts and projected trends in hospital utilization whereas the former are calculated for the base or calibration year.

The last of the three input variables is the accessibility costs, c_{ij}, and, as with the other variables, there are different approaches for measuring it. Essentially, it represents the average difficulty a person in area i experiences in accessing facilities in area j. Suitable measures used in past applications include distance, road distance, adjusted road distance (see sections 4 and 5), or travel time; however, which of these is most suitable would normally be decided according to which gave the better results.

The normalization factor, B_j, in equation (2) also requires justification, since it reflects a basic assumption of the model, which is that health care facilities tend to be fully utilized. Whether or not this assumption is justifiable for all types of health care systems is still a question which is keenly debated. Its validity depends on the pressures on resources within the system of interest, on the efficiency with which hospitals admit and discharge patients, and on other factors. Nevertheless, experience gained from applying the model in several countries suggests the assumption that demand tends to rise to meet supply and provides a robust working hypothesis. However, in the USA, where resource levels are traditionally higher on average than elsewhere, the assumption needs more careful evaluation. Much depends on the type of service being offered, the population affected, the status of the hospitals concerned, and the areas in which they are located. In the present application, which is intended as the first stage in a sequence of investigations, full utilization is presumed, but a further comment on this question is made in the discussion (see section 6).

4 Data sources, variable specification, and calibration methods
There are six health service areas in Massachusetts, which are broken down into twenty-three subareas. For this application of RAMOS, twenty-eight origin zones were used, consisting of the twenty-three subareas and five neighbouring states, and twenty-three destination zones also based on the

subareas (see figure 1). Table 1 lists the health service areas, together
with the respective number of hospitals and towns, and the sizes of the
populations contained in each. Four commonly provided hospital inpatient
acute services were selected for analysis—general medical and surgical,
obstetrics and maternity, paediatrics, and acute psychiatry. The total
number of deaths and discharges in each of these categories is given in
table 2. As is seen, they show considerable variation in terms of their
degree of specialization, but it is also of interest to note in passing that

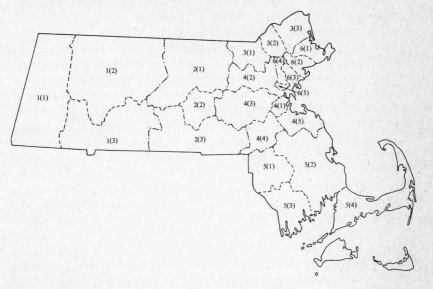

Figure 1. Boundaries of health service areas and subareas in the State of Massachusetts
(note: numbers refer to health service areas 1-6; numbers in brackets represent
subareas within health service areas).

Table 1. The Massachusetts health system (source: CoM, 1977, pages 3D-9D).

Health service area [a]	Number of subareas	Number of hospitals	Number of towns	1975 Census Bureau estimated population
1	3	16	102	822480
2	3	17	64	676766
3	3	8	23	478672
4	5	50	66	2225708
5	4	16	69	964953
6	5	15	27	647597
Total	23	122	351	5816176

[a] See figure 1.

the admission rates for the region for similar speciality groupings are considerably higher than in the United Kingdom. Such differences as these cannot be explained by a higher morbidity in the USA; rather, they are much more likely to be the direct result of a higher level of health care provision in the USA.

Accessibility costs in the model are based on road mileages and adjusted road mileages, where the latter are simply road distances weighted by an arbitrary factor to allow for road congestion in urban areas. Twelve of the 332 origin–destination pairs were affected by the weighting, which increased the average distance travelled by patients to hospitals from 7.583 actual miles to 9.581 adjusted miles.

Two calibration procedures (based on those given in Mayhew and Taket, 1980) were used to determine β, the model parameter; they are the slope method and the method of maximum likelihood. Briefly, the first is based on the regression of the predicted values of T_{ij} on the observed values. The model parameter, β, is then systematically adjusted until the slope of the regression is exactly equal to one. A check is then made on the constant term of the regression equation to ensure it does not differ significantly from zero. When both conditions hold, it means, on average, that there is a one-to-one correspondence between the predicted and the observed patient-flows (see also figures 2 and 3). The second procedure, which is more common but in fact less effective in this application, is the method of maximum likelihood, in which the objective is to select a value of β such that the predicted average distance travelled by all patients to all hospitals equals the observed average. Further details of the theory and the method, which uses a standard iterative procedure to reach a solution, are given in Batty and Mackie (1972) and in Mayhew and Taket (1980).

Table 2. 1978 discharge statistics for Massachusetts.

Health care speciality	Number of discharges, N	N as a percentage of total
Medical/surgical	658942	77.36
Obstetrics/maternity	88192	10.35
Paediatrics	84391	9.91
Psychiatric	20182	2.37
All patients	851760	100.00

5 First results

The results are presented in two sets for each speciality grouping and calibration method. The first, and most important, is based both on in-State and on out-of-State patients. This is because the Boston area in Massachusetts is a nationally known referral centre attracting approximately 50000 patients annually in all specialities from beyond the State boundaries.

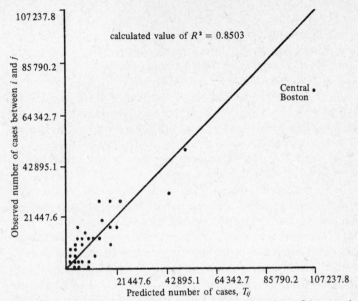

Figure 2. Comparison of predicted and actual patient-flows [the actual number of patients from origin *i* who are treated in destination *j* compared with the predicted number (23 × 28 observations). Medical–surgical discharges, Massachusetts, 1978 data; accessibility costs based on adjusted road mileage].

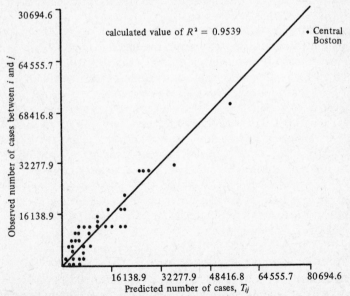

Figure 3. Comparison of predicted and actual patient-flows [the actual number of patients from origin *i* who are treated in destination *j* compared with the predicted number (23 × 28 observations). Medical–surgical discharges, Massachusetts, 1978 data; accessibility costs based on adjusted road mileage].

The second set is based on residents of Massachusetts alone. The main details are presented in table 3, which gives the parameter values of the models derived for each speciality and a measure of goodness-of-fit based on R^2, the proportion of variance in actual patient flows explained by the model. The table indicates that adjusted mileages significantly improve the goodness-of-fit statistic and hence the performance of the model. This can also be seen in figures 2 and 3, which are scattergrams of predicted flows on observed flows. In these figures, the position of central Boston is of interest as an example of one of the destinations whose mileage was altered. Prior to alteration, the intrazonal flow was being underpredicted, whereas now it approximates the actual value.

A further interesting set of comparisons are the variations in the values obtained for β by the respective methods of calibration for the in-State and out-of-State models. Using the slope method it is observed that β tends to hold its value more than in the method of maximum likelihood, for which the inclusion of out-of-State patients also increases the average distance travelled by about two miles. Also of importance are the differences in the value of β obtained between each patient category, since a relatively high value of β indicates that patients tend to use local facilities, whereas a low value indicates that they are prepared to travel farther afield. By this criterion, therefore, acute psychiatric care, obstetrics and maternity services, and general medical and surgical services tend to be obtained by patients locally, whereas paediatric patients need to travel farther.

6 Discussion and further work

Three general conclusions are apparent from the investigations to date and the brief description of the results given above. First, RAMOS provides a generally good fit to the data and hence description of the pattern of patient-flows in Massachusetts. Second, the differences obtained between different categories of patient for β, the model parameter, corroborates similar results from applications of the model elsewhere. Third, in spite of a much more market-orientated health care system in the USA, the model provides a similarly adequate level of description as compared with other applications to date. Nevertheless, more work is necessary to improve several areas of the model's specification, and there are also some pressing areas of policy that cannot, as yet, be currently addressed by the model.

The first priority is to validate the model by carrying out tests on its predictive capabilities. Thorough tests, for example, were carried out on the UK version (Mayhew and Taket, 1981), and these were subsequently extended by later investigators. These tests, which were based on back-predicting patient flows using a model calibrated on a different set of data, were successful in predicting reasonably accurately the changes that occurred in hospitalization rates and in identifying possible sources of systematic error caused by factors not incorporated in the original version. The model was subsequently refined prior to implementation by the regional health

Table 3. Calibration of RAMOS using 1978 in-patient discharge data from Massachusetts for all patients treated in the State and for in-State patients only (in-State patients are those who are treated in Massachusetts and have an address in the State at the time of discharge).

Category of patient care	Number of patient discharges in data base	Average mileage traveled by patient		Slope calibration[a]				Maximum likelihood calibration[a]			
				actual miles		adjusted miles		actual miles		adjusted miles	
		actual	adjusted	β	R^2	β	R^2	β	R^2	β	R^2
All patients treated in the State											
Total (all patients)	851760	10.024	11.984	0.1600	0.8407	0.2300	0.9531	0.11749	0.8577	0.13900	0.8585
Medical/surgical	650942	10.151	12.150	0.1600	0.8395	0.2300	0.9510	0.11505	0.7998	0.13613	0.8510
Obstetrics/maternity	88192	8.484	10.297	0.1900	0.8920	0.2700	0.9489	0.14082	0.8588	0.16368	0.8956
Paediatrics	84391	10.868	12.695	0.1500	0.7678	0.2100	0.9190	0.11116	0.7245	0.13309	0.8138
Psychiatric	20182	9.035	10.906	0.1900	0.8635	0.2500	0.9578	0.13924	0.8664	0.16412	0.8851
In-State patients only											
Total (all patients)	817892	7.553	9.581	0.1600	0.8524	0.2300	0.9559	0.13316	0.8385	0.17450	0.9202
Medical/surgical	632183	7.490	9.561	0.1600	0.8503	0.2300	0.9539	0.13321	0.8386	0.17583	0.9186
Obstetrics/maternity	85249	7.343	9.202	0.1900	0.8988	0.2700	0.9501	0.14337	0.8769	0.17577	0.9130
Paediatrics	80757	8.256	10.152	0.1500	0.7856	0.2100	0.9245	0.12432	0.7689	0.16478	0.8868
Psychiatric	19650	7.544	9.458	0.1900	0.8757	0.2500	0.9609	0.13380	0.8427	0.17145	0.9170

[a] β is the calibration coefficient; R^2 is the proportion of explained variance.

authorities in Southeast England. In the case of the USA, these tests should also act as a check on the utilization assumption of the model.

Apart from validation, one aspect for further investigation concerns more specialized categories of care, where patterns of referral can have a significant secondary impact on patient-flows. Although in the present investigations the number of such cases is small as a proportion of the total flow, the model should try to take it into account, particularly when this practice is likely to be prevalent. Another direction of progress is to stratify the demand side of the model according to the method of payment. This opens up a very important field of policy, since it is of considerable importance to be able to model the relative usage made of the public and private sectors of medicine, as well as the magnitudes of the patient flows under different financial incentives and constraints. A final but equally interesting set of questions concerns possible interactions between different patient categories, including the relative priority they are given and the effects on the numbers of patients involved as resource levels change. These then are some of the possible avenues of research, and the task ahead is to tackle them in conjunction with the health service agencies and hospitals of Massachusetts.

References

Batty M, Mackie S, 1972, "The calibration of gravity, entropy, and related models of spatial interaction" *Environment and Planning* **4** 205-233

CoM, 1977 *Health Data Annual* (Commonwealth of Massachusetts, Boston, MA)

Dhillon H, Giglio R J, 1977, "A computer model for planning locations, capacities, and schedules for outpatient facilities" report UMASS/IEOR-77-2 (United States Department of Commerce, National Technical Information Service, Springfield, VA)

Mayhew L D, 1980, "The regional planning of health care services: RAMOS and RAMOS^{-1}" WP-80-166, International Institute for Applied Systems Analysis, Laxenburg, Austria

Mayhew L D, Leonardi G, 1982, "Equity, efficiency, and accessibility in urban and regional health-care systems" *Environment and Planning A* **14** 1479-1507

Mayhew L D, Taket A, 1980, "RAMOS: a model of health care resource allocation in space" WP-80-125, International Institute for Applied Systems Analysis, Laxenburg, Austria

Mayhew L D, Taket A, 1981, "A model validation and sensitivity analysis" WP-81-100, International Institute for Applied Systems Analysis, Laxenburg, Austria

Morrill R L, Kelley M, 1970, "The simulation of hospital use and the estimation of location efficiency" *Geographical Analysis* **2** 283-299

Schneider J B, 1968, "Measuring, evaluating and redesigning hospital-physician-patient spatial relationships in metropolitan areas" *Inquiry* **5** 24-42

Shannon G W, 1975, "A method for evaluating the geographic accessibility of health services" *The Professional Geographer* **27** 30-36

Studnicki J, 1975, "The minimization of travel effort as a delineating influence for urban hospital service areas" *International Journal of Health Services* **5** 679-693

Zanakis S, Neas L, 1981, "A rational regional allocation of obstetric facilities in accordance with state health plan objectives" in *System Science in Health Care, Volume 1* Ed. C Tilquin (Pergamon Press, Oxford) pp 59-69